John Lyon's Dream

John Lyon's Dream

The History of Harrow's John Lyon School

BY

MICHAEL BURRELL

FOREWORD BY

JOHN BARNARD

MA FRCO(CHM) ARSCM

for Nicholas

with very best wishes

Michael Burrell

ALMYRIDA PUBLICATIONS

2013

First published in 2013 by
Almyrida Publications
44 Wertheim Way
Huntingdon
PE29 6UX

ISBN 978-0-9575277-0-6

Typeset in 11.5/13 pt Garamond
by Anne Joshua, Oxford
Printed in Great Britain by
Berforts Information Press Ltd, Oxford

On the education of young men:

. . . if they be trained up in good nurture, most commonly they resemble them from whom they come, and often times passe them, but if they have not one that can traine them up, they growe (as it were) wilde, and never come to their ripenesse.

Baldassare Castiglione
The Book of the Courtier, published 1528
Translated by Sir Thomas Hoby

From Preston farm and hollow
Where Lyon dreamed, and saw in dream
His race of sons to follow.

E E Bowen
Harrow School Song

I think this School approaches more closely to the ideal that John Lyon had when he founded the great school. . . . Had he been living, he would have been proud of the work that is being carried on.

G W Tallents
Harrow School and John Lyon School Governor and
Mayor of Westminster
John Lyon School Speech Day 1919

CONTENTS

ACKNOWLEDGMENTS

Sincere thanks are due to the following individuals, organizations and publications. Many of the people cited went to great lengths to help and to provide invaluable insights. I am grateful to them all.

The Beauties of England and Wales, by J Norris Brewer (London, 1816)

Harrow School and its Surroundings, by Percy M Thornton (London: W H Allen, 1885)

Harrow School, edited by E W Howson and G T Warner (London: Edward Arnold, 1898)

Harrow Through the Ages, by Walter Druett (Uxbridge: King & Hutchings, 1936, revised 1956)

A History of Harrow School, by Dr Christopher Tyerman (Oxford: OUP, 2002)

Harrow: Portrait of an English School, compiled by Robert Dudley (London: Third Millennium Publishing, 2004)

The Timeline History of Harrow School, 1572 to Present, compiled and written by Dale Vargas (London: Worth Press, 2010)

Harmony, handicap and houses, by Richard Upson (at JLS 1929–34) (Privately published)

The Public School Phenomenon, 597–1977, by Jonathan Gathorne-Hardy (London: Hodder & Stoughton, 1977)

Boys Together: English Public Schools, 1800–64, by John Chandos (London: Hutchinson, 1984)

Troublesome Young Men: The Rebels who Brought Churchill to Power and Helped Save England, by Lynne Olson (New York: Farrar, Straus & Giroux, 2007)

The British Olympics: Britain's Olympic Heritage, 1612–2012, by Dr Martin Polley (London: English Heritage, 2011)

'The foundation and survival of the Lower School of John Lyon.' An invaluable dissertation by Maureen Glynn (1976)

The Lyonian magazine from 1890 to 2009 and all its editors and their teams of assistants, including: Ernest Young, E H Butt, Frederick

Swainson, H Virgilius Black, D A Cowtan, Geoffrey Thornton, Robert Latham, Ian Whybrow, R S K Mearns, Rachel Reid, John Barnard, Nicholas Parsons, John Bell, Ian Read and Patricia Waldron

The Imperial War Museum and Angela Wootton of the Library Development Department
The National Army Museum and Justin Saddington
The National Archives
London Metropolitan Archive
The *Harrow Gazette* newspaper
The *Harrow Observer* newspaper
The *Independent* newspaper
The *Daily Telegraph* newspaper
The *Scotsman* newspaper
The Old Gaytonian Association website (http://www.jeffreymaynard. com/Harrow_County): a highly informative paper by Stephen Frost on the career of Ernest Young
The Association of Old Worcesters and historian Graham K Smith
The Old Mercers' Club website (http://www.oldmercersclub.org.uk) and the work of W E F Ward and R G Edwards
Minal Patel of Golders Green Crematorium
Tom Knollys and Clare Hopkins of Trinity College, Oxford

The constant help and encouragement of Brenda Allanson, one time Development Director and her Assistant Kathryn Harvey; and the equally great help and support of Michelle Gascoine, Alumni Relations Manager.

The help, too, of Rita Boswell and her successor Angharad Meredith as Harrow School Archivist.

The direct assistance and enthusiasm of Old Lyonians Professor David Reeves and Robert Cutts.

Personal accounts by, or interviews with: Stephen Adamson CBE, Dr Owain Arwel Hughes CBE, John Barnard, Francis Alan Bennion, Richard Berridge, Dr Michael Bogdanov, Frank Bogdin, Eric Boobyer, Ian Burrell, John Butt, Andrew Carwood, Professor Jagjit Chadha, Revd Canon Jonathan Charles, Richard Charles, Barry Cresswell, Dr Sadat Edroos, Roger French, Christopher Geelan, Mark Gettleson, Gary Gibbon, Mark Gifford, Christopher Glynn, Xuan-Zheng Goh, John Hayes(OL), Frances Impey, Stephen Janaway, Alykhan Kassam, John King OBE, Atish Lakhani, Lt Cmdr Geoffrey Lancashire, Keith Leader,

David Learner, the late John Learner, Terry Lyon, Ben Marsh, Ishil Mehta, Anek Mhajan, Stephen Pollard, Andrew Reed, Michael Rose, Peter Rudge, Nicholas Smart, Richard Symonds, the late Geoffrey Thornton, Robert Walker, George Weedon, the late Professor Paul Wilkinson CBE, Ian Whybrow, Revd Timothy Wright, and Old Gaytonian, Mehul Trevedi.

I am grateful, too, for more casual exchanges with numerous other Old Lyonians and members of staff; and to David Podmore for recovering material we thought to be lost. I am also especially grateful to John Barnard for his suggestions and for agreeing to write a Foreword and to Tony Sloggett for his invaluable help with regard to publication.

Photographs in the book were almost all commissioned by the School and are reproduced with the School's permission, the more recent ones taken by Graham Ryder, to whom, my thanks. Some originals and some re-photographs are by my son Mark. In instances where it has been possible to establish that other copyright exists, it is acknowledged in the individual caption.

Without the wholehearted support of John Hayes (OH), Chairman of the Governors who first encouraged me to undertake this project, and of Katherine Haynes, the School's Head who has gone out of her way to ensure I received all the help I needed, the book would not have been possible.

FOREWORD

In May 2012 I returned to the John Lyon School to present Old Lyonian ties to the Upper Sixth leavers. In front of me sat a group of boys I did not know; and yet in another sense I knew them well. They were the same intelligent, self-confident, engaging and gracious young men I recognized from my own time at the School. Although it was their final day before examinations began, they treated me with dignity and warmth, and their relationship with each other and with their Head of Sixth Form exhibited the same qualities. Some things do not change, and it is good to read in Michael Burrell's wonderfully researched account of similar relationships going back over decades.

Yet other things, not least the School's facilities, have changed and improved beyond recognition over the years since the Old Building was the sole school building, and Michael charts this development in fascinating and highly readable detail.

The John Lyon School has a unique and intriguing history, born out of its sometimes difficult relationship with the school at the top of the Hill. At times it has come close to having to shut down, yet, through the determined efforts of some heroic figures to whom we owe an enormous debt of gratitude, it has always pulled through and become ever stronger as a result. It is right that these men should have their contribution to the School's history and growing success recorded here for posterity. Many of them were, of course, Headmasters of the School, and Michael's account perceptively assesses the period of office of each one.

One is struck by the horrific loss of Lyonian life caused by the two world wars – some very fine young men died in these conflicts – yet also by the number of distinguished men on the current world stage who were educated at the School.

The John Lyon School has at several points been quite outstanding in the fields of drama, music and sport, and its academic record is no less impressive. It has attracted many excellent teachers whose influence on the young men in their care has been crucial and lasting, and it is good to encounter in these pages warm tributes from their former pupils.

We owe an enormous debt of gratitude to Michael Burrell for his painstaking work in assembling the material for this important book. No school is perfect, but the John Lyon School is indubitably a very fine one, and more than anything else it is a happy school, a place where people feel welcome and valued. May it long remain so.

John Barnard
Pupil 1959–1966 Assistant Master, later Head of
Modern Languages and Second Master 1974–2002

INTRODUCTION

The story of this remarkable School is not merely one of survival against the odds, though for its first sixty or so years it is just that, it is an account of a founding so contorted that is a wonder it ever saw its first day, let alone any later ones.

It is also a story of human determination, of pride and struggle, of selflessness, of profound and binding affection, and – from the beginning – of quite extraordinary achievement.

One of the epigraphs to this book is from Castiglione whose treatise on the education of boys and young men inspired Elyot and Ascham and the Renaissance founders of many English schools. The training of young males had previously been at the hands of the clergy or of private tutors. The new belief, as John Lyon makes clear in what he thinks should be studied, including archery, combines practical skills with book learning. It includes religion but is not limited to it. And it is a group activity to help a whole section of the community, rather than one or two individuals. A degree of social mobility is one of its prizes.

When *The Lyonian* magazine was started, nearly forty years after the embryonic form of the School had been launched as a semi-detached part of Harrow School, its editor, Ernest Young, wrote: 'we venture to predict [it] will last as long as the name of John Lyon is remembered in Harrow. It is to be a continuous chronicle of all the best efforts of our school, socially, athletically, and intellectually.'

A few years later, the first Headmaster, J E Williams, acknowledged the accuracy of Young's claim and added: 'When the time comes for the history of the School to be written, it may be that in our volumes will be found the materials for the chronicler, whose distinguished fortune it shall be to recount the brilliant achievements of a long line of Lyonians!'

That claim, too, and it was a brave one, has proved incontrovertibly true. I have had the advantage of speaking with a number of people connected with the School as pupils, staff or governors. The names of everyone who kindly gave their time to be interviewed are given in the Acknowledgments. I owe especial thanks to Maureen Glynn for allowing me full use of her excellent treatise on the early days of the Lower School. I am constantly grateful to my old friend, Professor David Reeves for his support throughout and for putting acres of research material onto CD-ROMs to make my life much easier. And to another old friend, Robert Cutts, who more than once drew my attention to material of which I was unaware and whose work to unravel into comprehensibility the complex Lyon family tree is happily shown in the Appendix.

But, from 1890 on, Mr Williams is right. I have not acknowledged the hundreds of times my source for information has been *The Lyonian* magazine, simply because it would become tiresome. I can assure all readers, it has been my distinguished fortune to have it as so rich and readable a source and I am happy to acknowledge my debt to all its editors over the years and to all its numerous contributors.

I hope I have done them, and this School, justice.

Michael Burrell

CHAPTER 1

THE LONG, LONG GESTATION
1572–1876

The John Lyon School, one of the three long-standing institutions that make up the Harrow Foundation, the others being Harrow School and John Lyon's Charity, stands on the side of Harrow Hill and about halfway up it. It commands a view across the neighbouring county and has grown over the years from a small establishment for some thirty boys to the high-achieving and popular public school which educates six hundred boys and is spread through several neighbouring buildings.

Its origins go back to the reign of Elizabeth I when a successful local farmer and substantial landowner, John Lyon, a yeoman born in the village of Preston not far from Harrow, obtained from the Queen a charter to found 'the Free Grammar School of John Lyon' to educate thirty local boys.[1]

John Lyon and his wife Joan were childless. It is sometimes suggested that they had a son who died young. However, the only candidate, Zachary Lionne, died at thirty–three and was still alive when the charter, which would have effectively disowned him, was obtained; and there is contemporaneous evidence in court documents that the benefactor John Lyon had no children. Elgar imagining a similar situation wrote his wistful *Dream Children*, its idea based on Charles Lamb's essay with the same title and springing from a comparable sense of deprivation. J M Barrie, in the same case, adopted the Llewelyn Davies boys. John and Joan Lyon, having considerable wealth, decided like others before and since

---

[1] John Lyon was not merely wealthy, his family had powerful connections. Eponymous relation Sir John Lyon was Lord Mayor of London in 1554 while cousin and exact contemporary of the School's founder, John Lyon of Ruislip, was a friend of Dr Caius, founder of Caius College, Cambridge. He probably aided in obtaining the Charter from the Queen and it can be no accident that this document includes the provision that £20 per annum be set aside 'for the support of four exhibitioners; two at Gonville and Caius College at Cambridge; and the others in any college at Oxford'. The great- (to the power of nine) grandson of the John Lyon of 'Ryslippe', Mr Terry Lyon, is alive today and resident in Virginia, USA. This John Lyon was, confusingly, also married to a woman named Joan, though four of their seven children survived. Both cousins, coincidentally, died the same year. A partial version of the Lyon family tree appears as Appendix 1.

that it would be used to benefit the young of future generations. They were to be their heirs.

In giving permission to found the school, however, the monarch took the opportunity to insist on another act of public generosity, at the same time. John Lyon, who owned farms in Middlesex and Hertfordshire, the proceeds of which were to fund the school, also owned some forty-eight acres in the area now known as Maida Vale and St John's Wood. As part of the same Charter, the profit from this land was to be used to maintain the roads that led to London from his home locality, namely the Edgware Road and the Harrow Road. For two centuries the money did just that. Then, by stages, the roads became the responsibility of other authorities until in 1991, after representations by the Harrow School Governors, the Road Fund was legally transmuted into John Lyon's Charity. This, in turn, has supported numerous good causes, from sports scholarships to a new hall for the City Literary Institute, benefiting with tens of millions of pounds individuals and organizations based in any of the districts crossed by the two major roads. What it cannot be used for is to benefit either Harrow School or the John Lyon School. In the course of time, John and Joan Lyon's beneficence has gone far beyond anything they can have conceived.

The 1572 Charter was not acted upon immediately. When John Lyon died twenty years later everything was left to his wife Joan. On her death in 1608, the promised school in his name was founded on Harrow Hill and a start was made on a building where the teaching could take place. This, known today as the Fourth Form Room, opened in 1615 and was subsequently incorporated into other fine buildings on the crest of the Hill, as the school grew in numbers and fame.

The process of growing, however, changed the nature of the school. From, in the words of the Charter, a place for 'the perpetual education, teaching and instruction' to be given gratis to the sons of local farmers and tradesmen, with a few paying 'foreigners' – that is boys from outside the parish – it became something more ambitious. Those who ran it saw financial advantage and more prestige in increasing the numbers of those from further afield. Gradually John Lyon's intentions were overlaid by a policy that not only attracted the wealthy who were happy to pay, but also the well-to-do who were equally happy to acquire property within the parish and, in consequence, have their sons educated free. By the late eighteenth century the genuine locals for whom the benefit had been intended, were almost entirely excluded.

While Harrow School, as it had come to be known, acquired increasing cachet, frustration among Harrow's parishioners mounted. In 1810 the Court of Chancery considered a complaint against the Governors and Head Master from several Harrow inhabitants concerned at 'the practical exclusion of the children of parishioners by the increase of the foreigners.' The Master of the Rolls, Sir William Grant, resisted the complaint. By the mid-nineteenth century when Dr Vaughan, Harrow's eminent Head Master, was in place, *The Times*, in one week alone carried three advertisements which appeared to subvert John Lyon's principal intention. They were cited by John Gloyn in his later commentary supporting pamphlets published by John Morris of Sudbury in 1854.[2] Two of the advertisements publicised the services of private tutors providing grounding (Gloyn himself uses the terms 'pre-instructed' and 'crammed') for the sons of noblemen or gentlemen wishing to enter a public school and both advertisements specifically allude to Harrow, one even going so far as to refer to Dr Vaughan in person. The implication is clear that the boys concerned would be seeking exhibitions, or non-fee-paying entry. The third advertised a house in the area as providing an 'opportunity for a family who may wish to avail themselves of the advantages of the School for their sons and whose admission into it can be obtained. . . . free'. In this case, the boy would enter the school as a local parishioner. Among those who did take advantage of this arrangement was the family of Anthony Trollope. They moved to Sudbury Hill and then to Harrow Weald precisely so that the future novelist and his two brothers could obtain a free education at 'the parish school that John Lyon bequeathed'.[3]

Complaints by now were becoming close to irresistible. Vaughan, the most notable Head Master of his day and in Harrow's history,[4] raised the matter with the Governors and, in 1851, suggested the setting up of an additional school to meet the local needs. The Governors demurred. More than thirty years later Percy Thornton, in his book about the

[2] John Gloyn: *Notes to Pamphlets printed for John Morris as to the Free Grammar School of John Lyon at Harrow on the Hill* 1862.

[3] Trollope's own words. He was far from happy at Harrow and wrote about the experience in *Orley Farm*, 'the grave of all my father's hopes, the cause of my mother's sufferings and those of her children'. Orley Farm was the fictional name he gave to Julians, the house his father built on Sudbury Hill, a name which lives on with the prep school existing there from the mid-nineteenth century. Trollope himself gave permission for the school to adopt the name. Orley Farm is now a feeder school for both Harrow and the John Lyon School.

[4] Vaughan raised 'Harrow from a state of depression near to death, to unprecedented heights of success and repute.' – John Chandos, *Boys Together*. 'In Dr Vaughan, Arnold seemed in the eyes of many almost to live again, and new boys came to Harrow. . . . on that account.' – Percy M Thornton, *Harrow School and its Surroundings*.

School, still shared the illusion that at this time 'there was little at Harrow out of accord with public opinion'.

In 1853 Vaughan succeeded in persuading the Governors to apply to the Court of Chancery to make the privileges of a free education at Harrow available only to residents of two or more years standing. This was agreed by the Court but simply resulted in the well-heeled arranging to move into the parish earlier.

The same year, at his own expense and to his own credit (and probably for his own peace), Dr Vaughan inaugurated the 'English Form'. This was to be a separate institution, though technically and legally a part of Harrow School, to educate up to thirty day boys according to the intentions of the original charter. The curriculum would not be the high classical one available at the boarding school, but one appropriate to the likely needs of youngsters intended for commerce or the professions. Most Old Harrovians were gentlemen and consequently strangers to work.[5]

The English Form

The Prospectus for the New School announced that every boy would learn Latin; that his family was to pay for all the books he used in the course of his education; that no boy would be admitted without previous examination by Dr Vaughan and those accepted would have to make application to the Governors of Harrow School to be entered on the Foundation. The hours of schooling were laid down as '9 to 12 in the morning and 2 to 5 in the afternoon' six days a week, with punctuality and Sunday church attendance insisted on.

Parents were required to pay £5 per year in three equal parts, so it was not quite free. And Rule 10 was to disabuse those attending of the idea they might think of themselves as part of Harrow School. It read: 'The boys will regard themselves as entirely separate in all respects from those of the Public School as at present existing. . . . and will on no account mix themselves with the games etc. of the Higher School'.

This was supposedly to protect the boys of the English Form and it illustrates the ambiguous, almost schizophrenic, initial relationship between what was to become in time the John Lyon School and the earlier foundation whose charter it more nearly fulfilled. For the boys of

---

[5] Not entirely true, of course. Many were destined for the Army, the Church or politics. But it was Trollope, again, who wrote of an upper class character's view: 'There were no doubt gentlemen of different degrees, but the English gentleman of gentlemen was he who had land. . . . and a family absence of any usual employment.' – *The Way We Live Now*, Chapter XIII: The Longstaffes.

the English Form appeared throughout its twenty-six-year existence in the Examination Lists of Harrow School; parental complaints were to be directed to its Head Master; so were boys seeking admission and those in need of punishment.

A single master was appointed to teach the boys of the English Form: Mr Henry Hutchinson, a nephew of William Wordsworth. Presumably he was an already known connection since the Head Master of Harrow preceding Dr Vaughan was Christopher Wordsworth, also a nephew of the poet.

The boys were housed in what had once been a coach house on Harrow High Street, near the top of Roxeth Hill, and was variously described as a shed or a stable and seems to have been known by the pupils as The Barn. Hutchinson, who had inspired, by his uncle's own account, his poem about the water lily as a result of the enthusiastic description he gave of the plant, remained teaching the boys in these Spartan surroundings, with the occasional help of M. Henri de Félice who taught French, until 1860. He was succeeded briefly by a Mr Robinson and then by one of the more important and more attractive figures of the John Lyon School's early existence, Charles John Gregg. He remained in charge of the English Form at the Barn from 1861 and then continued as Mathematical Master when an independent school was established in its place.

Mr Gregg enjoyed the support of a second master at The Barn, Mr de Witt, who taught French and possibly German. Subjects the boys studied ranged more widely than at Harrow and were prescribed as English, Latin, modern languages, history, geography, and maths. The conditions in which they studied were, to say the least, challenging.

The building was within a gated area with a climbable tree but not enough space to play football. If they wanted to try high jumps, the boys had to go onto the verge beside the roadway. The *Harrow Gazette* in 1868 described the room in which they were taught. 'At one end it is divided from a shed by a single unpainted matchboard partition; the size of the building is 43ft. in length by 20ft. in breadth with a tiled roof, two windows (similar to those placed over cucumber frames) on one side only with many broken panes. . . .' The newspaper, which published several leaders attacking the Governors of Harrow School for their snobbery and parsimony, continued, 'And this is all that is done out of John Lyon's noble fund!' There was a single stove which failed to keep anyone warm except the head boy who sat adjacent so, at intervals, Mr Gregg used to allow the boys to trot round the blackboard for five minutes in order to restore their circulation. Apart from candles, there was no artificial illumination despite the relative lack of light, which must have been a notable disadvantage in winter months. Nonetheless, a few parents thought it worth sending their sons there. Not the full complement allowed, but including boys from families some of whose names occur again and again in the century and more ahead.

One of the earliest remaining lists of pupils, that for the Easter examinations of 1858 includes, propitiously, an Arnold. There were three Greens, two Woodbridges – by 1860 there were five Woodbridges – two Thorntons, and two boys named Winkley. As the years go by the names of Perrin, and King, Parker and Cram join the roll of families whose attachment to the establishment is unshakable.

We know of the increasing number of Woodbridges from the historic ledgers kept for the first few decades, recording each boy, his dates of birth and of admission, his father's name, job and the family's home address. In this instance we also know it from a letter addressed to Mr Hutchinson from all the boys, asking for a day's holiday on Saturday 23rd June 1860, so that they could go to watch Queen Victoria review the Volunteer Forces of Great Britain in Hyde Park. Full of patriotic fervour, it was signed by every boy in the English Form, including A H Woodbridge, C Woodbridge, E Woodbridge, J Woodbridge, S Woodbridge and another boy whose surname will recur, J Parkhouse. What we do not learn is whether the petition was successful.

Given the testing environment of The Barn, it is perhaps not surprising that the boys who endured it, and survived, were tough both physically and in spirit. *The Lyonian* magazine, a later invention, contained in the first decade of the twentieth century a series of articles, written under a pseudonym, recounting life in The Barn by one of the survivors. Tom Brown's schooldays pale in comparison.

On the first day that I went to the old barn in the High Street, which then did duty for a school, I was duly installed as the sixteenth addition to the English Form.

I was first stripped to the waist, then held across a form, while the solitary washing-bowl used by the whole school was poured over my head and back, while a new godfather conferred upon me the fresh name of 'Sarah', and by this ancient and high-sounding cognomen I was known hereafter, until such time that I grew big enough to stop mouths with what the German Kaiser terms 'the mailed hand'.

More fights and references to bullying in ways he was chary of defining feature in the accounts he gave then and in an earlier series of articles, although he quite clearly survived not only cheerily but with a great sense of loyalty.

'Sarah' clung to the pseudonym in writing his memoirs as he was father of a boy attending the School at the time of their appearance. The father's schooldays included the translation of the English Form into the first occupation of the building on Middle Road. He describes this with reference to a boy known as Waggle who frequently came to lessons wearing hob-nailed boots and the swallow-tailed coat in which his father had married; and with a 'supreme contempt for punctuality, he usually arrived some ten minutes after prayers. On one occasion Mr Gregg opened the school-room door and discovered Waggle, to our admiring gaze, late as usual, but kneeling on the mat in the Hall, with both hands clasped and eyes closed, in an attitude of devotion, from which he was rudely awakened by a box on each ear.'

The move into the building on Middle Road occurred in 1876. Once there, Waggle met the end of his school career. 'An individual, long of nose and lank of body, who answered to the name of "Blinkers", was trying the stability of a gas bracket by the simple expedient of swinging on it, when it unexpectedly gave way. Waggle, who was swinging him by pushing his legs, was horrified at the rush of gas, and they both madly endeavoured to stop it up with wet clay culled from the playground bank, but all their efforts were futile until Waggle was struck by the brilliant idea of igniting it, but the "cure" proving worse than the "disease", it took the united efforts of the two masters to prevent the school being burnt down, and Waggle was informed that he would have to see Dr Butler, but Waggle thought otherwise, and obviated extreme measures by walking home and coolly informing his father that "he had got the sack" and he came no more.'[6]

The date given for the above comes in an article clearly written by the same hand and published several years earlier. The Old Building was, therefore, in use before the Lower School of John Lyon was officially up and running.

Later in his story, we are told about another contemporary, 'Malacca'.

He was, I believe, an Eurasian. His skin was of a dark copper colour, his features regular and handsome. He had been reared under the Indian sun,[7] and the ways of English boys were unknown to him. He had a pet monkey,

[6] Montagu Butler had succeeded Vaughan as Harrow's Head Master in 1860.

[7] 'Sarah' is a little confused. 'Malacca' may well have been of Indian descent as much of the population around the town of Malacca is. The town, however, is on the southwest coast of mainland Malaysia – or Malaya as it was then.

whose fur was black and shining, of which he was extremely fond and he would frequently bring it to school with him. He was a fine, sturdy specimen of boyhood and a thoroughly good fellow, combining an Englishman's toughness with the agility of an Indian. A certain youth who was 'Cock of the School' made a great mistake when he threatened Malacca with 'physic' at 'dinner time'. When the auspicious time arrived Malacca showed his white teeth and asked the nearest boy to kindly hold his monkey during the time he would be under the doctor's hands. Alas for the hitherto cocky and unconquered cock – during the extremely painful period he was in the hands of Malacca, the latter frequently shouted, 'Physic indeed!' 'I'll give you gruel' and when the cock at length emerged from 'chancery' I don't think his mother would have recognised him. Many other lads took heart from the easy way in which the bully had been beaten, and he afterwards suffered several other reverses, but Malacca's battle was certainly fought in record time.

Malacca's end was in keeping with his life, for a short time after leaving school he was bathing with a friend in the Straits of that place after which we named him, when his friend had cramp and was in danger from a shark, and Malacca made an heroic but fruitless effort to save him, with the result that they perished together.

Sad as the tale is, it is the stuff of G A Henty and R M Ballantyne[8] and all those Victorian schoolboy storybook heroes; for the forerunners of the John Lyon School it was their reality. And admirable in its way.

The Transition

The change from the English Form to an independent school was neither simple nor an isolated event.

The complaints against the Governors of Harrow School for ignoring the wishes of the original benefactor had been for many years replicated around the country. As a consequence, a Public Schools Enquiry Commission was set up by the government in 1861 to investigate the running of seven schools: Eton, Harrow, Charterhouse, Rugby, Shrewsbury, Westminster and Winchester.

The recommendations that resulted were, to the grave disappointment

---

[8] Robert Michael Ballantyne, was the Edinburgh-born author of some eighty well-researched boys' adventure stories, including *Coral Island*, which in turn was the inspiration for Stevenson's *Treasure Island* and Golding's *Lord of the Flies*. He and his family lived on Harrow Hill from 1878 until his death in 1894. His death was noted with regret in *The Lyonian* at the time. One of his sons became a professional soldier and it is possible that he is the same Ballantyne who attended the Lower School and is recorded later as being an army officer.

of many, designed not to reform the existing schools, but to provide solutions allowing them to continue much as before. The Commissioners made their report in 1864, noting that

The English Form offers the benefit of a cheap, though not wholly gratuitous, education to boys who would probably have resorted to Harrow School itself had it remained small and unimportant, and had not its course of instruction been classical. We are of the opinion that this institution which has hitherto been supported voluntarily by two successive Head Masters should engage the Governors of the School. While we consider that it would be unreasonable to sacrifice the interests of the Classical School to the claims of middle class parishioners of Harrow, who do not require a classical education, we think that some provision should be made out of the revenues of the School for the especial benefit of the class contemplated by the Founder.

The Report went on to suggest that a building should be erected to achieve this aim and a staff of teachers engaged to provide instruction in 'the common branches of modern education.' At the same time the Commissioners recommended that free education at Harrow for those residing in the parish be abolished.

The response from the local population was far from happy. Ablati Juris Vindex,[9] despite his classical pseudonym, wrote in barely contained fury, 'If the new school be part of the Free Grammar School. . . . let the children have all the privileges and advantages of the Free Grammar School and its noble foundation, and do not ask them "to regard themselves as entirely separate in all respects from the public school as at present existing."' He concluded his 'Observations' with the progressive suggestion that it was 'a consummation that may be fairly wished, that some of the high stations in the world shall hereafter be held by the sons of the poor inhabitants of Harrow; for be it remembered, oftentimes there are bright talents among the poor, talents of the highest order sometimes, and which only want direction and education'.

To the contrary, Harrow House Master Reverend F Rendall responded[10] proposing that, as class divides were now immutable, provision should be made for a 'thoroughly good and efficient Day School for those boys who are designed for a life of farming or trading, but no more.'

Dr Butler felt it wise to give a public address, making clear both his

---

[9] *Observations on the Present State of the Free Grammar School at Harrow on the Hill* 1863.

[10] *The Foundation of John Lyon: Remarks on the Present Distribution of its Funds* 1865.

own proposals and his reservations with regard to the Commissioners' Report. This he did in the Speech Room on 20th March 1865 as the Commission's recommendations were being debated in Parliament. He argued that the conflicting claims of the resident gentry, wanting a classical education for their sons, and those of the farmers and tradesmen wanting something more practical, were, by their nature, mutually exclusive. He agreed that the rights of the less-well-off inhabitants had been neglected and that John Lyon's intentions had been disregarded, 'since there are not at the present time those poor scholars in the Parish of Harrow who receive from his will direct benefit.' He proposed that a school should be provided 'on the Foundation of John Lyon which would precisely meet the wants' of those who had been ignored.

At the same time, a number of local people drew up a petition attacking the proposed Parliamentary Bill and pointing out to the Harrow Governors what their rights were according to the Charter granted to John Lyon. Principal signatories on the petition were the Vicar of Harrow and two men with close connection to the English Form and whose relations and their successors would continue the connection for well over a century ahead: William Woodbridge and Jason Woodbridge.

The complaints and the debates, which were especially lively from 1864 onwards, had little measurable effect on the Public Schools Act when it was finally passed in 1868. That handed the Governors of the schools in question the right, indeed the requirement, to vary their constitutions 'in such Manner as may be deemed expedient'; and to do so by 1st May 1869.

It allowed them 'to remove, wholly or partially, local or other Restrictions on the Class of Boys entitled to become Boys on the Foundation'. In other words they could continue, without hindrance, to ignore the terms of their charters or the wishes of their founders. The proper rights of the ordinary folk of Harrow parish were sunk. All they could now do was to continue to support the English Form, and battle as best they could for something better, something more nearly representing what should have been theirs under the will of John Lyon.

The bitterness felt at the Public Schools Commissioners' resolution was well expressed in a letter published in the *Harrow Gazette*. It also acknowledged the way the Governors of Harrow were moving in their thoughts and plans to assuage the situation.

In the Public Schools Act which has so ruthlessly set at nought this good man's intentions and confiscated endowments for the benefit of the rich, which were intended by him for that of the poor, it has provided probably a saving of conscience and a small instalment of justice, that the governing body of Harrow School may provide a subordinate school in connection with the existing school.

In response to the Act of 1868, fifty-four residents of Harrow and Sudbury sent a petition to the Governors, opposing any dilution of the original charter. They were builders, publicans, tailors, shopkeepers of all kinds, hairdressers, a butler and one schoolmaster, and they signed to make clear their firm opposition to the establishment of a new 'modern' school, in place of their sons attending the original foundation.

Although many writers despaired at the loss of their chance to send their offspring to Harrow, many others in the local population, on the principle of half a loaf being better than none, and after a great deal of negotiation with the Governors, did accept the establishment of a new school for their needs. It is worth remembering that the village of Harrow at this time was an island community on the Hill itself, surrounded by miles of farmland. The tollgate stood near the bottom of Peterborough Hill, and College Road and the shopping centre of today was then a gypsy encampment. The local residents' fervent hope became a viable possibility when Harrow School's income rose significantly in the early 1870s, and the Governors' concerns that a second school on the Foundation would be financially ruinous were allayed. One matter the locals did not accept, however, was the startling condescension of the name proposed: The Under-School of John Lyon.

In time the myth has developed, mainly as a result of a School Song written by Mr Gregg, of which more later, that the name actually adopted, The Lower School of John Lyon, was chosen in reference to its position further down Harrow Hill. It is an amiable idea, but false. The name was chosen to make it clear that this was a subordinate school, something less than Harrow.

However, even when the decision had been taken to erect a building for the purpose, with a handsome entrance, a hall and classrooms on the first floor, open cloisters below, the wheels ground slow.

The building was completed, initially with every window made from opaque glass, preventing any view of the outside. Happily, they had been replaced with clear glass by the time of the flag-bedecked official opening in 1876.

At the accompanying banquet, fifteen senior boys from Harrow School sang some of their School Songs, in particular 'Queen Elizabeth Sat One

Day', the song which links the Foundation inextricably with Spenser and Shakespeare and the granting of the original Charter.[11]

The John Lyon School dates its own commencement from this occasion. Certainly the boys, from then on, were Lyonians, although the title was always extended to even the earliest participants in the English Form. Mr Gregg, who was roundly praised for his sixteen-year leadership of the English Form, had magnanimously agreed to remain as an assistant master once the new school was in being and the promised Headmaster in post. In fact, however, he remained in charge for a further three years; and the boys he taught – although now in Middle Road and not The Barn on the High Street – were the boys he was already teaching. The tale of Waggle and the flaming gas, mentioned earlier, bears this out. The two masters who came running would have been Mr Gregg and M. de Witt; the avenging Head Master, whom Waggle avoided, Dr Butler of Harrow School. Only the location had changed. Some time later, Dr Butler himself recalled that the last name he had entered into the Register of boys joining the English Form was that of Owen Fisher and the date of his entry was 29th April 1879.

The first actual John Lyon boys, thirty of them, the same number as were envisaged for the original Free Grammar School in Harrow and, in turn, for the English Form, were admitted to the Lower School in September 1879. And that was the moment Mr J E Williams MA, graduate of Trinity College, Oxford and former teacher at Bedford Grammar School, took up his post as the first Headmaster of the Lower School of John Lyon. John Evans Williams, from a Glamorgan family, had been educated before attending university at Cheltenham College and in many ways he was a typical Arnoldian in his approach. One of the skills he developed when some kind of misbehaviour occurred

---

[11] They also sang Edward Bowen's rousing song, the opening verse and refrain of which run:

> When Raleigh rose to fight the foes
> We sprang to work and will;
> When Glory gave to Drake the wave,
> She gave us to the Hill.
> The ages drift in rolling tide,
> But high shall float the morn
> Adown the stream of England's pride,
> When Drake and we were born!
>
> For we began when he began,
> Our times are one;
> His glory thus shall circle us
> Till Time be done.

was to make clear the onus for improvement was on the boys themselves. He would report the infraction at Assembly and end by saying that it was a disgrace, adding, 'I can't stop it, but you can'. The recognised leaders among the boys would then deal with the matter.

A trivial note in passing: Harrow has always used the style 'Head Master'; the John Lyon School, invariably, 'Headmaster'. Until the time of writing, of course.

It took a little while, but the remarkable successes of this new school persuaded the Governors of Harrow, who were also the Governors of the Lower School of John Lyon, that their ugly duckling was, if not a swan, then a very lively lion cub, capable in due course of rivalling its older brother academically, at sport and in the quality of young men it produced.

Independent as both schools are, in the present day and for many decades the relationship between the two is and has been close and friendly, the rivalry entirely good-natured. And the two schools combine on a number of occasions.

A great deal happened, however, between the founding of the Lower School and the vibrant 600-student strong place it has become today.

CHAPTER 2

THE BIRTH
1876–1890

The official opening of what has for many years been known as the Old Building and was then, of course, brand new, took place on 29th June 1876. This new schoolhouse was not quite the shape it became later. The impressive entrance door and the protruding wing that houses it was sited differently from today, but the general appearance remains unmistakably the same. The building contractor, incidentally, died before its completion and the job was taken over by his son, a former pupil named Lander, who subsequently became a Congregational minister.

There were festive flags within and without and, as well as the small choir, Harrow furnished the occasion with the band of their School Rifles, playing assorted tunes. 'A goodly company of ladies and gentlemen assembled in the schoolroom', relieved no doubt to have achieved a tangible result from the long years of struggle and argument. They were to be further encouraged by the opening speech made by one of the Governors, Lord Verulam. He was at pains to make clear that this was the realization of John Lyon's original vision. That being taught in this place would lead to success in future life and that former pupils would be able to look back with pride and say, 'I began my life and education in the new School which was founded by John Lyon.'

This last is the view which the School itself, and generations of Lyonians and their parents, have held to firmly in all the years since. Its Governors were the same who governed Harrow School. It was (and remains) the only school to bear the Founder's name. And, among all the recent additions to the Harrow School family, the Harrow International Schools in Bangkok, Hong Kong and Beijing, it is the only one that fulfils most of the original benefactor's wishes.

Attendance at the School stayed at six days a week, with Wednesday and Saturday afternoons given over to sport. This remained the pattern until the latter part of the twentieth century.

The new institution was regarded as of sufficient importance that from 1879 events concerning it, including the annual Speech Days, were fully reported in the *Harrow Gazette*. Although, in July 1880 on the first anniversary of the School's opening, one of the Governors, Mr Charles Roundell, Member of Parliament and Old Harrovian, gave a speech saying they were still short of numbers, at the same time, he praised the quality of the results achieved by Mr Gregg, and Dr Butler added that he hoped the coming of the railway to Harrow might attract more boys to the School.

Two years later, Lord George Hamilton publicly stressed the closeness of the links between the two Schools on the Foundation and, in 1885, Dr Butler acknowledged the failure of the Governors in the past to support Dr Vaughan's efforts to start a new school, but said that now 'times had marched and the Governors had marched with them.' The same year, Percy Thornton wrote of John Lyon boys 'whether or not they rank as Harrovians proper it needs a lawyer to decide.'

As Maureen Glynn observes, there is a slight variance of view expressed by different speakers on the matter. 'Some like Roundell and Hamilton emphasise the closeness of the Upper and Lower School, others like Butler are somewhat more reticent and maybe more honest. Both are trying to appeal and placate, and enhance the Lower School in the eyes of the boys, parents and other parishioners whom it was hoped to attract to the School. Whether the School was seen for its intrinsic value or for its extrinsic value, that is its connection with Harrow School, it is difficult to say but it is no doubt true that it was probably a combination of both that caused the few parents that could afford the fees to send their boys to the School. The continued reassurances of the Speech Day speakers must have [had] some effect.'

It is fair to observe, as well, that the intentions of those in authority are often undermined by those they hope to command. Vaughan's stricture that the boys of the English Form were not to mingle with the boys of the boarding school was evidently not observed. Mr Roundell, at that first Speech Day[12], recalled the names of the boys with whom he had regularly played. He greeted them warmly as the familiar faces of old friends: Mr John Chapman, Mr William Winkley and Mr Timberlake, all his English Form contemporaries. 'I grew up with many friends like them in the six happy years I spent as a boy at Harrow, and I count it as one of my greatest privileges that it has been given me, as a Governor of Harrow School, to take part in establishing this School, and thus to render back a

---

[12] Although there had been no Speech Day for boys in the English Form, they were given prizes for good work, as the Examination Lists show.

portion of the deep debt of gratitude which I owe to the inhabitants of Harrow.'

By 1883, the number of boys attending had risen to fifty-three. While the boys were less than twelve years of age fees stood at £7 10s for residents and £9 for those from further afield, increasing once they had reached twelve to ten guineas and twelve pounds respectively.

Later, answering to the Governors, a Committee of Management for the School was established. It consisted of Harrow's Head Master, three of the Governors: Mr Roundell, Mr W H Stone and one of Gladstone's leading Ministers, the Earl Spencer; and two of the Lower School's most active and effective supporters, one nominated by the Governors, Mr T F Blackwell JP, High Sheriff of the County of Middlesex, and the other a nominee of the local School Board, County Councillor J W Paine.

James Paine had long campaigned on behalf of the local population and against its exclusion from the benefits of John Lyon's bequest, so his recruitment was astute, on the principal that it would be better to have him inside the tent rather than outside. As with Mr Blackwell, it proved of considerable, even crucial, benefit that he joined those managing the School.

Growth in the School numbers at this time was almost imperceptible: just two more by 1889, at which moment the Governors took more positive action. Action which was the direct result of propositions made by Mr Paine, fully supported by Mr Blackwell and Mr Roundell. They reduced the fees to a flat rate of £5 for all students. They increased the number of Lyon Scholarships, providing free education, from one to four each year; they advertised in the *Harrow Gazette* and, it might be thought a little late in the day, they produced the first Lower School of John Lyon Prospectus.

This said that the intention of the School was to provide 'a sound, liberal, practical education, of a commercial type, to boys intended for business'. Interestingly, Latin, previously announced as the first requirement was downgraded to 'under special circumstances only'. The range of subjects, though, was wide and certainly practical: writing, arithmetic, English grammar, composition and language; history, geography, French, German, mathematics (implying algebra and Euclid), natural science, book-keeping, shorthand, drawing, singing and scripture. These were not choices. Boys were expected to undertake them all. And to provide a minimum of one shilling each term towards the Games Fund.

The inclusion of science was not merely forward-looking, it was one of the major requirements of the Clarendon Commission appraising public schools and of the Taunton Commission a little later. At Harrow, a Scientific Society had been founded in 1865 and the subject became part of the curriculum four years later, with a building for the purpose being opened at exactly the same time as the building to house the Lower School in 1876. At the Lower School, rudimentary lessons in chemistry began soon after it came into formal existence in 1879.

Competitive sports at this time, and for some years to come, were generally conducted at the public Recreation Ground in Harrow. Informal games of one kind or another, however, including football, could be played on the field sloping down to Lower Road from below the bank which defined the western edge of the school yard. In wet weather, the open Cloisters were appropriated for the Lyonian version of the 'wall game'. The yard itself, often called the playground, and half the size it was to become later, was surfaced with clinker. On its eastern side stood the School Building and an opening onto Middle Road. The Cloisters looked out onto this yard and beyond, to the west, to a wide horizon many miles distant.

The recent changes made by the Governors resulted exactly as they wished. A rapidly increasing number of boys joined the School and soon structural alterations were needed to accommodate them. A substantial extension was planned and internal changes to the existing building, including the installation of a science laboratory, were carried through in time for Speech Day in July 1890. Headmaster Mr Williams was able to acknowledge significant help from the three most active members of the Committee of Management, instituted two years earlier, as well: Mr Roundell for providing shrubs to enhance the School grounds; Mr Blackwell, always financially generous, for helping to increase the number of library books; and Mr Paine for his constant support. He also paid tribute to two boys, Bentley and the School Captain, Tew, for their 'assistance in forming the tone and character of the School'. The anarchic ways of the English Form were being tamed.

So much so that Professor Pelham, Harrow School Governor, presenting the prizes, took the opportunity to remind the boys that 'they had a sort of right to a title of which he was proud – that of "Harrow boys" – just as much as the others on the top of the hill'. It is worth observing that this same year Percy Thornton, author of the then recent book on Harrow School, lectured at the Lower School on the history of the district.

1890 also saw another lasting change. In March, the young master brought in to teach science, Ernest Young, started a school magazine, *The Lyonian*. The sub-editors, it is interesting to see, are F C Tew and

W Bentley. Mr Williams welcomes the first edition 'with pleasure. . . . and we cannot but feel that the boys are alive to the responsibilities thrown upon them by the recently awakened interest shown in the school, and by the new and improved conditions under which it now exists.'

Mr Young, in his opening paragraph, is categorical, confident and – time has proved – correct:

March 1890 will be an eventful month in the history of our school. It is the birth-month of a school magazine, which, we venture to predict, will last as long as the name of John Lyon is remembered in Harrow. It is to be a boy's journal, supported and subscribed for by them. Its pages will be open for all matters of interest which any Lyon boy may care to discuss. It is to be a continuous chronicle of all the best efforts of our school, socially, athletically, and intellectually.

The magazine was to come out eight times a year.

It was not the first literary effort in the School's history, an Old Lyonian writing a letter to the May 1890 edition pointed out. There had been a fortnightly sheet produced by the boys for a time. And later Charlie Gregg, son of the popular master, had produced 'a very few editions' of a paper 'having a strong political character'.

The immortal 'Bottles' contributed articles upon the wrongs of the working man, whilst Major General Gogle Fox was to the fore in leaders upon the advantages of Socialism compared to the rule of a bloated aristocracy.

Those efforts were short-lived. *The Lyonian* started as it meant to go on. Within a few months, at tuppence a copy, a thousand had been sold. In the years since, the number of editions each year has, by stages, reduced to the current single production; at the same time it has grown and blossomed in size and splendour. What it has remained is largely true to Ernest Young's original recipe: it is a magazine of record for the School in all its activities, and it is a display case for the interests and creative efforts of any or all boys who attend. Stories, real and imagined, photographs, poems, jokes and riddles, contributed by the boys, and more recently as technology allows, artwork by them, too, fill its pages. The sense of vibrancy, of a proud community and of a positive, optimistic outlook are unmistakable from those first editions onwards.

From 1890 the Lower School of John Lyon was on the up.

CHAPTER 3

SPRING SUNSHINE AND UNSEASONABLE FROST
1891–1897

Evidence of the Lower School's self-confidence bolstered by enquiries from other schools, including Alleyn's at Dulwich and the thousand-strong British School in Darlington, who had appealed for advice on how to start a school magazine, was clear to see in the 1891 editions of *The Lyonian*.

An inaugural Sports Day was proposed and successfully conducted, while boys from the School were placed first or second in several races at both the Harrow Athletics and the Harrow Weald Athletic Sports competitions.

Various good public examination results were reported, among them that of Priest major who was one of only two boys in the country to be awarded a First Class Certificate in the Government's Practical Chemistry examination.

The number of boys at the School had risen to eighty-four and nearly all the newcomers were younger brothers of fellows already there. Hence Priest major was to be known in future as Priest maximus, there being three siblings now at the School. The pious editor hoped 'those elder brothers will set them a good example of genuine school-boy life'.

He also suggested that an annual reunion of Old Boys might be a good idea, strengthening those bonds of loyalty and affection which link pupils past or present as members of the same corporate body. Hardly was the suggestion made when it was taken up. As there was no organization of Old Lyonians at the time, it is proof of the magazine's wide readership that this first Old Boys' Dinner was well-attended by half-a-dozen different generations. Held at the Liberal Club[13] on the top of the Hill, it seems to have been a very lively – and very long – evening.

---

[13] Not as Harry Burcham, at the School at the time, mis-remembered, the King's Head which stood opposite the Liberal Club, where Byron Hill Road joins the High Street.

There were songs, including the National Anthem, toasts and more speeches than a modern audience might wish to sit through. But here they were greeted with unflagging laughter and applause. Mr C E Webb reported on the successes of many former pupils, now holding good positions in various branches of the Civil Service, at the Admiralty, in the Army and, referring to the same Charlie Gregg who once embraced political reform, in the Royal Navy. His speech was followed by Mr Chatham who announced, it was reported, ' "Speech is silvern but silence is golden", got up, replied quickly, and sat down. Let him be thanked.'

The evening was far from over, though. The Headmaster spoke at length and paid tribute, greeted in every case with enthusiastic applause, to the three most active members of the Committee of Management, Mr Roundell, Mr Paine and Mr Blackwell.

Thomas Blackwell JP, son of the joint founder (who bore the same names) of Crosse & Blackwell, was an outstanding philanthropist. It was the mark of his family who had been resident in the area since at least the fourteenth century, and who had donated the land that makes up both Harrow Weald Recreation Ground and Cedars Open Space to the local population. His father had started as an apprentice alongside Edmund Crosse in a food production company which, in 1829, the pair bought out and renamed, acquiring several royal patents in the years that followed. The Blackwell family lived in the house adjacent to W S Gilbert who once sent them a jocular complaint of their dog trespassing in his garden: 'please keep your pickles out of my preserve'. The Blackwells also donated the land on which St Anselm's Church, Hatch End is built and in whose churchyard the two founders of the company that made their fortune both lie buried.

As well as paying for the Church itself to be extended, Thomas Blackwell, the JP, gave generously over many years to the Lower School of John Lyon, supporting and extending scholarships, paying for building work and supplying needs as they occurred. Over and above this, Mr Williams made clear his gratitude for the sense of standing he had given the School. The connection, too, was a lasting one: Mr Blackwell's great-grandson was a boy at the School in the 1950s.

The response to the Headmaster's speech was made by Mr Paine, who was received with prolonged and deafening applause, having been praised for fighting for and obtaining many of the advantages the Lower School presently enjoyed. Councillor James Paine was a sharp and witty speaker and a political terrier who had championed the cause of the ordinary parishioners and of the Lower School relentlessly.

When, some seventy years later, new names were chosen for the School's Houses, it is a shame that the names of Paine and Blackwell were not adopted, along with Vaughan and Butler. Without those four, there would be no John Lyon School. That cannot be said of the other two men whose names were selected.

After Mr Paine there were several more speeches, including one from Mr Parkhouse, the early graduate from the English Form. With two toasts still to go at four minutes to midnight, it is remarkable that the occasion squeezed home just before the clock struck and coaches were turned back to pumpkins. The Dinner had had the desired effect, unquestionably, of cementing the bond between those who had been educated in The Barn and those who had taken their lessons at Middle Road. The feeling of a united community is palpable. The event's duration clearly did not deter, either: December 1892 saw the second Annual Dinner take place.

Before then Ernest Young, originator of *The Lyonian*, had left. An inspiring teacher, he had achieved remarkable results with the boys studying chemistry, eleven of them achieving successes this year in Practical Chemistry and twenty-one, a quarter of the School's population, in Theoretical Chemistry. Other successes included G Cram, holder of a Lyon Scholarship and B Langley, holding a Blackwell Scholarship, both achieving honours in the Cambridge Local Examinations.

Mr Young was leaving to teach at the 'Eton of Siam'. Afterwards he was to return to the Harrow Foundation. By a neat circularity, more than a hundred years later, Kevin Riley, Headmaster of the John Lyon School from 2005 to 2009 left when appointed Headmaster of the 'Harrow of Siam', but he did so without quitting the Harrow Foundation family to which the Harrow International School, Bangkok, where he took over, is related.

A regular feature of the School's calendar in the nineteenth century was Founder's Day, usually marked by a holiday. It was a movable celebration but always observed sometime during the month of October. Another regular event was the awarding of a prize for 'Schoolboy Honour'; this year, however, there were too few entries and it was withheld. The offering by one boy: 'always tell the truth, but if kept in, bunk when you get the chance', for some reason, failed to find approval.

A permanent loss to the School's staff came late in 1893. Charles John Gregg, grandson of a slave-owner in the West Indies, son of a schoolmaster, and himself the living embodiment of the Lower School's progression from ramshackle beginnings to a place of pride and achievement, died after a very brief illness at the age of fifty-four. He was remembered by one of his own schoolmates as 'the most amiable, pure, unselfish of all my friends' and these qualities had continued to personify his adult life. Ambition, in the normal sense, seemed to pass him by; after a brief period teaching at St Mark's College in Chelsea, he took over the reins at The Barn, aged twenty-one, and from then on he devoted his life to the boys of the English Form and the boys of John Lyon. His wife ran a small dame school where he would, when needed, supply some male authority if a child was becoming too difficult. His abiding qualities, however, were warmth and empathy. A Lyonian recalled that anyone caught misbehaving would be chastened by Gregg's grave and stentorian reprimand 'and then his features would softly relax, and with kindly spirit he would indulge in witticisms at the boy's expense.' A fellow teacher recorded that a firmer friend and a more sympathetic colleague never lived.

Most tellingly, perhaps, his former pupils clubbed together to found a scholarship in his name. And from respect they cancelled the year's Old Lyonian Dinner.

Mr Gregg's devotion to the School is apparent in the song he wrote to celebrate the place, the song which has been taken to say that the Lower in its title is a geographical reference rather than implying social gradations. Gregg, as can be seen, is rather more ambiguous:

> Not on the top, not on the top
> But halfway up are we,
> Fastorumque poeta, much read higher up,
> Says safest of all we be.
> Not at the bottom, nor yet at the top
> Tutissimus ibit he
> Who like us has climbed a good way up
> But is not at the top of the tree.

The next verses let us know that Virgil is studied at the Lower School, and Euclid, algebra, chemistry and physiography, otherwise physical geography, while the final verse celebrates the linguistic skills on the curriculum:

> In the garb of old Gaul
> If we are not arrayed,
> In its language we're versed – as you see.
> And Goethe we read in his native Deutsch,
> And Pitman's short 'i-n-g'.
> Then 'Stet Fortuna Domus!' Since

We live on the side of the hill,
May storms at the top and floods below
Immovable find us still.

Like all good teachers, Mr Gregg had an endless capacity to engage with his pupils. Even when they were in detention, they could tempt him into recounting stories which captured their imaginations and which would keep them enthralled until the time was virtually up. And, as with all good teachers, the boys loved to play tricks on him, most famously when they told him permission had been given for them to play cricket on Harrow's (rather sacred) Sixth Form Ground. Mr Gregg, naturally, joined them to oversee the match, only to be confronted next day by a furious Dr Butler who assured him no such permission had been either sought or granted. Nor would it be. But then, as other friends pointed out, Mr Gregg was a boy at heart himself, so having endured the discomfort of his interview with Butler, he probably quietly enjoyed the devilry that had put him in the line of fire.

One of the many letters of sympathy Mrs Gregg received on the death of her husband was from the same Dr Butler, now Master of Trinity College, Cambridge. The School marked his passing by naming all Mathematical Prizes after him. One of his last achievements, though, was in a different field. Hubert Cram, who was Head Boy, missed by one place winning the Royal Geographical Society's Silver Medal for the best paper in the Cambridge Examination for Physical Geography. Cram came second out of 4,766 candidates. The very last classes Mr Gregg had given were to him and on this subject.

It must have seemed a dark time when, after all that the staff and boys and supporters had done to establish the School, and just six months after Mr Gregg, Councillor James William Paine too died. His contribution had been immense. Only a month before his death he had made certain that a new Science Master would be appointed. It was he, more than anyone, who had influenced the Governors to halve the fees, to provide the scholarships, two for boys from Board schools, two for boys already at the Lower School, and so to turn its fortune. His voice had been the most persistent and most effective in lambasting the Governors when there was no Lower School. And like Mr Blackwell, he contributed from his own pocket in support of the place once it had come into existence.

The boys were not unaware of what he had done for them and Mr Paine's parents found the wreath they had collected for and sent 'as a tribute of affectionate regard and esteem to the memory of one who was their devoted friend and helper', the most touching they received.

The life of the School, of course, continued. Sport had become more organized and produced some fine performers. J D Hartley, a studious looking boy, one of the editors of *The Lyonian*, belied his appearance by also being for three years Captain of Football, being Captain of Cricket with a couple of centuries to his name, and, on the track, Champion Athlete of the School. Known as Dawson, and with more achievements to come, he was also Captain of the School.

More fine cricket results followed. In 1894 the School team defeated Pinner Commercial School, later to be renamed Royal Commercial Travellers' School, by an innings and 24 runs; and they enjoyed an even more comprehensive victory over All Souls Cricket Club, scoring 158 runs when first put in, one boy, Parker, making 93 not out, while the opposition managed just 29 runs in their first innings and 16 in their second. In the course of the season, the team played eighteen matches, winning all but four.

This was the first year that sports 'colours' are recorded. First to Titchener, King and Carter for football, where success seemed to follow the same pattern as in cricket: the School beat Wembley Reserves 14 goals to 1. With the same Parker scoring seven of them.

They handsomely beat the Commercial School on the football pitch, as well, and when the return match was played, the opposition conformed to the worst stereotype of commercial travellers: they reduced the size of the actual goals. They lowered the bar and shrank the width by 25 per cent.

They still lost.

It was also the first year that group photographs of the boys were taken. Oddly, this was done in December, presumably because this was when the peripatetic photographer[14] was in the area. A group of younger boys in caps of various designs clearly feel the chill as they sit outside the open Cloisters. Unsurprising, since the Christmas period was described as very seasonable, with plenty of opportunity to skate on the frozen Ducker, Harrow's outdoor swimming pool, and to toboggan on the fields below the School.

Mr E H Butt, who had replaced Mr Gregg, took over responsibility for the school magazine, and at this moment another man of lasting

---

[14] The photographer in question, Wilhelm Carl Stackemann, who lived a life of near and actual bankruptcy, moved with his wife and several children usually on an annual basis. He, and in later years his eldest son, specialized in taking school and other group photographs as they travelled the country. In 1893 the family was based in Catford, moving to Wandsworth in 1895.

significance to the School joined its staff of just four masters: Mr F
Swainson. At this time, too, the first seven boys in the School's history
were entered for the Cambridge Local Examinations and a boy named as
R H Bartlett, whose scholarship at John Lyon had been extended thanks
to Mr Blackwell, achieved a significant result in the South Kensington
science examinations, though falling short of winning one of the two
National Scholarships. He had earlier sat and passed sixteen science and
arts examinations, roughly equivalent to today's GCSEs, including one
for honours in chemistry. Mr Butt recorded that 'only those who have
done the same kind of work know what constant application has been
necessary for the purpose of obtaining even the amount of knowledge for
a pass in so many subjects'. All of this achieved after a four-mile walk in all
weathers from his home in Northolt and another four miles when he
returned at the end of each school day.

The first ever Gregg Mathematical Scholarship was conferred on the
Head Boy, C W Parkhouse, son of one of Mr Gregg's favourite pupils,
and Bartlett had his name added to the School's Roll of Honour, one of
four boys to enjoy the privilege. In the course of time, Bartlett was to
prove just how far a 'poor parishioner' could go.

These positives, such as they were, were welcome. Behind the scenes,
there were difficulties. The Governors were in straitened circumstances,
not for the first time in the history of the Harrow Foundation. Much of
the wealth bestowed by parents on Harrow School went, owing to its
historical structure, to the House Masters, rather than the School itself.
The income from the Lower School was not enough to cover its outgoings
and successive reports mentioned the very poor pay given to its staff.

At Speech Day 1895, Sir Archibald Geikie, presenting the prizes, spoke
of the financial limitations the Governors were suffering but thought that
they would be able treat the Lower School with more liberality in future.
When this was enthusiastically received, he had to backtrack immediately,
saying he had no authority or message from the Governors, this was just
his feeling. Mr Blackwell, speaking briefly after him, expressed his own
anxiety about this, making it clear that more rooms were needed for the
School to function at its best.

Meanwhile, sport continued well, with occasional reverses, but mainly
victories on both kinds of pitch. Notably, the School defeated the London
and Northwest Railway team by three goals to two, Mr Butt commenting
that it was 'distinctly encouraging, as the disparity in age and physique
was very marked'. Thereafter, they lost the next five matches, 'not quite
the form for the John Lyon School'.

Old Lyonians improved the sporting image. In May 1896, Dawson Hartley was awarded the *Harrow Gazette*'s cup as the best all-round footballer in the district, while the following month, the *Harrow Observer* started a series of articles on successful local cricketers by featuring Old Boy Mr H Woodbridge. He had shared in a record first wicket stand for Harrow Town of 275 runs and had picked up several centuries since. Then, back at the School, winning ways returned with all three cricket matches in the bag, two of them by more than an innings.

Another Old Lyonian, the perfect example of social and educational mobility, remarkable for his achievements and for the rarity of such opportunity, was Ernest Batchelor. Winning a Blackwell Scholarship from a humble Board School, he was admitted to the Lower School. From there, in time, he won a further Blackwell Scholarship taking him to Harrow School. Now, as an Old Lyonian and an Old Harrovian, he had gained 26th place in the list of 62 Indian Civil Service appointments. Not only that, he had just secured victory for Cambridge in the Varsity Athletics Match, by winning the long jump with a leap of 22 feet 7 inches. The current winners of Lyon Scholarships, the internal bursaries at the Lower School, were Grapes and Brown, 'with Memory coming a good third' – which you might think, was only to be expected.

The financial uncertainties underlying the School, however, persisted. The population of Harrow and Wealdstone – the political authority for the whole area being at this time Wealdstone Urban District Council – had grown to around 22,000. This naturally increased the pressure for more school places, but as things were, the Lower School had difficulty accommodating the number it already had. At Speech Day in 1896, Mr Blackwell outlined the Governors' historic problems regarding money, saying he had always found them sympathetic to the School's needs but often not able to respond positively. Now he could report better news. They were willing to make a grant for an enlargement of the School building, so that in future 120 boys could be taught in appropriate surroundings. What he did not say was that the bulk of the expense for this would be borne by himself. With his customary generosity, the High Sheriff may be thought to have forced the Governors' hand a little, by giving £1000 for the building work to be undertaken. The equivalent sum, in terms of the time when this is being written (2012), would be approaching half a million pounds.

The improvements were swiftly commenced.

The south end of the existing building was extended to include a substantial internal staircase, with the small wing containing the main entrance door moved to give onto it. From there the stairs led down to a groundfloor classroom and up to another classroom immediately above it, while narrower stairs led up further to a small study, above the entrance hall itself. This hallway also gave, to the opposite side, onto the existing high-ceilinged double room. The roof height, architectural style and choice of bricks for the extension so matched the existing edifice as to make it near impossible, as Eric Morecambe might have said, to see the join.

Away from the School it was noted that Queen Victoria had achieved the longest reign in British history while the weather had managed the longest rain anyone could remember, the same autumn. Bartlett was now working in the laboratories of Messrs Burt, Boulton and Haywood in Silvertown, while Charlie Parkhouse, about to leave, had his portrait featured in both the *Harrow Observer* and *The Lyonian*. The warmth of feeling between staff and boys, always apparent, was even clearer now that Frederick Swainson, or 'Cherry' as he was known, the newest of the masters, took over editing the School magazine: of C W Parkhouse's departure, he wrote, 'if anyone has ever obtained the suffrages of boys and masters alike, he has'.

The *Wealdstone Press* reported that 'the results of the Cambridge University Local Examinations last year showed the Lower School of John Lyon was well to the front, but this year they have done even better still and masters, boys and parents alike are to be congratulated'. For the first time boys had been entered for the senior examinations where candidates might be up to nineteen years old. Despite being substantially younger, two John Lyon boys had obtained honours. The juniors did well, too, and H B Gates, coming in the top section of the First Class was in a group of 140 who ranked highest out of more than four thousand entrants.

With Mr Young back from Siam and giving two highly popular talks at the School about his travels; with the Headmaster celebrating the joys of taking an interest in 'the glorious game' by entertaining thirty of the School's cricketers to supper in the Pavilion; with Batchelor now competing for his London Club against Cambridge University and helping to beat his alma mater; with the scientist Bartlett now winning a prize and the bronze medal for being placed second in the City and Guilds examination list; and with Mr Oglesby thanking the prize presenter on Sports Day by saying that his own son had profited so much by attending the Lower School that if he had a dozen boys he would send every one of them there; with all that, it might be thought that the sun was out and calm waters lay ahead.

Then, late in 1897, came the death of Dr Charles Vaughan, Dean of Llandaff Cathedral, iconic Head Master of Harrow and the one disciple of John Lyon who ensured his original intention came to fruition.

The Headmaster, Mr Williams, recalled in detail the encomium given to Dr Vaughan by Mr Roundell, the Member of Parliament who was a Governor and active member of the Committee of Management, back on the occasion of the School's first Speech Day, actually in 1880, although Mr Williams mis-remembered it as being in 1879. He had reminded boys that the germ of this School was the English Form instituted by Dr Vaughan, that the institution was looked on coldly by the then authorities, and that the effect of the Public Schools Act and Vaughan's persistence had been to ensure the Harrow Governors 'had given a permanent and statutory form' to the idea of the Lower School.

How permanent, however, was about to be tested.

CHAPTER 4

THE FIRE THAT PROVES
1898–1908

The School year opened in January 1898 with the physical changes to the building completed and enlarged photo-portraits of the three stalwarts, Charles Gregg, Thomas Blackwell and James Paine on the walls of the entrance hall.

J E Williams, however, the Headmaster who had steered the School from its formal beginning was suffering from stress and, later the same month, in something of a surprise, he offered his resignation to the Governors. Like Gregg, who had so determinedly kept the English Form going, he was a deeply religious man and this had informed, often quite overtly, his advice to the boys. One of his habits was to give a précis version of Dr Vaughan's sermons in Harrow School chapel the previous Sunday, to his listeners at the Lower School. An emphasis on moral rectitude ran through almost all education at the time and was a regular theme in the books written for children. It was very much in the air Williams had breathed at Trinity, Oxford, where John Percival, another keen disciple of Dr Arnold, had been elected President at exactly the same time that Mr Williams had assumed leadership of the Lower School. But Williams was always keen, too, to broaden horizons and saw sport especially as a way of helping boys to bond and to give them lasting pleasure. During his headship, he instigated extra-curricular activities that were not the norm: rambles, after-school lectures on a wide range of topics and, of course, he presided over a remarkable degree of academic success which for many Lyonians persisted in their subsequent lives.

If his going was a surprise, so was the choice of his successor. The appointment of Ernest Young, Bachelor of Science and Fellow of the Royal Geographical Society, just back from Siam, saw the beginning of what was to be a pattern lasting to the middle of the twentieth century. Each next Headmaster was a former assistant master. Unlike the two who followed him, Young had been elsewhere in two separate posts for six years; and he was, as his name proclaimed, remarkably youthful for the promotion. He was twenty-eight years old.

The advantage of appointing from within was that each next man at the helm knew the School's history, already knew the boys, presumably knew the problems and no doubt had ideas of his own as to how improvements could be made, where opportunities lay. For the School, too, there was the assurance of genuine loyalty, not to be undervalued in the Lower School's survival stakes. It was a survival, despite some of the public utterances, which came to be in considerable doubt.

Speech Day in 1900 heard complaints that the Governors had not followed Mr Blackwell's generous treatment of the School and that the formers' cry of 'no money' was becoming tiresome. Nonetheless, as the new century dawned, many things seemed to be going well. There was plenty of imperial trumpeting to accompany the war against the Boers in South Africa. A number of Old Boys were fighting there and a similar spirit informed a poem written by A P Kimber, a boy in his last term at the School. His final verse read:

> Then shall Lyon's name stand for England staunch and tried,
> Ne'er to Lyon's heart and muscle shall Right's battle be denied,
> Then in Lyon's dearest England, freedom great and good shall stay.
> British Lyons be her bulwarks, giants in sports and minds for aye.

In 1901 a School Cadet Corps was announced, with details of how it would be regulated, and although it did not properly come into being, a couple of years later a description of the boys doing arms drill under the orders of Mr Godwin, the master instigating the Corps, appears in the magazine.

At the same time, Mr Young was able to lead a school where academic results continued to improve. He formalized the wide-ranging after-school lectures into a definite programme, with a small charge to younger boys, but free to the older ones. He started a cycle club, and early in his reign, a very active boy, Oliver Gurney, one of several family members who attended the School, and whose father was organist at St Mary's and effectively Music Master at the School, began the Lyon Music Society.

Mr Young organized and took part in camping holidays in the summer to provide both adventure and a greater awareness of the natural world. They were advertised by Cherry Swainson with an insouciance no present day staff member would dare employ:

. . . mothers may remain easy, cradled in the thought that dear Arthur is taking no harm. His wants, foibles and failings have all been provided for, and if he does get washed out to sea on the broad flood of the Arun, it is perfectly obvious that he was born for that fate.

The annual Examiner's report was highly complimentary. When the Examiner begins by emphasising the pleasure he had in scrutinizing the School for a second year, you know matters are going well. He praised the fact that the 'prevailing features of worthy effort alike in duty and recreation, of sympathy which is not permitted to degenerate into slackness or over-indulgence and of admirable system and method in the general routine – of which the best instance is the monthly examination – were no less in evidence than before.' The Report then goes through each subject taught, mentioning the high achievers and recording class average marks with uniform expressions of satisfaction; and special mention is made of the fine example given by the sixth-formers.

Confidence was clearly high. Numbers increased to 145. After a spell in the doldrums, football results once more were impressive. In 1902 the First Eleven played twenty-three matches, winning eighteen and losing only three. Their goal tally was 115 for, to only 36 against. It goes without saying that the highest scorer, with 51 goals to his name, was yet another Woodbridge, Stanley 'the best centre forward the School has had'. Special blazers were awarded for members of the School's First and Second Elevens.

School caps became the first item of clothing to be prescribed for all boys. It was felt that the nature of jackets, trousers and shirts could not be dictated, but that an indentifying cap in Harrow blue cloth with a rampant lion in red silk embroidered above the peak would proclaim the School. This was described as a two-edged sword. In public, good behaviour would redound to its credit; poor behaviour would harm its reputation and knowledge of this should act as a restraint on the wearer. Caps had in fact been required somewhat earlier. Around 1890, a design of dark blue with red piping had been laid down, with the lion on its front only for boys in either of the First Elevens, but the photograph of younger boys in 1894 shows a disparity of design. It would appear that over the next few years, actually wearing a cap at all had fallen by the wayside.

News of Old Boys of course still features with the formation of the Old Lyonian Football Club and the mentions of H E Dyson taking First Prizes in both Theoretical and Practical Chemistry at University College, London, and R H Bartlett achieving more success, an Associate of the Royal College of Science now, with a languid comment recalling the time when 'he and Cram, C Parkhouse and Coombs used to take the cream of the prize list out of Harrow, for none of the quartet was a Harrow boy'. Just a hint of pleasurable triumphalism, perhaps.

Warm tributes were paid in *The Lyonian* to three of the leavers, the same Stanley Woodbridge already mentioned, another good sportsman Sidney Parker – with the lament that neither had a brother now to follow them – and to Joseph Gurney. He, wrote Mr Swainson, 'was no athlete, though he sometimes donned the Pinner colours, but in the School he made a good monitor and presided over the library as though he were Sir Richard Garnett and our collection the British Museum.'

The Library had recently increased considerably in size with donations, and sometimes purchases from the Library Fund, of scores of books. Some the sort that would clearly appeal to adolescent boys, many others either English classics or indeed classical texts, from Pliny to Lucian with a couple of dozen more obvious choices besides. Soon these were to be housed in the now fully enclosed Cloisters, so that the shelves should be easily accessible to every member of the School.

A substantial art collection was being garnered, too. Mostly engravings, but this year including a watercolour of cottages in Wealdstone, by a member of the Royal College of Art.

Both collections were remarked on by the School Examiner as valuable tools to enliven the often dry process of learning.

A museum was also begun, the collection added to term by term, of odd and interesting artefacts, archaeological items and natural specimens. Some are everyday, others esoteric and rarer, but the collection itself, augmented by the boys' own efforts, demonstrates a desire to discover, to examine, to note, which is almost eighteenth century in its endeavour. The same spirit that informed the decision, half-a-century later, that first formers should read Gilbert White's *Natural History of Selborne* as a set book. Although by then museum and art collections had vanished entirely.

The farewell to Joseph Gurney referred to his position in the School as a Monitor. This was a role given to certain senior boys, common to public schools from the days of Dr Arnold at Rugby, and now introduced at the John Lyon School by Mr Young. At this time there were rarely more than two, in addition of course to the School Captain, the most prestigious position. Introducing the rank had a twofold advantage. As numbers at the School grew, it took some of the disciplinary responsibility from the shoulders of the masters and it gave boys another target to aim for. As well as academic and sporting distinction, there was this reward for behaving maturely, for loyal commitment to the values and good running of the establishment. It provided an opportunity, as did being Librarian, or secretary of a society, or captain of a team, to understand the nature of management and to exercise varying degrees of judgment and authority, and to learn to do so in a responsible way.

If the tributes to succeeding Monitors and School Captains are anything to go by, the system from the beginning worked well.

While on all fronts the School appeared to be progressing handsomely, there were at the same time disturbing external pressures at work. A Royal Commission in 1895 had favoured, reasonably enough, the establishment of a system of state education. To this end, four years later, the government departments for Science and Art and for Education were merged with the Charity Commissioners to become the Board of Education. It was under the aegis of this Board that the encouraging inspections of the Lower School had been carried out.

By 1903, however, the tone changed.

The Inspection Report that year deemed the School accommodation unsatisfactory and a tussle between the Governors, who were struggling financially, and the Board of Education which was trying to force their hand began. It was to last for years.

The Board's underlying plan was that the School should become part of the state network. To this end, the Governors should immediately improve and greatly increase the facilities. Alternatively, this enhancement should be done in concert with the County Council. Given that this was a time of severe national recession with businesses failing, theatres closing and worse, the apparent choice was between the School closing, the Governors not being able to afford the improvements, or it continuing, having been taken over by the state.

Curiously, the origin of the Board's policy, indeed of the Board's own existence, lay in the very Public Schools' Commission which had brought the John Lyon School into being. The Commission's inspectors had revealed numerous instances of corruption including, as Jonathan Gathorne-Hardy has noted, thirty-eight schools in the north-east alone with endowments available to them for the provision of education in the classics, but without a single pupil between them. Not to mention many examples of institutions that did exist but where large amounts of their funds were being diverted from their proper purpose to line the pockets of a few individuals. The total sum of money being misappropriated one way or another was enormous and the Commission designed a detailed plan for it to be put to use. The proposal was for a national system of secondary education, paid for from this money, regulated by Parliament and free to boys and girls of all classes. It was this plan that the 1895 Royal Commission sought to bring to fruition.

Whether, in the light of this danger to their own School, the sight of the dagger that despatched Wat Tyler excited murderous thoughts among John Lyon boys when they visited Fishmongers' Hall is not known. It would not have been surprising if it had.[15] Considerable bitterness arose from the threat to a School which Harrow parishioners had fought so long and so hard to get. Extraordinary difficulties had been encountered and overcome in the half-century of its existence and considerable pride was taken in its achievements. Modest those achievements may have been, but to the ordinary folk of Harrow and Wealdstone, of Pinner and Wembley, they were nothing like as modest as the efforts of Parliament in supporting, or rather failing to support, their claim for the sort of school John Lyon had originally envisaged.

The Governors, despite their difficulties, proved both diplomatic and positive. They proposed, by renting the Baptist Chapel on Byron Hill, to increase the School's capacity to three hundred and they negotiated a grant from Middlesex County Council to help bring this about, while maintaining the School's independence. Sir Kenelm Digby, Under-Secretary at the Home Department and Old Harrovian, announced this at Speech Day 1904, while alluding at the same time to the prevailing 'tightness of money'.

The Education Board's view remained that the site of the School was incapable of effective development. Time has shown how lacking in imagination they were, but theirs was the leverage at this period and the tug-of-war was to continue.

The Board's view also ignored the fact that there was, in effect, a satellite establishment actually in existence at this time. Just around the corner, Byron Hill School took boys for the two years before they were admitted to the Lower School. Technically an independent institution, discipline was administered – and it was remembered as being severe – by the Headmaster of John Lyon: a replication of the arrangement that had pertained in the days of the English Form and the Head Master of Harrow.[16]

---

[15] A Royal Inquiry in 1382 into the Peasants' Revolt proved that Harrow people participated in the uprising. One of its victims was, according to Froissart, a merchant named Richarde Lyon, formerly Tyler's master, who was killed. He is likely to have been a direct ancestor of John Lyon since another John Lyon related to Richarde was already recorded as a property owner in the Harrow area.

[16] Remembered fifty years later by F E Woodbridge who was at the Lower School in 1905, and whose father was one of those original five Woodbridges in the English Form. See also Appendix 3.

Meanwhile daily life proceeded much as before. Edgar Rayner, one of three brothers, takes over from the second of John Parkhouse's sons as Captain of the School. Dr Dawson Hartley, erstwhile Captain of School, Cricket and Football, and Lyon Scholar to boot, cements dynasties by marrying Margaret Perrin, all of whose seven brothers had been at the School. In the same spirit, George Perrin of Sudbury marries Grace Parkhouse of Pinner, while the latest of the Parkhouse boys at the School captains the cricket eleven.

His fellows register their disappointment at the blazer awarded for cricket colours, described as 'begging-the-question' blue with orange-tawny trimming. The question begged was 'what's the good of struggling for those colours?' The School responds with a design which is more welcome and essentially remains the same today, though for all boys, not just the cricket eleven: the darker, more attractive, Harrow blue cloth with a red lion rampant on the pocket.

Sport continues with extraordinary success. A win of fifteen-nil at football is followed by one of fourteen-nil. Similar results, and these are against schools like Haberdashers', Royal Masonic, William Ellis, Mercers', schools often with many more boys to choose from and, at this time, far better facilities, obtain in cricket. The man behind these results is P L Godwin, who joined the staff in 1899 to teach the first and second forms. Clearly ambitious and something of a disciplinarian – boys had been known to hide in the boilerhouse to avoid the regular drill sessions he conducted – he nonetheless appears to have been generally popular. He had early taken an interest in athletics and shortly after took responsibility for all sport in the School. Mr Godwin held a commission in the Cadet branch of the Royal Fusiliers and had risen in eighteen months from Second Lieutenant to Captain, an unusually swift promotion in peacetime. He led the Fusiliers' shooting team at Bisley and was, in time, to teach musketry to both the Irish and the Coldstream Guards.

One of his regrets this year, 1905, would have been the departure of H A Neale. Known to everyone as 'Pocket', presumably as that was somewhere he could comfortably fit, he was an outstanding footballer, regularly eulogized in the local press as 'so many inches of solid pluck' and 'for his inches he is a little terror'. Thought to be the smallest boy ever admitted to the Lower School, he managed, on one occasion, to play an opposing winger who was six foot two inches (188 centimetres) tall completely out of the game.

Horace Neale was to remain, like so many Old Boys, in regular touch with the School in the years ahead.

Meanwhile, Mr Williams returned, not for the first time, to give a lecture on Canada, after which it is reported that 'we all wanted to emigrate'. And it is remarkable how many former members of the School had done so. Descriptions of their lives came back not just from Old Boys farming in Manitoba, in business in Ontario or serving with the Mounties in Edmonton, Alberta, but from Australia, South Africa, Hungary, Germany, Austria, Chile (with a strong plea to spell the country that way and not, as often then, Chili); from India and Argentina; from Casper, Wyoming and, from another Perrin, Robert this time, in Savannah, Georgia.

Foreign experience came, too, from the life story of the School's long-time French master, M. Belfond. In the previous century he had served as a volunteer in the Franco-Prussian War and had endured the privations of guarding Paris during the infamous siege of 1870. Hours standing in deep snow, having had no food all day and the only prospect of having any being horse if lucky, cat, palatable if well-prepared, or rat, not highly rated, bred in him a stoicism and patience evidently appreciated by generations of John Lyon boys. His remarkable claim was that in twenty years he had never had an argumentative word with any of the boys he taught. When someone misbehaved, one of his pupils recalled seventy years later, 'he reproved the culprit with the words, "Boy! Stand on the form. I will report you to the Headmaster." The threat, however, was never carried out for, if the footsteps of the Head were heard approaching the room, with a downward wave of the hand to the standing culprit came the words "Sit down, boy."'

As long serving was Mr Chaplin, the School caretaker. His earlier life had been, if anything, more colourful the M. Belfond's. After running away from an apprenticeship in Bradford and spending time working on a farm, he emigrated with his wife and two daughters as part of some project to colonize Paraguay. There, they nearly starved, living almost exclusively on maize, and with all three women ill, he brought his family by stages to Buenos Aires to take passage for home[17]. There a falling out with the ship's captain led to a fist fight, Chaplin's arrest and appearance before a magistrate who found in his favour, banning the captain from taking his next three voyages. After three years spent working in Buenos Aires Mr Chaplin, with his fully recovered family, returned to England, and settled in Harrow where, for a while, he took a job on Sheepcote Farm. After this he moved to his present post, and the boy writing up the

[17] The full and even more complex story is to be found in *The Lyonian* for March 1905, pages 10–13, written up by sub-editor Stanley Parkhouse.

interview attested from his own direct experience, he remained as hale and strong as when he began at John Lyon, two decades before.

Boys were constantly stimulated to look outwards. Not only by these many tales from foreign parts, but by a variety of trips and by other lectures. In one term alone these comprised visits to the remains of monasteries in London; to Stratford-on-Avon; the British Museum; the National Gallery; and talks on Alfred the Great, Paris, Shakespeare as a Londoner, the Press, and the British navy from the time of Alfred to that of Mary Tudor.

The following term began with a talk on one of the most celebrated of *Punch* cartoonists, John Leech.[18] Illustrated with slides, as many of these talks were, it went down well with its young audience. For one particular boy it would have had a special interest. He was often praised for his draughtsmanship and ability with a brush or pencil and a promising future was predicted for him. Born in the London area of an Austrian father and a French mother, Max Hofler did not disappoint. In later years he was famed principally for his landscapes and city views, mostly but not exclusively of places around England. He was a founder member of two groups of painters, the Harrow Group and the Wapping Group, was a member of the Royal Institute of Water Colourists and his work was hung several times at the Royal Academy.

Although the large majority of boys at the School were of historically native stock, there was a sprinkling, even in the early days, of boys whose parents originated elsewhere, among them three members of the Abbati family, the brothers Breukelman, Seah the Chinese boy, Dubois, Gossard and Percy Guterbock; not to mention F M Seifert, Eugen Koolz and of course, back in the English Form, 'Malacca'.

As the first decade of the twentieth century progressed, German returned to the syllabus, joining French and Latin as languages on the regular curriculum. As the decade progressed, too, more and more pressure was put on the Governors by the Education Board to increase the money spent on the Lower School or to close it. In 1907 the Inspectors' report declared the School of 'very doubtful value' because of its 'unsatisfactory and inadequate premises' and its 'underpaid and overworked teachers'. The next year the Board was demanding the number of boys attending be reduced, on pain of losing their grant. And so they were. From 159 the total returned to a mere one hundred and

---

[18] Leech's most celebrated cartoon is probably the one that depicts two rough-looking miners spotting an interloper. 'Here's a stranger. What shall we do wi' un?' says one, getting the reply, 'Where's 'alf a brick?'.

the extra space the Governors had been pressed to hire was given up. What benefit this was to the boys now excluded or to those remaining it is difficult to fathom.

At the same time, the School continued in its usual determined and positive way, recording that an earlier pupil had come 70th out of a thousand candidates in the Civil Service examinations; that Arthur Rackham, elder brother of the current School Captain, had won the Organ Prize at the Guildhall School of Music and had been made an Associate of the Royal College of Organists, while another Old Lyonian, C H S Duncan, had won the Lewis Organ Scholarship at the Royal Academy of Music; that Francis Tickle, a future School Captain, had delivered a paper on New Zealand at a Victoria League meeting; and, with what seems sublime irrelevance, that there were currently 17,499 cattle in the county of Middlesex.

It is possible that the last piece of information resulted from the same spirit of enquiry which kept adding items to the School museum and prompted the foundation now of a Scientific Society at the School. A Rifle Club, too, organized by the redoubtable Captain Godwin, comes into existence and holds an extensive Challenge Cup Competition with the Old Boys. The arts are not forgotten and the fifth and sixth forms go to see the great actress, Ellen Terry, in *The Merry Wives of Windsor*.[19]

The following year brought more quite apparent success.

For some years, members of the School had spent part of the summer holiday at camps which provided adventure and outdoor experience. This had been the time, after all, when Baden-Powell was formulating his ideas for an organization which would give a healthy and practical outlet for youthful energies along the same sort of lines. Ernest Young, the initiator of the School's adventurous holidays, was a friend of Baden-Powell's and in the 1920s was for several years editor of the magazine, *The Scouter*. In 1908, when B-P formally launched the Boy Scout movement, John Lyon boys went to Marchwood, to a camp run on naval lines, a change from previous years when they had attended at Army-run Bisley. This year, sporting competition between youngsters from a range of schools produced the following results. Norman Bowden of the Lower School took the Challenge Cup, as well he might, having won the Marathon, the mile, 440 yards, 220 yards and 100 yards races; Fraser, of the School,

---

[19] Keeping with esoteric facts: the part of the Page, Robin, in that production was played by a young girl, Audrey Cameron. Sixty years later when she was a widely respected, retired BBC Radio producer, she returned to acting and appeared at the Royal Lyceum Theatre, Edinburgh in *Toad of Toad Hall*, directed by the present writer.

came first in the high jump; first and second crews in the rowing race were predominately Lyonian and the John Aird Cup for the school with most points went to the John Lyon School.

Sport had a slightly more deleterious effect on one School event, however. At Speech Day in 1908 there was a marked absence among parents, particularly fathers. Perhaps the most famous Olympic Marathon of modern times, the one when the Italian runner Pietri collapsed after entering the stadium and was helped up, coincided with the occasion. With the temperature in the high seventies (26 degrees centigrade) the route passed through Pinner, along Lowlands Road, turning into Sheepcote Road and then on to White City. With misplaced priorities, many of the fathers found the temptation to applaud the runners, rather than their offspring, too much to resist. Speech Day, after all, came round every year; the Olympics once in a lifetime, if you were lucky.

What they missed was that the School's sporting success was matched in the academic field. In the matriculation results of London University where the School usually had three or four successes, eleven achieved that level of exemption, a larger number than was gained by any school in England in that set of examinations. To which could be added the achievement of W J Millar, coming top out of three hundred candidates for entrance to Finsbury Technical College and being awarded a scholarship.

While these successes must have been heartening for all directly concerned, they made clear that the Education Board's assessment that the School was 'of doubtful value' was itself wide of any mark and derived from a socio-political agenda rather than any objective assessment.

The anger felt by the good people of Harrow was about to reach boiling point.

CHAPTER 5

RUMOURS OF WARS
1909–1914

There were many irate responses to developments in the complex and debilitating negotiations between the Governors and the County Council with regard to the existing School and the proposed expansion of secondary level education. The two local papers, the *Harrow Gazette* and the *Harrow Observer* reverberated with angry letters and articles. In Maureen Glynn's words, 'Harrow was in uproar'.

Historically, the Governors had provided the Lower School with funding of £400 a year or more. Sometimes it had been £500, on occasion this had escalated for a particular reason to £800. Now the Council wished the four hundred pounds to go to the new school which would cater for all the local youth, whether or not that turned out to be an enlarged and re-sited John Lyon School or, as appeared more likely, a new institution altogether. The corollary to the latter alternative being the extinction of the existing School.

The Governors hoped that, in agreeing to this, they would discharge their duties under the Elizabethan charter and the requirements of the Public Schools' Act. They undoubtedly hoped, too, that they would rid themselves of a long-lasting notably unpleasant headache. They even went so far as to state they would provide that level of funding to whichever institution 'in perpetuity'.

They were then informed this would require the agreement of the Privy Council, since it was only possible after a revision of the original statutes. The Governors were prepared to proceed in seeking that permission, so long as the local people did not object. Whereupon two local Councillors got up a petition to oppose the action. Ironies here abound, since they were Labour Councillors and their action would be likely to stymie the move, in Harrow at least, toward the provision of nationwide secondary education. The number signing the petition was less than 250, but they were enough to persuade the Governors to withdraw their offer, for the very good reason that the latter could not afford a long-drawn-out legal enquiry to settle the matter.

Alderman Carlyon, who had been for some time a member of the School's Committee of Management responded to an article declaring the petition had caused the sum of money granted to the Lower School to be lost, and the fate of the School itself to be effectively sealed: he denied that this was so. He said that there 'was not the slightest case to declare [it] lost for ever' and that the parishioners need have no fear. A message hardly reinforced by his resignation from the Committee of Management almost immediately afterwards. Especially as he then accepted the Chairmanship of the Governors at the new County School, the site for which was selected at the beginning of June 1909.

The next month at Speech Day, Dr Leaf, Chairman of the Management Committee, announced a steep increase in the School fees of four pounds a year per pupil, since legal advice they had now received precluded the Governors from continuing to provide the annual subsidy of four hundred pounds or more.

Matters could hardly have looked darker for the John Lyon School. Soon a new school, well equipped and charging much lower fees (though not free as had been the original idea), would be launched. The Governors' plan was clear and logical. The John Lyon School would have to be closed, barely more than thirty years after its formal opening.

The blow must have seemed all the more savage when, in the summer 1910, with the County School finished and about to admit pupils, the Education Authority announced the appointment of its first Headmaster: Mr Ernest Young BSc FRGS.

With Shakespearean aptness, even the weather decided to offer the worst of omens. On 7th June a cyclone hit Harrow. The twister tore up trees and threw them fifty feet into the air, people walking along found themselves suddenly carried up to two hundred yards away. The upside was that, surprisingly, there were no fatalities. While on the School front, the Governors did their best to soften the impact of Mr Young's going by announcing they were, in future, committed to providing the four hundred pounds a year to create scholarships for the very local boys John Lyon had intended to benefit and that these scholarships would be 'tenable at Harrow School'. If an insufficient number of boys took up the offer, then the money would be available for scholarships at Harrow County School where there was already a link with Mr Young, or, if need be, at any other Middlesex school.

Young resigned from his old post that December and later in the month the parents of John Lyon boys were in for another shock. The *Harrow Gazette* carried a substantial advertisement for the County

School, inviting boys to apply and quoting fees that were less than a quarter of those at the Lower School. That was not the surprise. The surprise was that immediately below, there was another advertisement. The Governors of Harrow School had placed a similar one of their own, announcing Entrance Examinations for places at the Lower School of John Lyon, where boys might be prepared for scholarships at Harrow and quoting immediately beneath its title the motto shared by both schools: Stet Fortuna Domus. May good fortune remain with the house. The Headmaster of the Lower School was given as Mr E H Butt.

It looks as though the Governors were trying to ride two horses, waiting to see which would go on.

Doubtless attracted by the lower fees and the better facilities, some boys left to go to the County School and Major Godwin, as he now was, joined them at the new establishment. If, as must have been the case, the remaining staff and boys at John Lyon had a sharp sense of dereliction, betrayal even, they had the grace and self-control not to show it. *The Lyonian* magazine paid generous tribute and wished them all well. There were no letters to the press, no recriminations.

While these dramas played out, the internal life of the School continued in the best English manner, seemingly oblivious that anything untoward might be happening. At the behest of the Education Board, the school day had been reduced since 1908 to the hours of 9.00am until 12.30pm and from 2.00pm until 4.00pm and as a result of the required reduction in numbers, boys now entered at the age of thirteen.

As we have seen, achievements both on the field and in the study continued remarkably well. Drama flourished with Mr T C Martin 'stage managing' – the term used quite differently from today to signify that he directed the play – Shakespeare's *Twelfth Night*. One boy, Francis Tickle, scored a particular success in the part of Toby Belch and there was a substantial family input to the production: his father and sister performed in the orchestra that accompanied the performance and his brother, who had just joined the School, played a diminutive Sea Captain. Francis, or Frank as he came to be known, enjoyed an even bigger success a little later, receiving high praise for his performance in the title role of *Henry V*.

More tribute is paid to him as School Captain when he leaves for a career in business. Not one he followed for too long however. In the course of the next few years, he appears often in productions mounted by the Old Lyonians. Then he takes the plunge and becomes the first boy from the School to become a professional actor and as such enjoys a substantial career.

Other Old Boys do well. Rackham and Duncan, the organists, both become Licentiates of the Royal Academy. S E Parkhouse gains a First in Contract Law at LSE, Max Hofler achieving the same in Advanced Building and Architecture and winning the King's Prize at the Royal Institute of British Architects. Arthur Armstrong who had been at the School 1900–1904 makes progress in an area where few Lyonians in the School's history have strayed: he becomes Private Secretary to Cabinet Minister Lewis Harcourt. Several former pupils are now themselves teaching, for example at Loretto and King Edward VII Stourbridge; Percy Rayner is at Spalding Grammar and was to become Headmaster in due course at Pinner County Grammar, while R H Bartlett is already Headmaster at Ipoh in Malaya. Other Old Boys, too, are venturing abroad, one a poultry breeder in Los Angeles, one trying his luck in Siberia, another in the Gold Coast, a fourth in Gibraltar, while several more join fellows in Canada, Australia, Argentina and Germany. From the last, Clement Betts writes presciently, 'A new nation has risen up, hardworking, ambitious . . . determined to wrest from England her long commercial dominance.'

At the School we have sight for the first time, and briefly, of Deputy Monitors, later to be known as Prefects. It is surprising they were felt necessary given the small size of the population at that time. In advance of Captain Scott's expedition to the Antarctic, eighty-one of the School's ninety-eight boys contributed towards the three guineas he was sent to buy a dog. Scott sent a handwritten acknowledgment, saying, 'Will you please convey my personal thanks to the boys. I shall REALLY buy a dog with it and call him Lyon.' In the event, he named the dog 'Treasure'.

One of the small number of boys at the School, and a very able one, was J H Stillman. He was notably good at German, science subjects and as a visual artist. At the tender age of fifteen, he passed the Civil Service examination, taking 23rd place out of eight hundred candidates. He lives in Hounslow and staff calculate that in getting to Harrow, he travels 4,700 miles each year. He and Stanley Kipping – a name still remembered at the School – are among the 1910 matriculation successes. It occurs to the same staff that, up till now, the John Lyon School has not approached these examinations with the best strategy. Most of their boys have been entered at the age of fourteen. They are competing with pupils from other schools aged up to seventeen. The decision is taken to delay entry in future by a year, leaving them still disadvantaged, but not so much as before. The problem being, of course, the cost of keeping boys on at the School for a longer period.

As 1911 dawns, the new County School opens its doors. Despite the emigration of some, and the fears of many, the John Lyon School does not sink into terminal decline. From the School's records it appears that around two dozen boys made the move away. A little later two of them, both inevitably Woodbridges, chose to move back. The immediate dip, though, in the John Lyon total was no more than a dozen, suggesting there were other families happy to send their sons to the School, even at this parlous time. Much of this can be attributed to the energy and determination of the new Head – and old hand – Mr Butt. Regarded by one colleague, at least, as verging on the dull, there can be little question that it was his absolute loyalty to the School and his unremitting doggedness that saw the crisis through. The Governors feared for his health as he was spending so much time and effort on keeping the School alive. Tired, he may have been, but they need not have worried. The new Chairman of the Committee of Management, Mr John Lilley, described events this way: 'Some time ago we were in a very bad position, but – there was a "but" in the matter [loud laughter from his Speech Day audience] – Mr Butt came forward and said there was a possibility of the School being a success, and he was prepared to take over the duties. We have heard the result.' He rode out the storm and presided over the School for the next fifteen years, sailing it, as Dr Leaf described matters, into much quieter waters.

The same positive note is struck in the School magazines of this year. Warm and sincere tributes to Messrs Young and Godwin there were, and not only to them. The editor finds space to say, '. . . . I consider the 1910–1911 Sixth Form about the best set of real decent boys and hard workers that I have known. We shall look back upon the times of Tigar, Parker and Crundall and Co. as the halcyon days of our School.' Given the recent difficulties, the choice of the adjective 'halcyon' comes close to heroic.

Modelling the latest flying machines, Wrights, Bleriots, Farmans and Valkyries, a group of boys start an Aero Club. A Cadet Corps, with 25 members, is initiated by Lieutenant Stranders, the second such attempt in the School's history. Frank Tickle writes in to say he wonders why plays are presented by the Old Lyonian Football Club rather than having a dramatic club with that as its purpose; and another Old Boy, H W Rackham, brother of the organist and singing master, for the tenth time wins a prize offered by the London *Evening News*, in this case for the best description of a real football match.

Crucially, the School is now free of the strictures and socio-political pressures of the Board of Education and announces that it intends to adopt a wider and more adventurous curriculum. In the meantime, Parker of the exemplary sixth form takes fourteenth place out of a field of 660 candidates in the Civil Service Examinations; and a new Form Master is appointed, Mr O A Le Beau. A man of wide talents and catholic interests, Mr Le Beau had degrees in both arts and science and at sixteen years of age he had been elected to a Fellowship of the British Astronomical Association when he discovered a new star. His arrival on the scene must have been both welcome and enlivening as he shared with Mr Swainson a quirky and boyish sense of humour. One of his many favourite entertainments for a class was to recite:

> The boy stood on the shining track,
> The engine gave a squeal.
> The driver took an oily rag
> And wiped him off the wheel.

Le Beau also brought increased academic rigour. Where Young had organized a wide range of lecturers, Le Beau continued the programme, extending the number devoted to scientific topics and demonstrations, but not neglecting talks, illustrated with slides, on foreign countries.

It has been suggested that the continuing success of the School, after this difficult episode, was due to the opportunity it gave to be selective, no longer supporting working-class youngsters as the scholarships had been abolished and the County School would be looking after them. The appeal now could be to a more middle-class, more affluent demographic. In the longest term, this might be hard to deny, but looking at the School Register covering a period of seven years each side of the foundation of the County School, it cannot be supported.

The John Lyon School had, of course, always been selective, although the pool of choice may earlier have been quite limited. Even scholarships had always been awarded at the sole discretion of the School. The Register, which recorded, *inter alia*, the father's job when a boy entered the School, reflects no great differences between the before and after of the County School's emergence. There were doctors and dentists, many shop and business proprietors, the occasional journalist and accountant in the earlier period. Perhaps the biggest group was clerks, a designation difficult to define as it could as equally apply to the Town Clerk as to Bob Cratchit. What is noticeable is that the sons of this latter group tend to be the most achieving, several of them becoming School Captain, gaining commissions in the First World War and so on. In the period after the establishment of the County school the list offers no significant variation. There are as many sons of publicans and commercial travellers as before. There is admittedly the first son of a Professor of Philosophy, but he only lasts a year. And there is still the occasional boy whose father is a labourer or a gardener. Interestingly, again both before and after, where boys come from a home where money must have been difficult, they have very often been at a paid Prep school, indicating both a sacrifice and a determination on the part of their family. It is just this kind of commitment which will have cemented the John Lyon School's position at this time.

Two other factors must also have contributed. Again and again the School magazine lists the Old Boys who have come to visit, rarely fewer than half-a-dozen each month. That sense of solidarity, first evidenced at the Old Lyonian Dinners in the 1890s, has its importance. It is further supported by the School's attitude to the boys, and this runs right through its history to the present day. There is nothing impersonal about it. It is a relationship that is affectionate, demanding, amused, above all encouraging; almost guaranteed to build a sense of community, of belonging and hence, for the boy, of ownership. An ownership which the wider public of Harrow also felt in light of the School's rocky journey from being the dream of a local yeoman to the solid bricks and mortar of the building on Middle Road.

Early in 1912, the School makes its farewells to a boy named Dunhill in the warm terms already indicated. He is 'as straight as retiring. We are sure of his success in life.' It was a good assessment. The magazine also publishes a photograph of Mr Martin, elegantly dressed and with a finely waxed moustache. His successes putting on the annual School play are the more remarkable given that he designs, makes and paints the scenery at the same time. It publishes, too, a detailed account of the recent Indian 'Durbar' sent by Alec Anderson who had previously attended the School. *The Lyonian*'s readership was clearly widespread since shortly afterwards the *Daily Telegraph* borrows the description of this event for its own columns and the rest of the national press then follow suit. Meanwhile C W Pantlin (OL) is filing sports reports, in particular on the England v Ireland rugby international, for the *Evening News* and the *Weekly Dispatch*, leading to the possibility that he may have been the link.

Around the same time, the School heartily recommends a new magazine for boys with the title *The Territorial Cadet*. The suspicion that it is edited by Cherry Swainson is reinforced when the sub-editor is revealed as Thomas Ginever of St Kilda's Road, Harrow, a fifth-former at the Lower School. This particular magazine lasted only a year, being superseded in late 1913 by *The Imperial Cadet*.

Frank Tickle's earlier appeal bears fruit and the formation of an Old Lyonian Dramatic Club, separate from the soccer players, is announced with Tickle as its secretary. Almost immediately members of the new group are into rehearsal with Goldsmith's comedy, *The Good-Natured Man*, giving their performances in aid of two charitable causes: Harrow Cottage Hospital which nestled on Roxeth Hill nearby, and the Titanic Disaster Fund, raising just short of twenty pounds for each. There seems to have been little differentiation between current and former attenders at the School, given that Mr Martin again directs and Frank Tickle's father again provides and conducts the orchestra.

The organist and choirmaster of St Jude's, Hampstead Garden Suburb, Mr Arthur Gosling, takes over responsibility for music in the School, sadly to die of pneumonia less than two years later at the early age of thirty-eight. Perhaps a little surprisingly, in addition to fourteen Old Lyonians re-visiting the place in the month of March, the name of Major Godwin is recorded. Less surprising when you know that he continued to take the School's Army Cadets for drill. Despite his departure from the staff, the John Lyon cricket team remained overwhelmingly successful. The First Eleven easily beat Commercial Travellers' (twice), Ealing Grammar, Kilburn Grammar, West Ham Central School, Mercers', Headstone St George's and the Old Lyonians, their only loss being the first match of the season against the adults of the Roxeth Institute.

Football fared less well, about half the matches being won and half lost. The following season, 1912/13, began even less promisingly until the fillip of the first-ever match against Harrow County School for Boys. This the School won by five goals to one.

Confidence, based on realities, was gradually rising. New staff members joining are Mr Hanbury to undertake language teaching and in an additional post, Mr Fretwell. Mr Butt, the Headmaster, as if recent turmoils had not been enough to occupy him, had been using every spare minute to extend his own academic study and is able, by 1913, if not earlier, to be designated E H Butt BA.

A Boxing Club is launched, instructed by a trainer from the Société Athlétique de Dijon. At the same time, one of the School's young sporting heroes, George Mellor, leaves to complete his education at a school in Angers, where a juvenile Duke of Wellington had once taken the same path.[20] A Rifle Club, subscription one shilling a term, also opens, encouraged by the knowledge that John Lyon had wanted his boys to

---

[20] Not to the same schools, though. Wellington attended the Académie Royale d'Equitation, a military school; Mellor went to St Julien.

be proficient in archery and that the rifle was the modern equivalent of the bow. A sense here, too, with each of these developments, the Cadet Force, the Boxing Club, the Rifle Club, even the introduction of a military band to play at Sports Day, that there were international tensions and the young would do well to be physically and practically prepared. It is only a little later that Percy Guterbock, a previous School Captain, writes from Vienna that the Austro-Hungarian Empire is 'still beneath the heel of those twentieth century anachronisms, the priest and the soldier'. He foresaw European politics as being increasingly troubled and, as the century proceeded, Guterbock was, very publicly, to amend his name to Goodbrook.

Numbers of boys at the School are once more increasing. They had reached 105 and there was now a waiting list. The Governors planned an increase to 120. The surest sign of returning confidence was to be heard in the address given by Lord George Hamilton, Chairman of the Harrow Governors, on Speech Day. He happily acknowledged the one foundation of the two schools on Harrow Hill: 'The John Lyon School is a portion of Harrow School'. As if to confirm it, the Lower School's Sports Day was now, for the first time, held at the Harrow School athletic track. Hamilton praised the Lower School's eminently successful year and said it had weathered the storms and stood safe and sound in the harbour of popularity.

By coincidence, he cited the Duke of Wellington on the subject of schooling in his speech. Responding to a mother, the Duke had written, a boy 'must understand there is nothing learned but by study and application. There is nothing like never having an idle moment. If he has only a quarter of an hour it is better to employ it in some fixed pursuit, than pass it in idleness and listlessness.' That, Lord George – like all adults, at all times, when speaking to the young – thought was good advice. He had, however, the awareness a moment later to quote another tale. He knew, he said, of a mother who was worried about an unfavourable report on her son's studies and who had written the boy a four-page letter about it. A few days later she received this reply: 'My dear mother, I was so pleased with your nice long letter, but I have been working so hard I have not had time to read it.' With that, Lord George no doubt pleased both parties in his audience. The parents with the stricture; the boys with the smarter response.

In the late autumn of 1913, Arthur Parker wrote from Wealdstone to encourage fellow Old Boys to keep in touch, whether or not they were keen on football or amateur dramatics. His unstated intention succeeded admirably. Six months later, the Old Lyonian Association came into existence, separate from, and in due course embracing, the two existing specialist clubs. The Association acquired handsome premises on the Hill with a reading room, a smoking lounge, and committee, refreshment and billiards rooms, at number 102, the High Street.

A little earlier, the Cadet Corps, which had once again faltered, was re-formed. Vivian Stranders who had initiated it in 1911 remained at the School for not much more than a year. Then he left to join the full-time army, becoming, in due course, a captain in the Royal Air Force. Major Godwin features again, this time to be congratulated on his marriage to Dorothy Miriam Sholl from Sidcup. It is impossible not to believe, given the unusual surname, that she was not a connection of Harry Percy Gascoigne Sholl, a bright student and a nifty miler at the School, whose father was one of its benefactors.

As summer 1914 approaches a promising left-handed batsman is welcomed to the Cricket Eleven. His name is Victor Silvester. While over Europe the clouds gather, not to part for four long years.

CHAPTER 6

WAR ITSELF
1914–1919

But now on war's blood-spattered plain
They dare for England's need
And only know that England calls
For men, whate'er their creed.
God bless you! men with whom I played
And fought in days of yore!
Ah would that I could share this game,
As those I shared before.

Harold Tickle, the younger brother and the School's resident boy poet, reflected the contemporary reaction to the opening of conflict with Germany in these lines from his poem dedicated 'To the Old Boys Who Have Left Us'. As it was, he would in time be joining them, and fighting with some distinction. And, as it happens, he had penned some more percipient lines, before hostilities began:

I stood in the midst of a desert,
Beneath the Southern Cross,
And the sands lay around like the ocean
Till they met the sky beyond.
And I thought of those who had perished
On this vast, sad, lonely plain,
And the sound that arose from the desolate waste
Was the moan of departed souls.

At the declaration of war, a hundred and more Old Boys volunteered, many familiar names among them. Others like Temple and Victor Silvester, sons of the vicar of Wembley, left School early, lied about their ages and joined up, too.[21]

---

[21] It has been stated in some sources that Victor Silvester was expelled; in his own autobiography he says that he truanted. Neither is correct. He may have truanted from home to enrol in the army, but both Silvester boys left John Lyon by agreement and their leaving is recorded in the School Register as being from 31st December 1914. That was the normal end of the School year at that time. It is also recorded there that Victor was going into the army.

Dr Charles Vaughan, founder of Harrow School's English Form.

HARROW SCHOOL.

ENGLISH FORM.

Master,—MR. HUTCHINSON.

Examination, Christmas, 1859.

* Woodbridge maj. — *[handwritten] Sir T. F. Buxton*
* Thornton — *[handwritten] do. do.*
* Greenhill — *[handwritten] Ld Dufferin? Tryon?*
* ~~Smith~~ — *[handwritten] Irving? for Smith*
* Chapman — *[handwritten] Lord Clive.*
Parkhouse
Christie
Woodbridge ~~mi.~~ *jun.*
Fletcher
Winkley sen.
Chatham
Hoare
Walker sen.
Winkley jun.
Walker jun.

Armstrong } *not in the*
Woodbridge ~~min.~~ *sen.* } *Examination.*

* Prizes given to those thus marked.

[handwritten] Phillips | Ashton
[handwritten] Hubbard | Woodbridge mi
[handwritten] Joyce | Woodbridge min

Examination List of the English Form 1859. Winkley and Chapman were greeted warmly by Old Harrovian Mr Roundell many years later at Speech Day 1880.

The Lower School of John Lyon, seen from the Sixth Form Ground, around 1880.

Charles Gregg, Master of the English Form 1860–1879; Mathematical Master at the Lower School of John Lyon from 1879 until his death in 1893.

The School as it was in 1891. Note the main entrance position before its later move further south, when the building was extended. Note also the bell tower on the roof and the large chimney, both later removed.

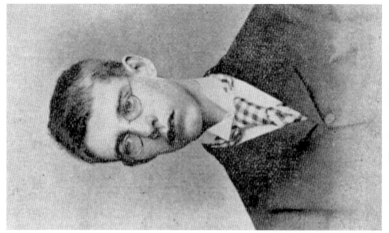

Dawson Hartley, at LSJL 1888–1893.
Captain of cricket, football, outstanding athlete
and later medical doctor.

John Williams MA, Headmaster 1879–1898.

J B Parkhouse, a boy in
the English Form 1857–1861.
Chairman of the Old Lyonian Dinner in 1892.

Advertisement for the School, 1893.

MAY 1890

VOL. I

THE LYONIAN

The Magazine of the
Lower School
of John Lyon, Harrow

Cover of *The Lyonian* in the year
Mr Young launched it.

Ernest Young, Assistant Master 1890–1892;
Headmaster 1898–1911.

Thomas Blackwell JP, High Sheriff of Middlesex, active member of the Committee of Management and a major benefactor.

A W Parker, Captain of cricket and football 1893–1894.

G A Cram, School Captain 1893–1894 and later a civil servant.

Lower Division boys, 1894.

Forms 3 and 4 in 1898. 'Cherry' Swainson is the master on the left; beside him in the back row is 'Pocket' Neale's brother; on the left of the second row is a young Edgar Rayner.

Edward Herbert Burt, Headmaster 1911–1926. He later, wisely, shaved off the moustache and looked far more cordial. This picture is courtesy of www.harrowphotos.com

Edgar Rayner, eldest of the three Rayner brothers as School Captain 1903–1904.

⁘ Lower School of John Lyon. ⁘

Report for the **Xmas** *Term,* **1905**

Name **S.P. Kipping**   *Form II.*   *Age* **10½** *years.*

FORM SUBJECTS.	Marks obtainable.	Highest Marks obtained.	Marks obtained.	Place.	REMARKS.
Religious Instruction.	50	50	28	19	*A year under the*
History, Geography, Literature.	150	147	128 ᶜ	6	*average of the form,*
Grammar, Composition, Spelling, Writing.	200	167	164 ᶜ	2	*he has had a consistent and*
Arithmetic.	100	100	90 ᶜ	3	*brilliant record this term, of which*
Freehand,	50	48	41 ᶜ	6	*he may well be*
French.	100	96	83 ᶜ	12	*proud.*
TOTAL	650	557	534	3	

Average Age of Form.

11½ *years.*

Form Promotion depends principally on place in Form Examinations and occurs annually.

Maximum Marks.
Arithmetic .. 100
French .. 100
Other Subjects 50 each.

Place in Form ....**3**.....   Conduct...**E**.......   Absent ....**0**.....half-days.

No. in Form ......**36**.........   Application..**E**.....   Late ....**0**.......times.

⁎⁎ E., denotes Excellent ; G., Good ; F., Fair ; M., Moderate ; U., Unsatisfactory.   C. denotes Commended for Work.

⁎⁎ Next term will begin on ___**18th Jan. 1906**___   **E. Cecil Blomfield.** *Form Master.*

Notice of unavoidable absence through sickness, or other urgent cause,
should be sent to the Head Master before School begins.   **E. Young** *Head Master.*

School report for Stanley Kipping 1905.

S. Page   C. Flinn   H. Prince   W. R. Abbati   J. A. Massey
H. Roberts   G. H. D. Higgins   A. R. Heard (capt.)   A. C. Bayley (vice-capt.)   G. Mellor
B. Mellor   G. Tigar

First XI Football team 1911–1912. Abbati was among the many young
Old Lyonians killed in the First Word War. Jack Massey was later President of the
Old Lyonian Association.

J.O'Brien   C. G. Welch A. Roberts   T. C. Martin   E. C. Baker   H. N. Fryer
F. C. Tickle   P. F. Thorp   V. Cole   G. G. Page   L. Tigar   E. C. Stearns
Miss M. Tickle   Miss D. Rayner Miss G. M. Tilbury Miss A. L. Tilbury Mrs. R. C. Solly

The cast of *The Good Natured Man*, 1912. Frank Tickle is second from the left.

Early days of the School Cadet Force. Captain Martin is to the right of the drum.

Rayner Sordes Ellis (Gallipoli) in 1915

William Williamson (Dardanelles)

Harold Tigar (Neuve Chapelle)

All three killed, plus Stearns on the next plate

O A Le Beau, Science Master 1911–1926; Headmaster 1926–1951.

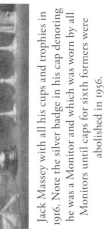

Jack Massey with all his cups and trophies in 1916. Note the silver badge in his cap denoting he was a Monitor and which was worn by all Monitors until caps for sixth formers were abolished in 1956.

Eric Stearns (Aberle)

The New Building going up, 1930.

The New Building completed, 1930.

John Lyon cadets at summer camp in the 1930s.

First XI Cricket Team 1931. The master is Mr G H Fairs. Boys with colours have the tasselled caps. Notice, too, the larger blazer badge than at later periods. The Monitor on his own in front is F Barnard, father of John Barnard.

First XI Football Team 1938. Mr A M Mitchell is the master. The captain with the ball is N J Payne and cross-legged on the left is a young Gordon Blyth.

The bell tower on the Old Building where a look-out bugler was posted during the Second World War.

Boyd Campbell, Test cricketer and later Bishop of Liverpool David Sheppard
and Colonel Wilson at the Easter Fair 1953.

Paul Wilkinson, wearing his Prefect's badge and working in the
War Memorial Library, 1953.

OLA President Mr Douglas Woodbridge presents new instruments to the Cadet Band,
as Corporal Michael Wright i/c Band and Boyd Campbell look on.

Field Marshal Earl Alexander addressing John Lyon cadets at the Annual Inspection.
Major Cummings is on the left and Captain Elgood faces the camera.

A class at work in a first floor classroom in the New Building.

Cadet Staff Sergeant John Allsop in charge of the School Armoury 1959.

George Weedon taking a class in the hall cum gymnasium in the New Building.

An aerial view of the School's buildings as at 1960, drawn by Don Allan. The bell from Bill Worman's ship can just be made out, hanging on the balcony of the New Building.

A scene from the production of *Morning Departure*, 1960.

The Motet Choir at London Weekend Studios in Wembley, 1970.

Anthony Grant MP and Headmaster Gordon Surtees as Oldfield House
is declared open, 1981.

The moment of impact: Motet Choir members greet the Dean of Peterborough's family
with unusual force.

Biology Field Trip, 1984.

Headmaster David Dixon.

Alan Woodbridge executing the Fosbury Flop, 1983.

The completed Lyon Building, seen from the lower field.

"Ma" Dillon, 1985.

S Marks in full flow, 1985.

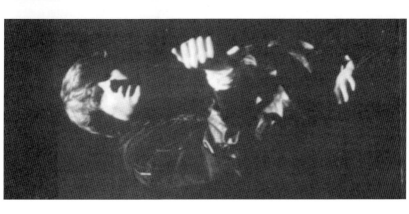

Julian Rhind-Tutt as Hamlet, 1984.

The archery team check their scores, 1998.

Rhodri James receiving the Massey Bat, 2001

JLS boy Samuel Steel who competed, with signal success, in the Solar Challenge
at the Olympic Pool in Munich, 2003.

Dr Christopher Ray, Headmaster 2002–2004.

Middlesex and England bowler, and later School parent and Governor, Angus Fraser in conversation with Headmaster Tim Wright in 1994. Mr Fraser had just opened the latest pavilion at Sudbury.

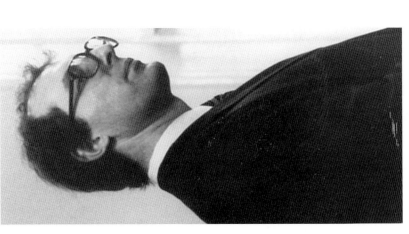

Music maestro Fred Goodwin.

The Model Railway Club 2004.

JLS supporters rival The Kop, 2006.

On 21st November 1914, the first to lose his life was twenty-seven-year-old Horace Muddock. Lewis Reid was posted missing, just weeks after he had quit as School Captain and as an editor of the School magazine. He had joined the London Scottish Regiment, where he served as part of General Sir John French's bodyguard at the first battle of Messines. Lewis was still listed as 'missing' when the war ended, his remains never found. He was seventeen years old.

Reports came in from young men with the British Expeditionary Force in France and from HMS *Lion*. A 'game' had begun which would mark all who lived through it. A pattern, which now appears tragically predictable but then brought unlooked-for news with arresting regularity, continued side by side with the School's own quiet progress. As was the case in schools and homes across the nation, it was news that ate at hearts and minds and came close, at times, to undermining the will to press on. Although of a different scale and significance, the struggle the John Lyon School had already undergone in assuring its own survival may, to a degree, have prepared it for the attrition ahead. Nonetheless, there are hints, as the war proceeds, of near despair at the continual loss and maiming of boys, so carefully prepared and educated for good, purposeful lives. More usually, a muted, stoical determination obtains.

Among the customary developments of school life, two masters leave: Mr Martin for the headship of Laxton Grammar School in Oundle, Mr Hargreaves for the armed services. Three new masters join: Mr Christie Tait, the wonderfully named Mr H Virgilius Black and, from Strathallan School in Scotland, Mr William Wilson BA, LCP. Mr Fretwell obtains a captaincy and takes command of the Cadet Corps whose membership soon approaches a hundred and is now established as a separate company, rather than as part of a unit within the Middlesex Regiment. Mr Wilson sets about forming a cadet band.

Numerous messages come into the School from Old Lyonians serving in France, Belgium and on the high seas. One is interned in Germany and more and more are shown as enlisting. There is news of commissions obtained, and before summer 1915 has fully arrived, there comes the news of more Lyonians lost on active service: a Sub-Lieutenant and a Midshipman drowned in separate incidents at sea; and three soldiers killed, variously serving with the Queen Victoria Rifles in Flanders, the Australian Expeditionary Force in the Dardanelles, and, ten days after arrival with his men at Neuve Chapelle, Lieutenant Harold Tigar. He had called at the School the night before he travelled to the Front, 'full of hope and enthusiasm'. Among the wounded there are head injuries, leg injuries from shrapnel or grenades and for Edward Chatham, from the third generation of his family to attend the School, the ill luck of a leg amputation.

Later in the year there is the oddity of the School celebrating its Tercentenary. This, of course, relates to the formal opening of Harrow School in 1615 and was another public affirmation of the day school's direct lineage. Mr Lascelles, Governor of Harrow, was at pains to explain the history in detail, making it clear once again that the English Form and the John Lyon School were, equally with the 'foreigners' of the boarding school, the intended beneficiaries of the statutes drawn up by the Founder.

On this occasion music was under the direction of Arthur Rackham, the talented organist, who had now returned to join the staff of his old School. The number of boys at the School had grown to 140, not including all four brothers Mackay who had left to join the Middlesex Regiment and the now two hundred Old Lyonians serving in the war.

The close of the year brought more untimely deaths: twenty-year-old Lieutenant Eric Stearns, with a host of tributes from his comrades, from his Colonel to his batman; Raynal Sordes Ellis at Gallipoli, just nineteen; Tom Lion at Bethune, a youngster in the Medical Corps, and bright and intelligent James Paterson, aged twenty-five, who had been taken prisoner and died of his wounds at Muenster, Westphalia. Raynal's parents wrote their own commemorative verse with the courage the bereaved had constantly to adopt. It concluded:

> Peaceful he lies with patriot comrades sleeping.
> The task performed that victory might be won –
> If Britain's cause be served and its upkeeping,
> We freely yield, though miss and mourn our son.

While the guns wrought destruction across the Channel and countless Old Boys wrote from their dug-outs and depots and rear resting stations graphic letters of their experiences, the School maintained as evenly as it could, the tenor of its way. The Scientific Society, in particular, kept up a lively programme; and one of two previously regular public events continued to be organized as it had been in the years before the war.

This was the Annual Conversazione. The title gives little idea of the nature of the event. Opening in the large school-room, the one that could be partitioned into two, the Headmaster and his wife, Ida, formally received everyone who was attending: parents, friends and former pupils. The place was garlanded with flowers and could scarcely hold the number who arrived. Then, with Mr Le Beau as Master of Ceremonies, a succession of demonstrations, staged in all the different rooms in the building, were given. Senior boys performed experiments in chemistry and physics, including the production of aniline dyes from coal tar, the liquefaction of gases, the operation of Rijke's Sounding Tubes – apparently very loud – and, sounding even more esoteric, Chladni's Plate and the Cryophorus. Many other experiments were on view, too. While elsewhere a London company demonstrated the production of prints using the Bromoil process and in another classroom the British Astronomical Association, of which Le Beau was a Fellow, had lent some remarkable photographs of the moon for display. In the Sixth Form Room one of the boys, A B Howe, gave a much praised illustrated talk on the topical subject of submarines.

When the guests had digested all of that, there was an hour of music to entertain them. Several songs, including the pertinent 'Until the Boys Come Home', were sung by Mrs McGowan. Piano solos and violin solos of popular classics given by visiting performers followed and the evening was rounded off with some uproarious monologues delivered by Mr Black, the English master, and the returning Frank Tickle. It was not much before midnight when the occasion came to an end.

For a small school to organize an event of this scope can have been no mean undertaking. Neither can it have been easy to stage the Annual Concert in the Public Hall in Harrow. This, too, had been a regular event until the war broke out and it involved a substantial number of professional performers, quite a few of whom returned over a number of years. Among them, two whose names have an anachronistic familiarity to the modern mind: Miss Kate Moss and the comedian Mr Harrison Hill, almost inevitably known as Harry.

Sports Day and Speech Day of course remained major occasions in the School calendar and matches against other schools, visits to places of educational interest, and an annual camp of two or three weeks all held their place. On the sports field, one young man was pre-eminent. He was regarded as the best all-round athlete the School had ever had, quite a claim, given the achievements of one or two of his predecessors. His name was Jack Massey and it was a name that still reverberated in the Lyonian world half-a-century later. Remarkably, Jack gained his First Eleven cricket colours at the age of twelve, holding his place for all five years of his School career and twice topping the batting averages and twice taking most wickets in the season; at football, he was a year later getting his colours and was a phenomenal goal scorer: sixty-five goals in twenty-eight matches during the 1913/14 season, for example. On the track he was a multiple winner on Sports Days and set records at both junior and senior high jump. The successes of individual boys like Massey or his fellow Monitor and member of both elevens, Leonard Dawson, must have raised the spirits at this time and although humour is less evident in the way things are reported, the odd sardonic comment slips through. A boy named Robert Loader, described as brilliantly clever, brings the observation that he was capable of doing great things – 'if he thought it worthwhile'. He went into advertising.

Many of the School societies atrophied, perhaps because of the concentration on scientific knowledge which clearly engaged many boys and the demands of the Cadet Force, to which the majority belonged. Most of the pages of the School magazine were given over to the news and the letters of boys who had recently left.

As 1916 dawned and with it the battles of Verdun and the Somme and the unimaginative command of Sir Douglas Haig and his colleagues, that news became increasingly sad. Norman Bowden writes an extended account from the mud of Flanders, concluding with an apology that 'this is so long and a dismal failure' while Ross Heard, also in the front line, observes that the infantry in the trenches wait twelve months for furlough while people at the bases and those who never see the line get leave every three months.[22] He adds the dry comment that war cannot last much longer as Belgium is nearly all covered in sandbags.

The brittleness of life is even reflected in a remarkable piece of verse written by a French boy at the School. Punningly titled 'The Pierrot's Life', it is by Pierre Reau and looks – at length – at the brevity of existence and the deceptiveness of seeming joy. The sophistication and skill in the writing might call the authorship in doubt, but it was indeed the creation of a boy in the School named Pierre Reau, and as a reflection of the mood at the time it seems spot on, summed up in its perky concluding lines:

> How short is life!
> Some sweet delight
> Some hope – some strife,
> And then – good-night.

Another of the correspondents is former School Captain, Lieutenant K J P Asher. Kenneth Asher writes from the trenches of the foreboding

---

[22] Neither young man was of a wilting nature. Ross Heard had been School Captain in 1912, captain of both elevens and athletics champion, while Norman Bowden was to be one of the many young officers produced by the School to be awarded the Military Cross.

that goes with being sent out on a working party. Life in the war zone, he says, is usually very dull. 'When, however, it is not dull it is too exciting to be pleasant.' Less than six weeks later, he is dead. So, too, is Second Lieutenant Alan Paterson whose brother James had been killed nine months earlier. The list goes on: Lieutenant Eric Fryer, Lieutenant Bill Abbati, brother of twins who had also attended John Lyon; Roland Naylor known in the 1890s as a good scholar and one of the quietest boys ever; Rifleman Fred Slade follows his elder brother George in being killed in action, another brother, Harry, being wounded; two more notably quiet boys, an ambidextrous artist William Oliver and a fine essayist, Arthur Fillimore, are killed late in the year; so too, Thomas Candlin, once a keen swimmer and soccer player. Frederick Mason, and Jasper, brother of the first Lyonian to fall, Horace Muddock, and himself the third member of his family to die in this single year, join the number of the slaughtered.

There is much news of postings and promotions and of wounds. Then, as if to set the seal on an appalling year comes news of one man dying in his bed. J E Williams, the first Headmaster, had breathed his last. From the many tributes paid to him, it is clear that the boys had held him in some awe; interesting, given he had a horror of administering corporal punishment and resisted the use of sarcasm which he felt was essentially unfair from someone in his position. It was said that he had been as keen to learn as to teach and had a gift for seeing both sides of a question. Like almost everyone connected with the School, he had remained in regular touch right up until his death, attending many events and seeing former pupils.

Tributes are paid, too, to Bob Mellor who leaves the School for a post at the Admiralty. In what had clearly been a golden period for sport, he is saluted as a rival to Jack Massey as the finest all-rounder ever. Three years as Captain of both Cricket and Football and, uniquely, two years as School Captain amount to an unsurpassable record.

Other positives in 'this time of wholesale death' are the promotion of two young Old Boys to the rank of captain and Military Crosses awarded to Lieutenants Bolton, Watson and O'Brien.

At the same time, Ernest Young, who has left his post at Harrow County School in the pursuit of yet another quest, qualifies as a barrister. He never, in fact, practised at the Bar and later stood for Parliament as a Liberal in the 1918 elections, coming second out of five candidates to the successful Conservative. The element of restlessness in his character made the farewell present the School had given him on his first leaving in 1892, a travelling clock, peculiarly appropriate. Not many years later he edited *The New Era in Education* and was appointed Assistant Secretary for Higher Education for the county of Middlesex. He maintained his links with the Lower School, however, keeping up his membership of the Old Lyonian Association until his death in February 1952.

Meanwhile, early in the summer of 1917, Mr Tait and Mr Wilson were called into the armed forces. The news continues to be of promotions and wounds, and descriptions of life, such as it was, on the Somme. In later years Mr Wilson described one of his own experiences at the front. He was called with his men to find why one of our artillery batteries was out of action. Arriving where the battery was, they were confronted not by a scene of carnage, but of statuesque stillness. All the soldiers were in place, unmarked and unmoving, caught like the victims at Pompeii, in mid-action, apparently frozen for eternity. One, he recalled was in the process of loading a shell into a field gun. A huge explosion nearby had simply sucked the air, and the life, from all the members of the unit, eerily leaving them in exactly the pose they were in at the moment of death.

More cheerfully, there are now fourteen former boys at the School serving as officers in the Royal Flying Corps while another, Victor Silvester, is currently with the Red Cross. His story is mirrored, in one respect at least, by quite a few underage volunteers. A month after leaving John Lyon, when he was fourteen years and nine months old he had volunteered for the London Scottish Regiment, adding four years to his age. Due to institutional myopia he, like many other juveniles, was accepted for service and saw action in France. Later, at the battle of San Gabriele, he fought with distinction and was awarded the Bronze Medal for Valour by the Italian government. On this occasion he was wounded and invalided out of the army. So instead, he set to work with the Red Cross.[23]

Shortly after this, the School Cadet Corps formed an Ambulance Section. It only lasted briefly. Lieutenant Roy Matthews, a boy at the School commissioned to run the Corps in the absence of the staff who had previously done so was now, himself, called up.

As 1918 progresses, the toll of lives, if anything, increases. Most of the boys are young subalterns, the most risk-intensive role whether infantry or cavalry. Arthur Parker, a superb sportsman and a school hero in the early 1890s is perhaps a little older, but among the more recent leavers,

---

[23] Again, one source has suggested the Italian episode, the wound and the decoration were a fantasy devised for Victor Silvester's much later autobiography. The truth is all three events were publicly announced at the time.

Lieutenant Joe Taylor of the Royal Naval Air Service and another pilot, Lieutenant Berry die in flying accidents; in ground assaults Lieutenant Eric Green, Lieutenant Victor Gillings, Lieutenant John Hamilton, Lieutenant Harry Boreham and the outstanding scholar, Lieutenant Hubert Cram lose their lives in a single month. While 'Tinker' Ashford dies at Passchendaele and Sergeant F B King is killed in Palestine, as the latest 'in the interminable chain of tragedies of this most horrible war', as Fred Swainson records it.

That war, for good or ill, continues to dominate. Lieutenant George Barter is taken prisoner, as earlier in the year Lieutenant Harry Waters had been. Claude Hook dies of wounds and his brother is missing, not to be found. Boys in the Cadet Force are inspected in the Mall by the Duke of Connaught before marching to St Margaret's, just by Westminster Abbey, for a Brigade Service. And the RFC officers are joined by Douglas Kinsey, all of them now commissioned into the newly founded Royal Air Force.

The effect on families where more than one son is serving must have been intense. The Best family, all three of whose sons were captains in the army, faced an unenviable mixture of emotions: Jack had been killed at Armentières; the eldest, Albert Frank, has been awarded the Military Cross; while Ernest, having fought in France and Palestine is now with the Indian Army. The Higgs family's situation is not so different: their eldest boy is severely wounded; the middle one also receives the MC; while the youngest, with the war still going, is permanently discharged from the forces which carries the suspicion that he may have been suffering from shell shock. He works as the Assistant Rate Collector for Harrow.

As hostilities at last come to an end in November 1918, the Higgins family mourn their middle son, Captain Arthur Higgins, who dies of wounds in Serbia just two weeks before the Armistice. Their eldest son, Donald, a lieutenant, is still stationed at Woolwich. Gurney, the youngest, visits the School.

The Parkhouse family, central to the Lower School's history, must have entertained conflicting feelings, too. In 1917, Frank, a lieutenant, was killed in action. Now, Charlie, another lieutenant, is Mentioned in Dispatches. The two elder sons, Jack and Stanley, are both Lieutenant Colonels and both decorated with OBEs, a particularly high honour when awarded in the field.

More honours come the way of other Lyonian soldiers. Frank Start from Stanmore was the one Old Lyonian to be awarded the Military Medal, the equivalent of the Military Cross, awarded in those class-conscious days to those who did not hold a commission. Major Reginald Stanton, already holding the King's and Queen's Medal for the Boer War and another from 1906 when he had faced the Zulu Rising, is awarded an OBE, the Distinguished Conduct Medal, the Distinguished Service Order and, having fought with the Russian Army, the Croix de St George, the Order of St Stanislas and the Order of St Anne. Captain Harold Roach in the Royal Air Force receives the Air Force Cross. Military Crosses are given to the outstanding sportsman Captain Stanley Woodbridge, though he sadly dies soon afterward of appalling wounds; to Lieutenant J McFarlane, Lieutenant Norman Bowden now serving with a Canadian regiment, to Lieutenant Leonard Walson and to Second Lieutenant Alfred Dunhill. Likewise, Second Lieutenant Harold Tickle is gazetted 'for conspicuous gallantry and good leadership', and receives the MC, too.

While the war's end is greeted, naturally enough, with a tremendous lightening of the spirit, H V Black, who has taken over from Cherry Swainson the editorship of the magazine, dryly quotes, 'sufficient unto the day is the evil thereof.' And perhaps the final word should be left to Mrs Stillman of Tiverton Road, Hounslow. Her son, John Humphrey Stillman, was the boy who had travelled so far to get the best education he could. Good at German, and art, after leaving school a brilliant student at London University, who managed to pass the examinations for Membership of the Institute of Bankers at the same time as studying for his degree, late in 1918 he died of wounds in France the day before his parents managed to reach him. He had served there for three long years. This was the letter his mother wrote:

To the Headmaster of John Lyon School

Dear Sir, I thought it well, though late, to send you the news of the death of an old scholar of your school; illness has prevented me doing so earlier. We feel certain he did his best, as he always tried to do with everything he undertook. He volunteered for the Army quite unknown to us, the day after he was 21, and came home and told us what he had done. Not anything this world can give will replace his loss to us, his parents, and sister. We loved him very much; he was always so kind and noble in the home. We must not be too selfish, as many others have met their death in doing their duty. We had hoped his education would have been a greater blessing in the world, but we have to leave it. Once more expressing my gratitude for all the help the masters at your school were to him, our dear son.

Yours sincerely,
ANNIE E STILLMAN

CHAPTER 7

DOMUS REDIVIVUS
1919–1926

There are now few letters from the front since, as the magazine notes, Johnny has come marching home, and the School takes on something of its old complexion. Mr Wilson returns to his post and briefly, Mr Hargreaves too, who will be reviving the Boxing Club he earlier started.

There are extraordinary results to report. In the London University examinations taken the previous December, all six of the John Lyon boys competing, half of whom were only fifteen years old, succeeded in gaining matriculation, three of them with honours. Between the six they gained fifteen distinctions and one special distinction. In each case it was the boy's first attempt. Of the other 128 candidates in this particular set of exams, seventy-seven were re-sits and exactly one other individual obtained honours.

It would have seemed as though Spring had come at last, were it not that the early months of 1919 saw the longest spell of snow anyone could remember. Mr Butt generously extended lunch and break times so the boys could enjoy snowballing. This contrasted with the view taken thirty-odd years later when one of his successors, Boyd Campbell, expressly forbade snowballing in similar circumstances and one boy at least earned himself a caning for choosing to disobey.

Of course there is still war news trickling in. Alfred Dunhill, despite his MC, was wounded just two days before the Armistice. The War Office is seeking lists of former students who served, of those who were decorated, and those who were killed, and the School puts out an appeal for everyone to send in details of anyone they know about, from which a full, and hopefully definitive, account can be collated. Within a year the design for a memorial to the young men from the School who had given their lives was agreed.[24]

---

[24] Sadly the memorial was to contain two errors: the name of William Abbati was misspelt and, worse, that of Horace Muddock was missed out, despite it having been reported in *The Lyonian* both when he was killed and, later, when his brother also fell.

Alfred Dunhill, incidentally, returned to the small family tobacco firm and, in the course of time, built it into a global business, diversifying initially into smoking accessories and then into upmarket items of clothing; it became a company always associated with style. A century after he left the School, the annual presentation of the Alfred Dunhill Cultural Icon Award, organized by *GQ* magazine, was an event widely reported in the press.

The greatest blow to the improved sense of well-being at this moment came with the news that Cherry Swainson, with Mr Gregg probably the two most popular masters in the School's history to date, had died of pernicious anaemia. Although he had originally been appointed to teach mathematics, it was soon recognized that his real strength lay in writing, a talent which extended beyond the bounds of the schoolroom. As well as switching to teach English and edit *The Lyonian*, he became a popular author of boys' fiction contributing to the *Pall Mall* and other magazines and constantly to *The Captain*, where he also became sub-editor. His one full-length book, *Acton's Feud*, was so popular that the copy in the School Library fell apart and had to be replaced.

When the news of his death spread abroad, the response was quite remarkable. A subscription fund was opened and soon a hundred pounds was collected, a substantial sum at the time: it equalled, and then surpassed the sum the entire town of Stratford-upon-Avon gave for the rebuilding of the Shakespeare Memorial Theatre when it burnt down a little later in the decade. Two valuable Swainson Memorial prizes, for English in the fifth and sixth forms, were instituted from the fund. A memorial plaque designed by former pupil Charlie Prince, and which long remained there, was placed on the wall inside the main entrance door to the School. The fund, meanwhile, continued to grow.

A new master arrived whose responsibilities were to include cricket, a very necessary move as the previous year things had reached such a pass that the First Eleven lost to a team made up of their sisters. Improvement was not immediate. Another step in the collaboration between the two Harrow Foundation schools came with the junior boys being allowed to play their games on the Philathletic Ground.

School societies remain depleted in number. The Cadet Force, unsurprisingly, continues to be active and the Scientific Society has never ceased to be lively, but it is not until early in 1920 that the Debating Society appears to get going again, arguing the case for and against there being a Monitor on duty in the Cloisters during the lunch hour. It is reported that minutes of the previous meeting were read, although there is no evidence of a previous meeting being held for some years. Largely because the report is a spoof, disclaimed at its end by the magazine's editor. The same year, Middlesex and London Cadets, including John Lyon boys, are inspected at St James's Palace by the Prince of Wales, and that really did occur.

The School is once more recognized by the Board of Education, with what degree of shamefacedness on the part of the latter is unknown. Either way, a rigorous two-day Inspection is satisfactorily survived. By neat irony, the prizes on Speech Day are presented by the first Old Lyonian to be a qualified school inspector, former Head Boy R J Bartlett. This is the earliest recorded use of the term Head of School, rather than School Captain, which is how he would have been described in 1894 when he held the position. And his fiefdom now as Inspector of Schools is Singapore and Malaya, making a tenuous link to that courageous boy so many years ago in the English Form, described in the first chapter.

The Board of Education also increased their representation on the Committee of Management, providing three additional members, and the School's future security was further helped when it was recognized as qualifying for a grant under the Teachers' Superannuation Act.

Given the difficult economic situation in the country in the years following the First War, with many businesses failing, farming having an unusually tough time and austerity the rule of the day, it must have been encouraging to see that the School was not merely full, and the total attending had been increased by ten to 140, but that it had become necessary to create a long waiting list. Relations with Harrow became demonstrably closer with Speech Day being held for the first time in the Speech Room rather than in the Public Hall. Dr Walter Leaf, giver of many scholarships for boys to continue their education, presented the prizes. And in the summer holidays that followed, Harrow School's swimming coach gave a series of training sessions in life-saving to John Lyon boys at Ducker. The boys had to be keen: the sessions were held at 7.30 in the morning.

At the same time, trees along Middle Road in front of the School were felled so that, close to the Old Building, a ditch could be dug. On this lower level, holes were then knocked through the wall and two substantial windows put in to provide more light in the Cloisters. Here, the first-formers were now in residence. A little later the school yard was doubled in size and, for the first time, asphalted. Previously it had been clinker which makes the Cadets' highly-praised drill all the more remarkable.

Two contrasting events occurred in 1921. First, the unveiling by one of

the oldest living Old Lyonians, Mr F Greenhill, of the School's War
Memorial. The fifty-eight names, which should have been fifty-nine, a
startling proportion when you consider that the school which produced
them seldom had more than a hundred boys on its roll and that most of
them were contemporaries or near-contemporaries, were engraved on a
copper sheet, set in a wood surround and surmounted by the School's crest
in full colour. Its production had been in the hands of Jack Massey. The
two principal funeral directing companies in Harrow were Massey's and
Ellement's and the sons of both families were educated at the School. The
Memorial was placed on the wall of the large schoolroom, immediately
over the Cloisters, a very present reminder to all current Lyonians. For the
unveiling, the walls were lined by Cadets in uniform, the parents of the
boys who had been killed were present and the School Choir sang two
hymns. The Memorial itself was moved much later to be on the wall of the
consecrated War Memorial Library, where it hangs today.

In a different field of activity, there was a blazing row over the London
University English examination. Details are hard to come by, but it seems
clear the questions were perverse and not designed to give candidates a
reasonable opportunity to show what they knew. The row was not
confined to one or two schools. It ranged across the country and the
examination paper was denounced in the press as 'nothing short of an
outrage upon the pupils'. A year later things had improved and it appears
likely that those responsible had been replaced. In the meantime the
disappointment for those studying the subject may, or may not, have
contributed to the dearth of creative contributions to the School
magazine. There were none.

Then, in 1922, virtually the first original piece by a boy, as against
simple reports, is printed. The first, that is, since the War ended. It is a
tongue-in-cheek article by Geoffrey Corder, son of the Clerk to the Royal
Courts of Justice, attacking the falsity of theatre performances as a genre.
It evokes from *The Lyonian*'s editor a lengthy, mock-pained response,
concluding '. . . pretence is the charm of the stage. Did you never play
soldiers, Corder?' It also causes the editor to reveal that he started life as a
professional actor, which may account for his decision to use as his first
name Virgilius, rather than whatever the 'H' stood for that preceded it.

Corder, however, was not done. The following edition, as he left school
having matriculated, contained another spoof piece from him, this time
written as a Frenchman. It, of course, proved the editor correct: Corder
enjoyed pretence more than most. What the younger brother of Pierre
Reau made of it is unknown. He was busy breaking the School's junior

high jump record which had stood for some years, clearing 4 feet 5 inches at age thirteen.

Very soon after, Mr H Virgilius Black was appealing for another school wit to emerge, although one of the serious reports the magazine carries almost qualifies as black comedy. Leslie Smith, having quit the Civil Service to serve in the forces during the War, has now gained his law degree and married. Not before a chequered time in the army. There, he had been wounded and spent six months in hospital. After this he rejoined the service and was wounded again, a bullet remaining in his knee. Unabashed, he returned to the trenches, only to be wounded a third time, the bullet passing through both cheeks. 'Through all this he kept up a brave front . . . and played a good game of football for the Old Lyonians'. With a bullet still lodged in his knee, it is hard not to wonder how desperate the Old Lyonians were at the time, or how much more phlegmatically British Mr Smith could have been.

At the School, the Army Cadets were in good form. They began a series of successes which were added to year by year. If ever proof were needed of the value of good teaching, the work of Mr Wilson and Mr Le Beau provides perfect illustration. Wilson did all he could for School sport and both football and cricket results had started to look up. Although, technically, the Headmaster Mr Butt was commanding officer, he also had full responsibility for the Corps and with his frontline experience had a good deal to bring to the task. The first reward was that the boys won the Colonel Phillips Shield, awarded to the company which was the smartest in the Middlesex Battalion. They were also judged to be the best at drill, the best at musketry and to have the highest average attendance. The secret of great teaching is not merely the possession of knowledge and the ability to impart it, it is to know how to enthuse the taught so that they want to learn, so that they try their utmost. The evidence of Mr Wilson's ability in this sphere was that the team from the Lower School also won the county-wide Lady West Memorial Competition for physical drill: physical training or physical education as it would later be termed. With boxing and shooting competitions within the School also being organised under the aegis of the Corps, the School shared victory in the Battalion Boxing Tournament with Kilburn Grammar School, each team winning five bouts in the final. Rhys Trevor Peace won at his weight for the third year running and was rewarded with a medal specially struck to mark his achievement. Then the School's Company Sergeant-Major, Barrie Bennetts, was appointed Battalion Sergeant-Major, the most senior NCO in the whole of the Middlesex Cadet Battalion.

As is so often the case, boys who achieve well in one field also succeed in others. Both Peace and Bennetts contribute in other areas of school life; Peace writes an interesting article as a Tudor character shocked by what he finds in twentieth century England; Bennetts wins praise for his delivery in the Speech Room of a recent address given by Winston Churchill at a Press Fund Dinner.

In sport, the results in cricket are generally pretty even. The beginning of a resurgence shows when Lionel Kitton sets a School record, scoring 149 runs and taking seven wickets against Marylebone Grammar School. The final tally was 225 runs for John Lyon, 24 for Marylebone.

When the military competitions come around again in 1923, the School retains the Phillips Shield and wins the Lucas-Tooth Shield as the best in the county at both physical and company drill. A year later the boys sweep the board: they are the Lady West county champions, the Lucas-Tooth county champions, take the Phillips Shield again, win the County Shooting Shield and receive the Battalion Boxing Cup.

Mr Le Beau, meanwhile, continues to inspire the scientific curiosity of John Lyon boys. He regularly arranges visits to different factories and process plants and there is a significant success for the School in an essay competition open to every school in the country and conducted by the *Educational Times*. The subject is My Favourite Hobby and the School selects three boys to enter: E A Holder, secretary of the Scientific Society, A W Russell and W I Todd. Extraordinarily, in that order, they take the first, second and third prizes, against all comers. There must have been a feeling of buoyancy infusing the place at that time and it is not a surprise to find that in the 1924 examinations the Lower School achieves more distinctions in chemistry than any other school in the country.

The Scientific Society visits the Great Exhibition at Wembley and the works of the *Sunday Pictorial* newspaper, and Alger Gregg, grandson of the great man and currently a boy at the School, gives a talk he has researched on the wonders of the world.

The sense of well-being can only have been enhanced by the Town staging a pageant in which one of the scenes was of Elizabeth I granting the charter to John Lyon, a role undertaken by Old Lyonian Douglas Woodbridge, with sixty current pupils also taking part.[25] The same spirit

---

[25] In 1951, as part of the Festival of Britain, another large pageant was staged by the Town on Wealdstone Football Ground and the same scene was enacted again. This time just one John Lyon boy took part. The full event concluded with a credible look-alike for Winston Churchill slowly walking the length of the pitch, picked out in the darkness by a follow-spot, as Elgar's *Pomp and Circumstance March No. 4* ('All Men Shall Be Free') ensured an emotional response.

would have informed the Whizz-Bang Concert Parties organized by the four Monitors (for some eccentric reason they were suddenly termed Prefects, but as one of them was School Captain, they were certainly Monitors). The four were Lionel Kitton, School, Cricket and Football Captain; Edward Holder, a fine scholar and an outstanding Librarian; Donald Harries, Cadet Sergeant-Major and Vice-captain of both Football and Cricket; and Colin Rose who was to succeed Kitton as School Captain, only to fall seriously ill with typhoid when he left to go to University College, London. The concerts were orchestral events, punctuated by piano solos, violin duets, singing and Colin Rose playing 'an amazing number of instruments'. The School was clearly flourishing again and as if to confirm this the magazine once more started to contain a variety of inventive and original contributions.

News of former students continues to appear and it is reported of Captain Sidney Daw, whose home is on the Kurfurstendamm in Berlin, that he has recently married. He would have been resident in Germany as a member of the Allied Control Commission. The successes of Temple Silvester, presently appointed to Guy's Hospital having gained his MRCS and LRCP, are also reported. Two other men with connections to the School, and both having the initials V S are – curiously in one case, at least – ignored.

Temple's younger brother, Victor Silvester, having studied briefly at Oxford's Worcester College had then spent time reading music at Trinity College, London before concentrating seriously on dance. In 1922, partnered by Phyllis Clarke, he won the first World Ballroom Dancing Championship and embarked on the career that would make him world famous. A year or two later, he was one of the founders of the committee formed by members of the Imperial Society of Teachers of Dancing which sought to codify the different aspects of ballroom dancing and in 1928 he published the first book to define and describe them, *Modern Ballroom Dancing*. It went through numerous editions and was last reprinted in 2005.

He opened first one, and eventually more than a score of dance studios, teaching many celebrities including Hollywood star Merle Oberon. He formed his own dance orchestra, their recordings, which sold in the millions, always observing strict dance tempo. Many of these recordings are still available on compact disc and other media. Through most of the twentieth century he featured regularly on radio and television the world over, so that when his autobiography appeared in 1958 he was described as the most famous dance band leader in British history and for his work he received an OBE three years later.

The other VS was part of a very different story. Vivian Stranders, founder of the School Cadet Corps back in 1911 was, like Captain Daw, now part of the Control Commission in defeated Germany. It was a position from which, however, Captain Stranders was hastily dismissed around the time Silvester was winning his world championship. The reason was his scandalous private life. Thereafter, Stranders only occasionally returned to England, spending most of his time on the continent. Then, in 1926, he was arrested in Paris. The British were about to bring criminal charges against him both under the Official Secrets Act and for bigamy. The French were quicker and did charge him with spying, of which he was convicted, and for which he spent two years in prison. After serving his sentence he returned to Germany and he was to re-emerge in an even less palatable guise some dozen or so years later.

Back on Harrow Hill, as the General Strike paralysed much of the country, the School continued its examination success. All sixteen entrants for School Certificate made the grade, fourteen achieving matriculation standard with many distinctions in specific subjects, especially chemistry and maths.

The Gurney Shield, for which cadets from the four School Houses competed, was inaugurated the same year, as was the first annual School Swimming Sports. Cricket results improved markedly as the summer term progressed, with several strong wins in the latter half of the season, while football results in the autumn saw an even more signal improvement. All but three of the sixteen matches were won and by margins such as 13–1 or 11–1. Confidence breeds confidence breeds success.

Before the football season of 1926, though, in the July, Mr Edward Herbert Butt announced his retirement. He had guarded his Christian names a close secret, and possibly his age, too. He was seventy years old. He had been with the School from the days of its first Headmaster, J E Williams, and had served for thirty-three years. He had steered it through the stormiest years of its existence and brought it to a time of remarkable achievement on many fronts. He must have felt, and deserved to feel, a sense of real accomplishment.

His position as Headmaster was quietly handed to the multi-talented and energetic O A Le Beau whose philosophy saw finality in no undertaking: each achievement, he said, was merely a milestone along the way. The School magazine never even announced his appointment. He was simply there.

CHAPTER 8

DIGGING IN
1927–1938

The next dozen years saw a period of entrenchment. There was growth in the numbers of boys and staff, additional School buildings and additional facilities, but perhaps more importantly, it was a time when there was no threat, apparent or cloaked, to the School's future. It was a time when the foundations could be strengthened.

On the face of it, it is surprising that this should coincide with a period of recession and slump, of unemployment and a return to international tension and foreboding. Equally, it may have been that those external pressures were seen to increase the worth of what the John Lyon School stood for: a link into the nation's long history, a code of decent values and an ambition to succeed through work, through energy, through commitment.

The period opened less than propitiously with the unexpected death of Virgilius Black, English master, editor of *The Lyonian* and for eleven years responsible for the boys' singing on Speech Day and on other public occasions. Shortly after, Dr Walter Leaf, who was on the platform at many of those Speech Days and who was a generous benefactor of the School, also died. He had joined the Committee of Management as far back as 1893 and had chaired it for the ten years from 1903. Dr Leaf was the unusual mix of a highly successful businessman – Chairman of the Westminster Bank – and a famous and widely-respected authority on the classics. The scholarships he gave to enable boys go on to university had helped many Lyonians to successful careers and they continued to do so after his death.

Editorship of the School magazine fell to the new head of English, Donald Cowtan, and the style which had been evolving over the years, now became blander and more impersonal. Little emerges about the characters of individual boys, except in the pieces they, themselves, write. Extraordinarily, given a Headmaster who was a keen photographer and who produced scores of slides to illustrate different talks, photographs cease to appear in the magazine. Humour is largely absent, too. For a long

time every Spring Term is greeted with the same formula of words; so too
every Summer Term and every Winter Term. There are appeals, as there
had been from Mr Black, for original contributions and as the years
proceed these increase impressively. The quality of these articles is often
impressive, too. But some of the liveliness *The Lyonian* had historically
shown seems to have seeped away.

There is also some confusion over the title to be given to the most
senior boys. For some years the School Captain is designated as such in
the magazine but referred to as the Head of School on Speech Day after
Speech Day. Monitors suddenly disappear from the honours list to be
called Prefects in 1927 and 1928. Then, the following year we find a
School Captain, one Monitor and four Pro-Monitors. Then three
Monitors and four Pro-Monitors until in 1930 we return to having a
School Captain and five Monitors. After that the number of Monitors
increases, only to decrease dramatically in 1932 with the result that not
one House Captain that year was also a Monitor. A little later, however,
the pattern that was to obtain into the next century was established, with
the number of Monitors varying from around eight to a dozen. In 1935
we finally arrive at a consensus that the top boy is to be called the Head of
the School or Head Boy, while House Captains remain, as they do today,
House Captains. Although even in 1935 the Captain of West House is
still not a Monitor. The same year, for the first time, there is an official
Deputy Head Boy.

John Learner, who had entered the School in 1926, remembered the
staff as being limited to Mr Le Beau who combined his Headmastership
with teaching all science, 'Froggy' Thomas so-called for the plain reason
that he taught French, while 'Bruiser' Thomas succeeded Mr Black in
teaching English. He appears to have lasted only a term before Mr
Cowtan replaced him and maybe his nickname gives a clue why. Mr
Kearsey taught history, Doctor Ewbank, commuting daily from
Southend-on-Sea, taught Latin and produced the famous and widely
used textbook on the subject, while the redoubtable Willy Wilson was
responsible for maths, the Cadet Corps and organizing end-of-term
concerts and Sports Day, for which he was sometimes known as Pooh-
Bah, the minister for everything.

There were around 35 boys in each year, although out of the two
hundred candidates who sat the entrance examination in 1927, forty were
in fact admitted, so that the School's population was around the 180
mark. This must have made the demands on the academic staff of six
quite unremitting. At this time music, drama, geography and biology

were not taught. From 1922, regular sport was overseen by Mr 'Johnny' Williams, but there was still no sports ground for the exclusive use of John Lyon boys. There was, however, the unofficial School tuckshop lower down Middle Road, known as Missus. Very soon, there were two such popular resorts for the boys: the one in Crown Street was immediately called Top Missus and the one in Middle Road then became known as Bottom Missus. There were no School meals so boys either went home or brought a packed lunch. After a time Bottom Missus, spotting the gap in the market, supplied simple meals at midday.

The lack of an exclusive track or pitches did not mean sport was not being taken seriously. Sports Day, as before, was held at the Harrow School track. The Boxing tournament, with the usually victorious Peace whose father was the principal coach, only managing a draw with Dave North, was conducted in 1927 at the Old Lyonian headquarters in Pinner View. The following year it was in the Harrow School gymnasium. Swimming Sports were once again at the Harrow Baths.

Cricket meantime continued its exceptional run of success. Of twenty-one games played in 1927 by the First Eleven, eighteen were won and two drawn. On three occasions, centuries were scored and most of the victories were comprehensive. The Second Eleven, playing fewer matches, achieved a comparable level of success, with eight wins and only one loss from their ten confrontations. This was a pattern which held for several years. As is almost always the case, good sportsmen do well whatever the game. School football showed similar positive results. The previous season the team faced thirty-two opposing sides and was victorious on twenty-six occasions, including every single home game; next winter they found themselves playing twenty-seven games and losing only three; then the following season, playing twenty-six matches, winning eighteen of them and drawing four, with scores varying from the dramatic, Royal Commercial Travellers' School 1, John Lyon School 19, to the not-quite-so-satisfactory John Lyon School 1, Mercers' 3.

This level of achievement, which lasted until 1932, is the more remarkable in the light of a second-former's letter to the School magazine, four years earlier, pleading for year-round sports facilities so that boys could *practise.*

Throughout this period, too, the Cadet Force continued its winning ways. The Lady West Championship for the county was held continuously by the School, until in 1936 all other schools had given up. Encouraged possibly by the Harrow Rifle Club donating a cup to be competed for by the best shots in the School, the John Lyon squad nearly as often won the Battalion Shooting Cup. Almost immediately on leaving, one of the boys involved, R W Gregg, won the Silver Cup at Bisley as the Territorial Army's best shot, before emigrating to take his degree at McGill University in Montreal. At the same time Colin Rose, back from Tanganyika, gave a lecture about the country at Middle Road and then went up to University College where he straightaway became London University's Captain of Shooting.

From the early 1930s, the John Lyon contingent continued to take the Lucas-Tooth Competition as well, holding it for five years without a break. They then took to winning the Walton Shield, presented for target shooting, to depress their rivals even further.

It can hardly have been a surprise, therefore, that Field Marshal Lord Allenby, one of the principal military leaders in the Great War, elected both to conduct the Annual Inspection of the Corps and then, in 1934, to present the prizes on Speech Day. Nor would it have been a surprise that Mr Wilson was promoted to Major and, in 1937, awarded the Coronation Medal for his services to the Cadet Movement. At Viscount Allenby's funeral a representative group of boys from the School responded to the invitation to attend at Westminster Abbey.

To go back, though, to the earlier days of Le Beau's reign there was, as is not unusual with a new person at the helm, a sense that fresh challenges were to be embraced. Much of the established pattern of School life went on, of course, as before: trips by parties of boys to a range of places, to Parliament, to HMV, Nestlé's chocolate factory, a waterworks, the Public Record Office, the Royal Mint, the Royal Tournament and more; then the beginning of a series of visits, often several each term, to see Shakespeare at the Old Vic, run by the inspirational Lilian Baylis.[26] Junior and Senior Debates continued, but now they focused on international, and even in one instance, interplanetary subjects rather than domestic ones. Familiar names could be spotted on the School register: the latest Perrin joining the first form as a Parkhouse and a Breingan set off from the fifth into the world. At the new Headmaster's first Speech Day the prizes were presented by Sir Frank Dyson, both of whose brothers had been educated at the School.

Among the innovations, Credit Marks were awarded on a termly basis to selected boys. This continued for some decades although it was never

---

[26] Lilian Baylis CH, 1874–1937. The present day Old Vic, Sadler's Wells and National Theatres, the Royal Ballet, Sadler's Wells Ballet and English National Opera all owe their existence to the pioneer work of this extraordinary, plain-spoken woman whose determination, energy and eye for talent were second to none.

quite clear what the criteria for the award might be. By the name it was given there was an implication that good work had been done and that there was a loyalty and commitment to be saluted. At the same time, it was quite possible for a boy to be a regular prize winner and captain of his form but not to enter the list of the anointed. Apart from the mention in the School magazine, there did not appear to be any advantage in the award, either.

It was announced that a School Orchestra and a Drama Society were planned. The orchestra soon came into being, described by one boy, Richard Upson, as Mr Cowtan's 'pride and joy'. Young Upson joined it to play all the lower scale brass parts on his uncle's euphonium. This experience so overcame his shyness that by his last year at School he helped form a dance band fronted by Steve Statham, a boy who modelled himself on the cavorting of 'Snakehips' Johnson. Playing at the School concert, 'it was a riot'.

A Chess Club was started. Most significant of all, Dr Cyril Norwood, Head Master of Harrow gave news in 1928 that the School was to be enlarged and the age range of its pupils to be extended to eighteen years.

The next year came reports of the New Building, as it was logically known, going up. It was to incorporate an assembly hall doubling as a gymnasium, a physics laboratory, and enough form rooms to enable both post-matriculation studies and a substantial increase in the School population. Academically the School was still achieving some remarkable results. J A Shaljean and R H King, for example, took First and Second Prizes, respectively, for mathematics in the senior examinations of the London School of Commerce. Brian Pearce, described as our 'precocious history scholar'[27] won the Bronze Medal and First Prize given by the Royal Empire Society for an essay on Livingstone. His interests were wide and around the same time he contributed an excellent article to *The Lyonian* on the history of the thirteen islands of the Dodecanese, and later a perceptive piece on contemporary cartoonists. In adult life he was to become a distinguished Marxist historian, three times winner of the Scott-Moncrieff Prize and to write several significant histories, including *How Haig Saved Lenin*, refuting some of the Soviet claims made for Russia's achievements in the First World War. It was published in 1988. His works are held in the Pearce Archive at Aberdeen University.

By the April of 1930 the New Building was complete and photographs

[27] The phrase was quoted from the 1929 edition of *The Lyonian* in the *Guardian* newspaper's obituary of Pearce when he died in 2008, aged 93. There were numerous tributes to his brilliance at that time.

were reproduced of its exterior and some of the rooms. John Learner rejoiced that his fifth-form year was to be 'spent in all this luxury'. Sixth-formers must have rejoiced, too. Barry Cresswell, who joined the School around 1927 remembered his first-form year being spent in the Cloisters, while the sixth form were 'wherever they could find a space!'

While these positive steps were being taken on the Hill, something was going awry among the Old Boys. A group of fifty, very soon to be ninety and then more, formed their own John Lyon Association and in 1929 had held eleven meetings at the School. They organized their own Annual Dinner, formed their own Dramatic Club and then their own football team. There was obviously some kind of rift with the Old Lyonian Association. Each group played a football match against the School and each was well beaten.

The situation lasted for a couple of years with the supporters of the John Lyon Association returning to the Hill for all sorts of meetings, including billiards matches and a second Annual Dinner. Then, as suddenly as it came into being, it is heard of no more. The Vicar of Harrow, the Reverend Eric Stogden says he is glad there is now harmony about all former pupils joining the Old Lyonian Association.

Individual Old Lyonians continued to distinguish themselves. One of John Learner's contemporaries and friends, Terence Spencer, did notably well at university and in due course became the Professor of English at Belfast and then held the same chair at Birmingham, going on to be Director of the Shakespeare Institute at Stratford-upon-Avon. D J Gold, who had only recently ceased to be the assistant editor of the School magazine, won the Gold Medal for Higher English in the London Chamber of Commerce examinations. Norman Goldhawk, a former School Captain, added a Theology degree at Cambridge to the Philosophy degree he already held from London, while Vivian Varcoe, who had been at the School in the early years of the First War, received the Silver Medal, the highest award the Royal Humane Society has to give. It is rarely awarded. Dating back to 1775, it recognizes the recipient for 'putting himself in extreme personal danger to save the life of another.'

School examination results at this time held up extremely well and, the New Building not being improvement enough, the Governors announced that they had acquired ten acres of land at Sudbury, adjacent to Harrow School's Sanatorium, to be a sports ground for John Lyon boys. Almost exactly coinciding with the news, the fine games players came to the end of their school careers, and John Lyon's sport slid into a period of distinctly poor results. Nonetheless, the news was exciting and the next task was to raise money for a pavilion. Ironically, in their hour of need but not too much ability, boys now had the opportunity to practise for which young Ronald Deeks had once begged.

Mr Le Beau repeated his hardy annual Lecture on Liquid Air several times more. Donald Cowtan gave regular piano recitals and, under his baton, the newly formed orchestra, which had grown from a string combination to a symphonic thirty-seven players, gave concerts mixing classical pieces with carols. Mr Wilson organised and, with a mixed cast of staff and boys, played the principal role in a play entitled *Grumpy*. Later there was a production of *The Ghost Train*. All went down well. All raised sums towards the new goal. A specific Pavilion Fund was set up and among the early donors, following their generous family tradition, were Mr and Mrs Blackwell, parents of boys currently at the School.

One sport that fared well, better possibly than previously, was athletics. The Gymnasium Class – gymnastics were seen as extra-curricular – now came under the aegis of the Corps and displays were put on, but in athletics a number of records were broken and matches with other schools started to take place. The first brought a victory against Harrow County. By the middle of the decade competitions in a single season included the Public School Sports at White City, the Middlesex Inter-schools Championships at the same venue, and matches against Harrow County again, Acton County School (another victory) and a narrow defeat by the Old Lyonians.

With the enlarged buildings to house the School, the numbers of the taught increased substantially. So, naturally, did the number of the staff. John King, joining as a first-former in 1937, the latest in a long line of Kings in the School's history, recalled that there were two classes of around twenty-four boys in each year, giving a total in the region of two hundred and fifty, to which should be added those who stayed on into the sixth form. Before that, in 1933, the staff had been increased by three new masters who included J W Walker and W F Cummings, both of whom stayed to the end of their careers, more than a quarter of a century later. Mr Shelley, a descendant of the poet's family[28] had already joined the staff. His responsibility was art. Eric Boobyer remembered the subject as not being taken too seriously. His view was possibly influenced by the fact that it was not an examination subject. Shelley was an able practitioner and teacher who devoted close to twenty years

---

[28] It is a quaint reflection that his forbears were, we know, good friends with the forbears of Mr Hutchinson, the original master in charge of the English Form and nephew of William Wordsworth.

of his life to the School where, from its inception, drawing and visual art had always been part of the syllabus. In the course of time many boys had been noted for their ability in the field and not a few went on to be architects and the like. In the mid-thirties, one of the School's bigger events was the exhibition Mr Shelley organised in the Art Room and which included, among many drawings, models and paintings, a complete scale model of an aerodrome, watercolours on rice paper and a painting executed on the inside of a narrow-necked bottle. All were the work of boys, but unfortunately *The Lyonian* fails to reveal the name of even one of them.

From its earliest years, the School had recorded the details of each boy joining in ledger-like Registers. Noted there was the boy's date of birth and when he entered the School, his previous place of education, his father's name and the home address. Sometimes later information was added: achievements at John Lyon, subsequent employment or success, and always the date he had left. Of particular interest is to see the feeder schools involved. They vary enormously. Some, of course, because boys have arrived from other parts of the Kingdom. There was always a measurable number from what were called Board schools, later called National schools, then Council schools, later still, State schools. At the beginning several dame schools featured. Most regular, however, were Quainton Hall, Lyon Hall and a small establishment in Pinner, Reddiford. Although the record continued to be kept beyond this date, the Registers have unfortunately been lost. The last existing record is for early 1935. The final entry is for Gordon Slater Blyth, from Sudbury. In due course he became Captain of North House, and when he returned as a member of Staff after war service in the RAF, he became House Master of North House, before going on to be Headmaster of Downham Market High School in Norfolk. One whom the Register missed, possibly because he joined the School marginally too late for it, or perhaps because the Register itself is these days in tatters, was Malcolm Shepherd. His father was national agent for the Labour Party and one of the architects of the 1945 landslide election victory. He was ennobled and became the party's Chief Whip in the Lords. Malcolm, educated at the Lower School and a Quaker school in Saffron Walden, in due course succeeded to the title and followed his father as Chief Whip. He became Minister of State at the Commonwealth Office, a Privy Councillor and, at different times, Deputy Leader and Deputy Speaker in the House of Lords.

Back in 1935, the long-promised Ambulance Section is formed. For boys in the senior forms, the Scientific Society is revived and so is one of the keen pastimes of Ernest Young, rambles, by the newly formed Nature Club. Shortly afterwards there is a Pedestrian Club committed to exploring the urban landscape. Someone, not before time, thought to invite a professional coach from the Football Association to work with the boys, as well. There is a definite sense that it was important for things to move on, for activities to be expanded. As Sir Alfred Hurst had observed at Speech Day in 1933, 'We need a rising generation of greater training, wider experience and easier adaptability than has characterised this nation in the past.' Sir Alfred, who lived in South Hill Avenue and was Under-Secretary at the Treasury, began a long association with the School, encouraging boys to study longer and take all the opportunities they could in preparation for life in a competitive world.

A Geographical Society comes into being for the first time and then, without preamble, more building is announced. The north end of the New Building is to be extended towards Crown Street and westwards down the slope towards the Sixth Form Ground. The building style would match the existing edifice and the three, stepped blocks would provide a chemistry laboratory, several more form rooms, showers and a cloakroom and, at its furthest and lowest reach, a space which could double as a small gym when required. The construction was swiftly accomplished and the extension opened in 1935. In a unique flash of humour for this time, *The Lyonian* observed, 'we believe VIth formers made their first acquaintance with colloquial Italian while the parquet floors were being laid.'

Inter-school swimming competitions were entered into, with successful matches against RCTS and Kilburn Grammar, but a loss to Harrow County.

The sense of moving on and of a changing world was reinforced by Leo Amery when he came to present the prizes in 1936. He marvelled at the changes seen in the last fifty years. English fliers, he said, could now reach Australia in three days! But he added that this was nothing to what tomorrow's prizewinners would see. Leo Amery was the Head Boy at Harrow whom the young Winston Churchill had unwisely shoved into the water at Ducker. He had become a distinguished politician, and he was to serve in Churchill's war-time government. He was also, in the future, to withstand a near-unbearable personal and family tragedy. On this occasion he concluded by saying that after the Great War 'elderly men hoped they had settled the map of the world on lines that might endure. . . . It looks as if they were mistaken.' He was not wrong. And he was well ahead of many of his Parliamentary colleagues in his concern.

In the Coronation celebrations of 1937, Cadets from the School paraded at Horseguards' as part of the Review by the Director-General of the Territorial Army, General Sir Walter Kirk. The band was formed by players from Christ's College and the Lower School of John Lyon. Two former pupils, Horace Dive and Squadron Leader Harold Roach, received OBEs in the Coronation Honours. Among other recent successes, Brian Pearce who had contributed many fine articles to the magazine, took the Dolley History Prize at University College, London and, remarkably, at the age of sixteen H N Hunt, who was Head Boy, won an Exhibition to the same college. Peter Hargreaves, who was of an age with Hunt, was awarded the highly valuable Duddell Scholarship by the Institute of Electrical Engineers.

The contributions by boys to *The Lyonian* had been of an increasingly high standard. It proved all too easy to parody Longfellow and the rather irritating rhythms of *Hiawatha*, though one or two of the pastiches were very funny. Other individual poems, often by very young boys like second-formers H R W Rady and H J Cook, showed impressive talent. There were well-thought-out articles on a huge range of subjects and a number of short stories well-crafted for teenagers, or adolescents as they would have been called then.

On their visits to the theatre, which now extended to regular trips to Regent's Park as well as to the Old Vic, the boys had seen the greatest actors of the period at work: Olivier, Gielgud, Ralph Richardson, Edith Evans, George Robey as Falstaff, Robert Atkins as Bottom, Sybil Thorndike – the stellar list goes on. In the later thirties H J R Tickle, known as John, next generation of his family to be connected, entered the School and he was surely in the party that went to see yet another production of *A Midsummer Night's Dream*. It was 1938 and the cast at the Old Vic was led by Ralph Richardson as Bottom, Vivien Leigh as Titania, Robert Helpmann as Oberon and, as Quince, the 'rosy rotundity' of his Old Lyonian uncle, Frank Tickle.

This same year the Headmaster's Testimonial Fund, raised from dozens of gifts to mark Mr Le Beau's quarter century of service, was put to good use. The money purchased for the School a grand piano and cover, a film projector, honours boards for the Hall and a roller for the cricket pitch. It is amazing how far £183 went in 1938.

There was more news of academic success. At UCL, A K Hudson took a First in English and with it, the Rosa Morrison Memorial Medal as the best final-year student, the Morley Medal for English and the Quain Essay Prize, while D W King took the Morris Prize for Geology.

Mr E Lloyd Thomas, the senior French master, retired from the School. H J R Tickle gained a credit mark, School Certificate and Matriculation.

Continuing the process of digging in, in the light of the worsening international situation, masters and boys of the John Lyon School took spades to the field below the School. There, as in towns and villages the length and breadth of the country, they dug trenches against what might come, while younger members of the School, envious of their elders, sat inside sewing pieces of hessian into bags and filled them with sand.

CHAPTER 9

KEEPING CALM AND CARRYING ON
1939–1945

As the old year ended and new one dawned, the School was doing well. Boys of that time spoke of strict discipline, firm but fair, mostly imposed by Monitors and Prefects. On occasion, as Robert Walker, who at eighty claims still to have the broken teeth to prove it, the punishment handed out in the boiler room by senior boys went well beyond the acceptable. Among the staff, it fell principally to the Deputy Head, Mr Wilson, to ensure good behaviour. At Assembly, he would take an offender by the ear onto the platform to give him a public dressing-down. He also had a good line in warnings. Two of them remembered by generations of pupils being, 'If I come down there, there'll be nothing left but a grease spot and a trouser button' and the other the threat, 'I'll warm your onion!' Corporal punishment by the Headmaster was occasionally applied, but Mr Le Beau was generally mild in his dealings. The cane was reserved for serious offences committed off School premises and Eric Boobyer recalled it being used only twice in his time at the School, once for shop theft and then on an occasion when a boy was caught selling bayonets belonging to the Corps, down in Harrow. After castigation, he was expelled. John King experienced a couple of more domestic physical punishments while Geoff Lancashire, who joined the School in 1935 and liked to avoid sport if at all possible, found himself in detention for skiving on a Wednesday afternoon and choosing the cinema over the pitch. Generally behaviour was orderly and the view usually expressed was that there was great spirit in the School.

In those days, no one came to School by car. It was public transport, the bicycle or walking. School uniform was well established as a navy blue blazer with the School crest on the breast pocket. The shield was of the unusual shape long associated with Harrow.[29] Boys wore long or short

[29] The identical design with blunted top corners to the shield and bulging sides, surrounding a lion rampant, and with crossed arrows above, is depicted low in one of the windows of a side chapel

grey trousers, according to age, a white shirt, diagonally striped blue and maroon tie not unlike the Guards tie, grey socks and black shoes. Monitors and those with sports colours wore a different, much larger blazer badge. The shield, lion, and the letters which proclaimed the distinction (set between two red lines), were in gold. The letters were M for Monitor. A for Athletics, B for Boxing and so on. Later, when Shooting colours were awarded, members of the shooting eight had a Roman VIII on the badge, to differentiate it from the S for Swimming colours. Eric Boobyer remembers Monitors wearing a single-coloured tie signifying the House they belonged to, but a little later those were reserved for boys who had been awarded House Colours, who might or might not be Monitors. Prefects were distinguished by a small red lion rampant, exactly as on the blazer badge, but minus the surrounding white shield outline, worn on the left lapel.

The advantage of this prescriptiveness was that adolescent rebellion could be, and from time to time was, registered by wearing yellow socks, without any need to hit an old lady over the head. Or, indeed, to set up as an arms dealer in central Harrow. Not that this entirely stifled juvenile invention. 'Joey' Cummings regularly attracted attention on arrival in a form room by banging his case down on the master's desk. On a particular occasion, a boy positioned that desk so that its front legs protruded over the dais on which it was placed. The consequence of a hefty blow from above does not need to be described. Nor does the pleasure the whole form derived from it. A little milk on the board rubber also provided satisfaction: it rendered the blackboard afterwards impossible to write on.

Books which, from the original days of Lyon's charter had to be purchased by parents, in addition to the fees they paid, were obtained from Shepherd's Bookshop in Lowlands Road. A little more than a decade later they were available from the excellent Harrow School Bookshop on the High Street, just along from the Head Master's House. At Shepherd's it was possible, and quite usual, to buy the set texts second-hand. 'If you were lucky you might get one with helpful marginal notes added by previous owners, but you were more likely to inherit schoolboy graffiti.'[30]

in King's College Chapel, Cambridge. It is clearly the John Lyon/Harrow School arms since adjacent, for no apparent reason in either case, are the arms of Eton College. Both are monochrome and very small, maybe six centimetres high.

[30] These recollections are drawn from Eric Boobyer's private memoir, 'A Very Personal Account of Life at John Lyon School 1938–43'.

Following the presentation of three one-act plays, including Chekhov's
The Proposal with D Kapamadjian in the role of Stepan Stepanovich the
previous Christmas, boys and staff prepared for the 1939 summer
production. This was to be *Busman's Holiday* by Dorothy L Sayers and
M St.Clare Byrne and it proved to be the last play staged at the School for
some time. Previously there had been a number of full-scale productions
and, at each Speech Day, a scene from an English play and a scene from a
French play performed in their respective languages by the boys in the
Speech Room.

1939, however, with Mr Paul Vellacott,[31] Head Master of Harrow on
the platform, was to see the last Speech Day, and the last awarding of a full
list of prizes, for some years. On Government advice, the occasion was
cancelled thereafter. It proved to be a wise decision. In 1940 the Speech
Room suffered a direct hit by an incendiary bomb and was seriously
damaged.

The accent now, understandably, was on the Cadet Corps. Mr Wilson
was promoted Lieutenant-Colonel and given command of the 1st
Battalion, Middlesex Regiment Cadets. The School's contingent rose to
220 members reducing only when large numbers were evacuated in the
ensuing years. One of the boys, N J Payne, was appointed an Under-
Officer and another, encouragingly, to be Sergeant (Cook). The latter role
was not subsequently repeated, though whether because the appointee's
food was so good that no one could follow him, or so appalling that a
repeat could not be risked, is not revealed. Once again, the School won the
Lucas-Tooth Competition. Then that, too, seems to have been dropped.

With the outbreak of war and the imposition of blackouts, a number of
regular activities had to be ended or curtailed. The Signals Section of the
Corps had to reduce its activities, while the Ambulance Section extended
the training it undertook, with visits to Harrow Hospital and with Section
members manning Air Raid Protection Posts. The School had set up its
own ARP scheme just before war was declared.

On War Office orders, the annual Cadet Camp was cancelled. Re-
sources were needed for more immediate demands. The School, early on,
had become part of the Public Schools' Cadet Association. At the height
of the Battle of Britain, boys debated whether membership of the Corps
should be compulsory. Their verdict was 51 to 4, against. The other big
debate around this time was on the motion 'That Hitler is Mad'. No vote
was taken since, presumably, it was felt to be unnecessary.

---

[31] Later, a popular Master of Peterhouse, Cambridge's oldest college.

Gym classes, which were still an after-school activity, could only function in the summer months. A planned display had to be cancelled. Neither these classes nor boxing practice were fully restored until 1941, when presumably effective masking of the lights in the Hall had been achieved. This may seem a little odd, since the Hall was equipped with ropes, wall-bars, a beam, vaulting horses and the like, and these could have been used during normal daylight periods. It appears the timetable was not adjusted to allow for this, perhaps for fear some more vital part of the curriculum would have to be sacrificed when everything had to stop at sundown.

All sporting activities were restricted. The reduction in time for boxing must have been especially galling, given that in 1939 three John Lyon boys reached the semi-finals of the Public Schools' Championship. Sports Day the following year, an occasion much looked forward to as boys decided in which events they would compete, was cancelled and the separate contests had to be staggered over several days. Football matches for the First XI were reduced to just three, two of which were victories. All rambles were cancelled. Instead, on the 'Dig for Victory' principle, boys worked on the School allotments, sited on the lower field, alongside the footpath up from Lower Road. There, they would come in at weekends as well to tend their vegetables and take them home, Mr Le Beau digging with the best.

The Lyonian suffered a drastic reduction of its contents, in response to the economic situation. As it had a quarter of a century before, it became in part a record of deaths and decorations. In doing so, it once more found a greater and welcome measure of emotional involvement.

Normal schoolwork was affected, too. With periodic daytime air raids, as soon as the siren went classes would be interrupted and everyone would troop to the New Building's lowest room, its windows blocked with sandbags. Gas masks had to be carried at all times and their cases were, on the evidence of one boy, used to secrete sweets and, even worse, forbidden magazines which might beguile the juvenile mind during the *longueurs* before the all-clear sounded.

Early in the war a small bomb scored a direct hit on the bicycle shed, beside the New Building. Form 2B were in the divided hall being taught by Joey Cummings when the explosion blew in the windows on the hall's western side. The glass had been heavily taped and caused little damage, the shed was destroyed, but the blast was such that boys, desks, papers and books were blown in a heap across the hall. At the time no one seemed to be much hurt. After tidying up, Joey even managed to continue the lesson. Keith Leader and one of his friends later found they had lost the hearing in their right ears. It was not immediate, but it was lasting.

After this, a boy would be posted on the playground, and later perched in the bell tower on the roof of the Old Building, to spot incoming enemy planes, so as to reduce the interruption caused when sirens sounded for no readily apparent reason, but to give due warning when needed. One of the ablest of the spotters was Colin Sorenson. A talented painter, he went on from School, once the war was over, to the Royal College of Art and enjoyed a successful career as a painter, social historian and as an outstanding Curator at the Museum of London.

As in the Great War, scores of Old Boys, many of them recent leavers, volunteered for the services. The first of them to die was Pilot Officer John Grimes, killed in action on 6th December 1939, remembered as 'full of youthful energy and charm'. With the passing months the numbers of those joining, the numbers of those killed, the numbers of those honoured, multiplied. And, as in the Great War, the numbers of those returning to spend an hour or two at their old School before going off to the bitter fray increased dramatically.

Another death, from natural causes this time, ushered in 1940. E H Butt, aged eighty-four, who had not retired until he was seventy and who had remained in close touch during the intervening years, was recalled in the warmest of tributes. His amazing versatility, his brilliance as a teacher, especially of maths and French, and his musical gifts were all acknowledged. The statement that his passing 'leaves an aching void in our tradition' recognized his greatest achievement and his most lasting legacy: without him, his determination and his perseverance, the John Lyon School would not have continued to exist. *Si monumentum requiris circumspice.*[32]

Later in the year, in almost exact replication of some of the losses in the First War when exemplary students like Hubert Cram and John Stillman were killed, H N Hunt, known by his middle name of Norman, died in action. A Pilot Officer, twenty-two years old, he had been an outstanding scholar. At thirteen, he gained his School Certificate with Matriculation Exemption, the necessary qualification for university entrance and designed to be achieved by bright sixteen-year-olds. At seventeen, he had acquired Higher School Certificates and Intermediate qualifications in both science and the arts. 'Inters' were equivalent to completing the first year of each degree. He was awarded an Exhibition at UCL where he

[32] If you wish to see his monument, look around you. Borrowed from the inscription on Sir Christopher Wren's tomb at St Paul's Cathedral.

gained a First and the College's Diploma in Engineering. When he gave his life, he was one of two hundred and sixty former pupils serving in the Armed Forces.

Other young men were still doing brilliantly. Among the many Old Lyonians taking degrees, H K Hardy gained a First Class BSc and a First Class Associateship of the Royal School of Mines, the Bessemer Medal and the Bessemer Prize and the Edward Ernest Glorney Scholarship awarded to the Royal School's top student.

Still others were honoured for conspicuous bravery: Lieutenant Bernard Wing RNR, commanding a Minesweeper Flotilla, received the DSC; Harold Roach received the AFC, G R Ross and J C Davidson both received the DFC, pilots all three of them; and the Military Medal was given to F A Waters, only for him to be killed shortly afterwards. The School magazine, noting yet more visits from former students, added 'We can no longer leave the records at this, as happily once we could. They must be seared now with reports of casualties.' To Waters' name was straightaway added those of Howard Forster, a navigation officer in the Merchant Navy and Pilot Officer Horace Hewlitt. The war clouded every aspect of life. It darkened the mood and defined the possible.

At Middle Road, by December 1941, the War Savings target of £1500 had been surpassed by fifteen shillings and sixpence (77.5p). Thanks to the successes of the Royal Air Force, daylight raids were few and several activities could be resumed. A concert was staged with three professional entertainers. Gymnastics, boxing and swimming were all back on the calendar. More cricket matches had been played in the summer, though the results were uninspiring apart from a victory by eight wickets over Merchant Taylors'. Restrictions, however, meant that prizes for school-work were limited to one for Science, two for History and ten Swainson Memorial Prizes for English, plus a Donald Maisey Memorial Prize for the boy making most progress.

Two other responses to the national emergency were highly practical. In early 1942, around the time the Army Cadets were able to shed their First World War uniforms with peaked caps and puttees wound round up to the knee and to replace them with contemporary battledress, twenty-four boys from the School formed Number 1573 Flight of the Air Training Corps. They wore standard RAF uniforms and were lucky enough to camp at Bovingdon airfield and to enjoy flights in Avro Ansons and Handley Page Hampdens as the war continued.

The Air Cadets combined with their counterparts at Harrow School for instruction, the two units having been formed jointly. At the same time four of the School's Army Cadets represented the Corps at Buckingham Palace where they were inspected by the King.

The second innovation, brought about by two boys in particular, was to start a canteen in the Cloisters. Involved in both these recent developments was Eric Boobyer. In the latest, with his close friend Eric Willis, he managed to acquire food coupons (canteens for the use of), as he described them, with which various sandwich fillings, including the inevitable spam, were bought. Along with the sandwiches they concocted, the two Erics brewed tea and made soft drinks which they sold at break-time and lunchtime to their schoolmates. Their enterprise continued long after both boys had left.

The same kind of initiative galvanized sixth-formers in 1943 to ask if they could set up their own social club. While, unlike during the First War, almost all School Societies and activities kept going strongly once the blackout problem was overcome, there was almost nothing available where senior boys might enjoy simple relaxation and fun. Their idea was immediately accepted and various masters took it in turn to unlock and lock up on Saturday evenings so that the boys could organize their own entertainment.

Only a few months later, an Inter-Schools Sixth Form Committee was formed, involving only the young people themselves. It included all the local County schools, except Harrow County for Girls, whose staff would not allow the girls to attend without being there to chaperone them. The rest, Lower School boys among them, all met at Pinner County, where the Headmaster was Old Lyonian, Mr Percy Rayner, for an evening of music and discussion. Future events planned included dances and a political conference.

Historically, poetry had been a regular feature in the pages of *The Lyonian* and, tight as space was, room was still found for some excellent contributions. One that stands out is an updated version of Cowper's 'The Loss of the Royal George', to mark the sinking of HMS *The Prince of Wales* off Singapore. It was by sixth-former R F C Ward and written while he was fire-watching. The Duke of Wellington would have approved of a young man who filled each unforgiving minute with such positive activity.

The magazine's rediscovered emotional centre allows a tribute to a leaver to appear, someone still alive, the first of any substance for years. It is a farewell written by P A L McHenry and seconded in print by sports master Johnny Williams, to John King, Captain of Boxing: 'John has worked unceasingly training and teaching the juniors and encouraging us seniors. As captain he has worked hard, but as a boxer he has fought even harder and we are very sorry indeed to lose him'. John had won the London Public and Secondary Schools Championship. He went on to take a degree and enjoyed the hard struggle to succeed, a habit he was sure he acquired at the Lower School, where he had also been Captain of Gymnastics. Later he entered the construction industry. Asked recently if there were any particular projects he was pleased to have carried through, he mentioned being in charge of the reconstruction of London Bridge to Lord Holford's design, after the nineteenth-century predecessor was sold to Arizona, and then he added as an afterthought, being responsible for the drilling and building of the British side of the Channel Tunnel. This, of course, was one of the most complex and risk-filled engineering feats of the twentieth century. He received the OBE for his work.

Examination results at the School still held up well, despite several members of staff being called up and replaced by others who often stayed only briefly. Among the first to leave were Mr Paine, Mr Shelley who joined the RAF, and the caretaker, Mr Roach, whose successor known as Beery Bill was regarded as geriatric and given an uneasy time by the less biddable elements in the School. It may be that the record number of Monitors appointed, sixteen, was in response to this unruliness. Mr Mitchell, the physics master, also left, summoned to use his skills at the Admiralty.

One of the newcomers, too old for military service, but who stayed until his retirement nine years later, was the avuncular Mr Watterson. He taught French and looked after one of the first forms.

With success on the playing field still tending to languish, Johnny Williams began to arrange sporting lectures for the boys. One of his coups was to persuade Patsy Hendren, described in Wisden as one of the greatest cricketers ever, to be among the speakers. Hendren had scored 170 first class centuries, a record only beaten by Sir Jack Hobbs and, playing between 1919 and 1939, he had brought off 725 catches. His racy stories were reported as going down very well with the boys and he may have been the inspiration they needed. Next season the results were impressive: the eleven matches played brought just one defeat and the victories included contests with Malvern College and Merchant Taylors'. Football, unfortunately, did not manage to keep pace with the cricketers.

The canteen, now that its originators had left and were to be found along with several contemporaries holding commissions in the Royal Engineers, was in the hands of a committee of boys. Its standards were praised by Head Boy, W D Rushworth. The service became more comprehensive, too. No longer merely offering morning and lunchtime snacks, teas were supplied on Monday afternoons for the Boxing Club, Tuesday afternoons for the Gym Club, and on Thursdays for Cadets taking Certificate A. Full parades of the Cadets were on Saturday mornings.

Boxers were still doing well. Of the three boys entered by the School in the Army Cadet Force tournament, two reached their finals and one, H M U Dabbs, came out the winner of his.

A talk of a more sober kind, on the task of being an Army Chaplain in North Africa after the Allied landings there in 1941, brought home the bleaker realities of war. It was given by the Reverend G H Woolley VC OBE MC MA, a man whose relationship with the School was to grow close over the coming years.

There was glory of sorts, too, to be sure. As a beginning to the end of hostilities came into view, many were honoured. Colonel Wilson was awarded the MBE; for Captain J L Powles there was a Military Cross; Air Commodore Roach as he now was, Air Vice Marshal Roach as he was to become, received the CBE, and in due time was made a Companion of the Bath. There were DSCs for Lieutenant C T Finch RN and Squadron Leader D P White. For Wing Commander J Woodroffe, the DSO; for Flight Lieutenants F W T Andrews and Roy Merrifield the DFC; for Squadron Leader Graham Ross, a Bar to his DFC. His original decoration had been for scoring a direct hit on the German battleship the *Scharnhorst* when, in 1941, he volunteered to make a low-level attack on Brest Harbour, where she was holed up.

There was also always a price. Oliver Handscomb, who in July 1944 had been an Under Officer in the Cadet Force and had then joined the Army as a career officer, by July 1945 was dead. He could have been no more than nineteen. In his memory, his family donated the Handscomb Cup, awarded to the outstanding Cadet for as long as the School had a Corps. The number of fatalities among Old Lyonians was mounting and continued to mount until both wars, that in Europe and that in the Far East, finally ended. News of the 'missing', Tickner and Cheetham and more, trickled in and confirmed they would not be returning. Nearly seventy years later, Barry Cresswell remembered with great sadness that Ralph Ball, RAF pilot and his best friend, was in that number. News from Japan revealed that three more former pupils had died in the horrors of the prison camps there.

The total number of John Lyon boys who gave their lives was sixty-one. Among them, Peter Bigg, who with all his classmates had signed the back page of a copy of *The Lyonian* the School still has; and young John Tickle who, like the others, had not yet had the chance to make his mark. Proportionate to the size of the School, a smaller percentage had been killed than in the previous conflict, although the total was slightly greater. But each death was a lasting tragedy for family and friends. Geoff Lancashire at eighteen had been commissioned into the Royal Navy and one of his last commands, as the war neared its close, was HMS *Christopher*. With her, he combed the seas of the West Indies for U-Boats that were trying to hide there. Earlier he had commanded coastal convoys. His most vivid memory, however, was that of the thirty-two boys in his form at School, sixteen did not return. Virtually all of them, aircrew.

One bereaved parent, who wished to remain anonymous, sent to the School the kit his son had worn when keeping goal for a junior eleven. He wanted it to be used by the boy now filling the same role.

And it was.

CHAPTER 10

AFTERMATH AND AFTER THAT
1946–1951

As at the end of the last great conflict, the peace brought relief, elation, austerity and unexpected revelations. For the Lower School, the situation was surer and steadier than it had been in 1919. Three masters, Messrs Worman, Shelley and Howard, were warmly welcomed back to the staff room after their war service, and Mr Jackson, the friendly and effective groundsman, was welcomed back to Sudbury. Among the rewards for service were a DFC for Old Lyonian P Upson and a knighthood for Norman Kipping. As Director-General of the Confederation of British Industry, Sir Norman Kipping GCMG KBE JP, was deputed by the government to report on the needs of India after independence, as a result of which 'Kipping Aid' was instituted. In the sixties, he served as vice-chairman of the committee appointed to look into recruitment and training in the Home Civil Service.

The mixture of negative and positive feelings abroad in the nation so soon after the war was neatly illustrated by two talks given as 1946 began. The first, a sermon almost, was given to the School by the Headmaster and examined the idea of God through the ages and the significance of scientific advance in light of the atomic obliteration of Hiroshima and Nagasaki. 'What purpose can there be in a universe whose destiny is annihilation?' was the question Le Beau posed. While he found counter-balances in faith, the doubt and pessimism of the question coloured political life generally for decades to come.

The Scientific Society, on the other hand, found positives in science itself. Mr A L Bacharach addressed boys on the advance made, and advantages gained, by the discovery of penicillin just a few years earlier.

Among the signs of a return to normal life was the re-forming of the orchestra, thanks to the efforts of Mr Jack Walker. At the same time, a young Malcolm Ames, sitting the entrance exam soon after hostilities ended, noted the houses on Lower Road, opposite the School field, had been 'kissed away by a flying bomb'. That bomb, or another dropping in a similar area, was remembered by Robert Walker. As a boy he was in class in the Old Building when the intermittent engine noise of a doodlebug was heard going over. No warning had been sounded. But then came the awful silence as the engine cut out and it started to fall. The master in charge yelled for boys to get on the floor and they huddled as best they could under the desks as the explosion blew in the windows. There were so many air raids that, as mentioned earlier, it was the habit to post a senior youth on the playground, or in the belltower atop the roof of the Old Building, to spot when genuine danger was actually approaching. Otherwise teaching was disrupted impossibly. On this occasion, unfortunately, the boy had failed to blow his bugle until *after* the event.

In the early days of peace, bomb sites were everywhere. It was to be two years before the damage inflicted on the School by Marshal Goering's Luftwaffe would be repaired. Whether this referred to the small bomb which, early in the war, eliminated the bicycle shed or the much later V1 flying bomb, just described, which destroyed three houses around four hundred metres away, killing three people and blowing in the glass of both School buildings is uncertain.[33] Most likely it was the more lasting damage from both.

Speech Day was held once more, the first since 1939. Under the baton of Colonel Wilson the choir in the Speech Room sang, perhaps unsurprisingly, 'England' by Parry, 'Jerusalem' by Parry and Edward German's 'Fishermen of England'. As Battalion Commander, Colonel Wilson had been the inspecting officer of the Corps, all sections of which were busy. Cadet NCOs went on courses to Wellington Barracks while Sergeant Jewkes of the Grenadier Guards gave a taste of the real army to boys back at base. All would have been mightily surprised had they known about the subsequent career of the man who founded the John Lyon School Cadet Force back in 1911.

Vivian Stranders had left the School in 1914 to fight in the Great War. He served as a Captain in the Royal Flying Corps and remained on the continent after the conflict ended. His job at this time was to oversee the disarmament of the German air force, a job from which he was sacked because of some scandal. Then, in 1926, he was arrested in Paris and charged by the French authorities with spying. He was convicted and gaoled for two years. Once released, he settled in Germany.

When the Second World War broke out, Stranders like William Joyce, if less famously, became a Nazi propagandist, broadcasting to Britain

---

[33] The account of the V-bomb comes from Dr Douglas Model who had joined the School as a boy shortly before it came down.

under the name of 'Mediator'.[34] By a curious concatenation, there was a sickly Harrow Foundation link in this. Another broadcaster on behalf of the enemy was Old Harrovian, John Amery, son of the leading politician and arch opponent of Chamberlain's policy of appeasement, Leo Amery. Leo was a staunch, though sometimes argumentative, supporter of Winston Churchill. He was, of course, the senior boy Winston had once pushed into the water of Ducker. In adult life, Mr Amery was a member of Churchill's cabinet during the war, serving as Secretary of State for India,[35] but when his son's treachery became known, he offered his resignation. Churchill's response was, 'Good God! I wouldn't hear of such a thing.' Loyalty was repaid with loyalty.

Stranders went on to volunteer for the *Waffen-SS* and, in 1943, he joined again with John Amery, attempting to recruit prisoners-of-war into the *Britisches Freikorps* to fight for Hitler. Happily their efforts were a miserable failure and their *Korps* scarcely reached even platoon strength. Its membership varied between one and twenty-seven.

When the war ended, John Amery was put on trial in Britain. He pleaded guilty to treason which allowed no mitigating circumstances to be considered, and was hanged: 'the bravest man I ever had to execute', according to Albert Pierrepoint. British Intelligence, which had many matters to occupy it, never quite caught up with Stranders. Their files at the time describe him as a 'notorious British civilian renegade'. He was, in fact, neither British nor a civilian. From 1933 he was a naturalized German. He became in time a *Sturmbannfuehrer* in the SS and was as guilty as John Amery or William Joyce, who was also hanged. Stranders lived the rest of his life unmolested, dying of natural causes in 1959 in the Ruhr.

On the Hill, the Stranders story remained unknown. Young men, as they left the School, were all called up to do their eighteen months' National Service, later extended to two years, and a number of them elected to make the forces their career, among them J T Treglown who entered Sandhurst as did several Old Lyonians, G L Askew who went to Cranwell and Philip Hayhoe, commissioned into the Royal Navy.

The boy-run School canteen continued, despite bread rationing; just

---

[34] Joyce was known to all British listeners to the war-time wireless for his braying broadcasts as Lord Haw-Haw; and even in 2012, there are still people who recall Mediator.

[35] Leo Amery had been born in India and spoke numerous languages, including from the age of three, Hindi. The post, at first appearing something of a backwater, turned out to be of extraordinary importance as the war extended to the Far East. Amery, unlike his PM, recognized the desirability of Indian postwar independence.

before he left, Philip Hayhoe who had been its latest organizer, described the canteen as satisfying 'seething multitudes . . . with fill-void studge' (sic). He went on to give his double-edged thanks to 'most of the Lower Sixth for helping both me and themselves.' D A Sidey (IVa) added his own implied criticism by offering a full-blown tribute to the tuckshop down the road, Bottom Missus, in the same edition of the magazine.

Other Old Boys were making their mark at university. At London, K H Griffin won the Drew Gold Medal and M Mather took the Brewer Prize for History. Francis Bennion, who had been elected President of the Balliol Law Society, won the Jenkyns Law Prize and the Oxford University Gibbs Law Scholarship, later adding the Paton Memorial Studentship and the Robert Younger Prize as well. Usually known by his second name, Alan, he was called to the Bar three years after coming down from Oxford and was to become a noted constitutional lawyer. His impressive career was to include advising the governments of several countries, serving on numerous committees and trusts, usually as chairman, drafting the constitutions of Pakistan and of Ghana and publishing a large number of books on the law and politics, some of which are now set texts for legal students.

As a boy at the School in the years leading up to the war – where he served as an RAFVR pilot – he was something of a favourite of the Headmaster. One of the benefits of this, as many boys discovered over the years, was the receipt of various gifts. Cakes and the like sometimes, to some boys penny blacks, the Victorian postage stamps, but most often, books. In Alan's case, a series of heavily illustrated 'Wonder' books – the *Wonder Book of Astronomy*, the *Wonder Book of Science* and so on. After the war, Mr Le Beau took delivery about once a month of a large box from Hatchard's and would dispense from it the works of Captain W E Johns, volume by volume, to passing boys. It was possible over time to accumulate the entire pantheon of heroic tales featuring Biggles, Gimlet who was a commando, or the rather forbidding senior WAAF NCO, Warrender, if you were in the right place at the right time, often enough.

Those not so lucky, or not so favoured, used the Library where currently the most popular books were the adventure tales by Percy Westerman and the classic, *Lorna Doone*. Here Mr Le Beau gave a number of other adventure books written by G A Henty, and soon after, Leo Amery donated two of his own publications: *Days of Fresh Air* and *Days in the Rain and the Sun*.

As it happened, the winter of 1946/47 was one of the harshest in living memory, made worse by the frequent but unpredictable power cuts and the serious shortages resulting from a cripplingly expensive war. Most visits to firms and factories by School societies had to be cancelled, since they had closed down. The 'ice age' wiped out all football fixtures which, given the previous season's poor results might be regarded as less than a tragedy. The only bright spot then had been the record of the Under-12s, captained by J E Sloggett. They drew with Orley Farm and enjoyed a comprehensive victory over Ealing Priory in their only two matches. Football remained uninspiring for the next few seasons. The Gym Club was doing well, with a hundred members – gymnastics was still extra-curricular – and the annual display had a record-breaking attendance: 'at least we got here – some of us – and got home again', as one contemporary recorded.

Before this, cricket had got off to an encouraging start, although after the winter their results were as disappointing as the footballers'. The games were described by another contemporary as being 'good rowing practice for batsmen: in – out, in – out, in – out . . .' The only exception was, once again, the Under-12s. Captained, again, by young Jolyon Sloggett. At Speech Day in 1948, Mr Le Beau announced that twenty cricket elevens a week were being fielded and neatly avoided mentioning that, having been fielded, they were almost all swiftly returned to the pavilion.

Athletics meanwhile, under the aegis of the Corps, had done remark-ably well. One of the School's Companies won the Middlesex Brigade's Senior, Junior and All-Round Championships. Four boys, R W Digby who was Head of the School, Woodgate, Fincher and Sorrell were selected to represent the Brigade at the All-England National Champion-ships and Woodgate also won, for his weight, the London Command Boxing Championship. The Air Training Corps did well, too, with their members taking first and second places in both the 100 yards and the 220 yards races at the Divisional Athletic Competition. A little later, Woodgate again, together with Lambert and Watson reached the finals of the national Army Cadet Force Boxing Championship.

When, however, an athletics match between the School and Harrow School's Beetlers was instituted, J R F Mills reported the School to be rather outclassed. John Lyon boys registered several seconds and thirds, but only Staple in the 880 yards was a winner. This remained the pattern for the next few years until it was possible to announce, in 1957, that the Harrow School track had seen an overall victory for the Lower School. But by then, sport in all departments had noticeably improved.

Ironically, as the weather became better elsewhere, a number of boys went on a walking tour of Snowdonia where they enjoyed a combination of gales, mist and rain. At least adventures, if uncomfortable, were possible again.

With the generally improved conditions, visits to factories resumed, the Scientists making for Benskin's Brewery and the Geographers, more puritanically, for the Colne Valley Water Company. Harvest Camp was restored to the calendar and the Band, whose instruments were not a little battered, started their recovery by having the mace re-conditioned. Later the bugles were sent away for similar restoration. At the cadet Summer Camp boy bandsmen were further inspired by the Corps of Drums of the Second Battalion, Coldstream Guards, beating the tattoo and giving a marching display. Following which, at the 1948 Speech Day, it was Major-General Allan Adair, the war-time commander of the Guards Armoured Division, who was on the platform as guest of honour. He, too, knew how to inspire. His opening words can hardly have failed to please: 'It is a great pleasure to come here and realize straightaway that this school is a great school'.

One of the announcements on this occasion was that an Association Day was being added to the fixture list. Variously held on the Philathletic ground or at Sudbury, every summer several teams of boys play cricket against Old Lyonian teams, all at the same time. This has continued every year since and is a wonderfully English, mellow occasion. The competition is genuine and often hard fought, but the atmosphere in which it takes place has something of a romantic, nostalgic feel to it. It is a celebration rather than a fight.

Another change announced was that the Army Cadet Force, formerly for a time the Officer Training Corps, was now to be part of the Combined Cadet Force. The re-structuring would mean the absorption of the Air Training Corps into the CCF where it would in future be known as the RAF Section. Clearly there were administrative advantages in this and a practical one would be that recruits all trained together in the army section then, at fifteen, would opt for the blue uniform if they wished.

The process of change began in early 1949 although the new shoulder flashes took a little longer coming, so that the bright red and white ACF flashes continued to be worn for a few more months.

As always there were changes among the staff, too. Johnny Williams, the sports master, was off ill. The eminent head of classics, Dr Ewbank had, after twenty years at the School, reached his retirement. With him went Mr Mogg, the master who had introduced biology to the syllabus and Mr Shelley, the art master, soon moved on. A little later Dr B J J Hirst, whose doctorate from a French university clad him in a magnificently bright gown on Speech Days, left after several years' service and so did the avuncular J G Watterson. As the master in charge of 1A he knew well how to talk with small boys. When one of his class had a birthday, he mentioned it during the lesson and enquired of the boy whether, now he was twelve, he felt any different from when he was eleven? The boy thought for some moments and then replied that he didn't, really. 'No,' said Mr Watterson. 'I'm sixty-five next birthday and, do you know, I don't feel any different from when I was eleven, either.' The ability to empathize in that way is what makes great teachers.

At the end of the year, the pattern of nearly a century was adjusted. The academic year at John Lyon had always run from January to December, increasingly out-of-step with most institutions. With the dawning of 1950 a short 'year' was announced. Come September, boys would move up a form so that progress through the School and the time of principal public examinations for pupils would coincide with other educational establishments. Nationally, the General School Certificate and Matriculation were being replaced by Ordinary Level examinations, and Highers by Advanced Levels. So it was a sensible moment for the change.

A measure of humour was evident again in *The Lyonian*. A contribution appeared having fun with the absurd conversational gambits offered in traveller's handbooks. 'The ticket collector is suffering from ptomaine poisoning' begins a series of ever more dire and ludicrous exchanges, supposedly designed to provide a handy vocabulary. The young wit at work here was one Timothy West. When a party of boys made a trip to Nestlé's chocolate factory, the account of the visit read, 'Ample scope was given to observe John Lyon boys make the most of their opportunities. The following week it was reported Nestlé's failed to meet their export target.'

Rationing, still in place, made factories producing confectionery popular destinations for School visits, although many more mundane establishments were visited, too, on a regular basis. Added to the list with the arrival of a new head of Classics, Philip Suggett, were trips to archaeological sites, the first ones being the Roman remains at St Albans and an early Iron Age site at Stanmore. A further addition to the staff in 1950, and one which had a profound impact, was Olympic gymnast George Weedon.

The previous season, 'the innovation of hot water in the pavilion' at Sudbury, reported by Tim Jones, captain of most things, seemed to have had an encouraging effect on results. The footballers managed to lose only half of their matches and the cricketers won more than half of theirs. On the athletic track, too, Harrow again managed to beat John Lyon, but John Lyon beat their own Old Boys. The advent of a current Olympian, seen practising every day on the bars, the horse, the floor, the rings, impressed every boy in the School and began to fan the glowing embers of sporting ambition into something of a flame.

Mr Weedon represented Great Britain at Wembley in 1948 and in Helsinki in 1952. He is probably the only veteran of the previous English Olympics to be involved with the Games of 2012. In his nineties and exuding fitness, he gave personal coaching to members of the volleyball team wearing the GB vest.

Gymnastics at John Lyon now became part of the syllabus. All boys up to the fifth form spent two periods a week doing callisthenics and apparatus work, in addition to their games afternoons. Failing to have your gym kit on the right days was an offence. After the long absence of still ailing Johnny Williams, the Gym Club, a post-School activity on Tuesday afternoons, was given new impetus. Almost immediately, the first public display of gymnastics for three years was staged. The Weedon philosophy was 'challenge yourself all the time'. His own constant practice bore this out underlined by the fact, not widely known at the time, that he had been operated on to have a kidney removed not long before Olympic competition. Illustrated, too, by a particular experience he had practising on the rings, one of George's specialities. He had purchased the highest quality rings – Olympic standard – and had them fitted in the School gym. In the event, one of them proved faulty. George was suspended in an aerial handstand when it gave way and he plummeted to the floor, landing face first. Such was his stoicism that most boys were quite unaware of the accident and George simply had the rings replaced and continued practising. Indeed, photographs of him, inverted in the air and with another athlete suspended horizontally from his neck featured largely in the national press as he prepared for the Finnish Olympics.

The renewed emphasis on fitness turned out to be only one of several far-reaching changes to occur in the period 1950/51. One small tradition that continued unchanged for many years yet was charring. In every form room, in the bottom corner of the blackboard, two names would be chalked up. The names changed each day by a simple progression through the alphabetic list of boys in that class. At the end of the day, the two concerned had to tidy the classroom and bin any rubbish left on the floor.

They then awaited their form Prefect or Monitor to descend from on high to approve their efforts. After that, they were free to go home. It worked as an effective leveller and bred a lifelong habit of disposing of litter responsibly.

Not long after the war, a fund had been started to raise money for a library to commemorate the Old Lyonians who had given their lives. The amount needed was realized through donations and money-raising activities and on Remembrance Sunday, 12th November 1950, what had been the form room of Vb, elegantly converted with polished parquet flooring, matching pine bookcases, study tables and comfortable pine-wood armchairs was opened as the War Memorial Library. The service of dedication was conducted by the war hero Vicar of St Mary's, the Reverend G H Woolley. It commenced in the School yard with hymns, prayers for the peace of the world and a lone bugler playing the Last Post followed by Reveille. Then the parents and relatives of those who had been killed proceeded to the Library for the dedication of the room itself. The pale furniture chimed well with the light and airy atmosphere of the room, large windows each side, between the open bookcases. In the centre at the further end of the room there stood a casement with an illuminated book of remembrance, showing the names of all boys and staff who had fallen in both world wars. It was the first thing you would see on entering the Library and each day a Librarian turned one of the pages.

The smaller room adjacent was the Monitors' common room and the Library became a popular place for quiet study among senior boys.

Chess was now taken more seriously and half-colours were awarded to boys who distinguished themselves in matches against several schools, including Harrow County and Haberdashers'.

Other developments included the first instance of House Colours being awarded, West House with five, having the most. Colours, too, enlivened the covers of the School magazine for the first time. *The Lyonian* now was faced with the full arms of the Harrow Foundation, the rampant lion on the shield, surmounted by the crossed arrows and with the School's single motto on a scroll below. All this printed in white on a blue ground for the end of the Michaelmas term, green for the Easter term and pillar box red for Summer.

Among the young men going on to university, two went to Queens' College, Cambridge, M F Proctor as a Foundation Scholar and R Moulton as an Exhibitioner. Here they joined two others already distinguishing themselves, T L R Jones, playing football for the university and Ian Mortimer who had just won his oar, both undergraduates at Fitzwilliam. The current Head Boy was Jolyon Sloggett, easily the most popular to have held the post for some time. Always quietly immaculate and quietly spoken he commanded respect without any apparent effort. Other notable boys at the School at this time were Tad Kopanski, the equally immaculate Drum Major of the Band who was about to depart for Sandhurst, and R W Perry who was an able sportsman, captaining School Boxing and who was joint winner of the School's Art Prize. This proved an apt combination, if surprising in one aspect. Roy Perry was awarded his colours for boxing, football, swimming and for gymnastics, which he also captained, but not for cricket. Ironic, since his later career saw him a highly successful painter of landscapes and especially of cricket scenes. His pictures, widely reproduced, were collected by, among others, the Duke of Edinburgh, Prince Charles and the Lord's Taverners. Like Max Hofler who had been at the School in the early 1900s, he exhibited at the Royal Academy and at the Royal Institute where he won the medal given for the best watercolour. He died, sadly young, not long after the Falklands war where he had been an official war artist. A number of his paintings are in the Imperial War Museum.

It is interesting to notice, too, that among the new crop of prefects, the name J R Silvester appears. Both his uncle and father, Victor and Temple, were members of the Old Lyonians.

On the sporting front, matters continued slowly to improve. The School won a cross-country race in which teams from four other schools were competing. The Gymnastics team lost two matches against Sutton Adult School by the slenderest of margins. The first by just half-a-point with 121 points; the second by a whole point despite John Lyon boys Blackman and Michael Bogdin (who later reverted to his original family name, Bogdanov) coming first and second. Football was also looking up, with eight convincing wins for the First XI and only two losses, each by a single goal.

Sadly, the much loved former sports master Johnny Williams, who had been ill for so long, died. Shortly after two new staff members arrived to teach modern languages: D L Hunt and Philip Davies. While Phil was to become something of an institution, another such was to bring his own era to an end. Oscar Le Beau, forty years at the School, quarter-of-a-century as Headmaster, retired in the summer of 1951. By another irony, this keen photographer did so just as one of his pupils, J K Jasper, founded a Photographic Society, open to every boy in the School.

The tributes to him were many. Among the warmest being, 'it cannot be that many boys have crept "unwillingly to school" during Mr Le Beau's rule; and they certainly cannot have traced "the day's disasters in his morning face," for there have been no disasters.' In his time as Headmaster he had broadened the curriculum to include Latin once more, biology and physical training; he had presided over the increase in the facilities so that the single building to house the School was now adjoined by the substantial New Building, itself extended by a further wing and then by the annexe, while games, once confined to the public recreation ground, now took place on the fine playing fields at Sudbury.

While he was Head, the staff had increased in number as had School societies, only one of them traceable back to the reign of Ernest Young.[36] His own broad interests and enquiring mind were rightly expected to keep him busy in what was only a partial retirement. He continued to teach astronomy at Harrow School and added the study and translation of Sanskrit and ancient Persian documents to his many hobbies.

If he was the personification of Mr Chips, his successor was of quite another genus. R F B Campbell had, at a young age, attained the rank of Lieutenant-Colonel during the war. With a Cambridge degree he had returned to his own old school, Berkhamsted, to teach, in due course becoming a House Master. He was thirty-eight years old, partially bald, crisp, strict and – a quality he shared with Le Beau – energetic.

The School bell, hanging on the small balcony of the New Building and rung by a duty Monitor to mark the end of each lesson, was in a state of decline after years of use. Appositely, at this moment, it was replaced by the bell from the ship on which Bill Worman had served as an officer.

A new era was to be rung in.

[36] The Geographical Society. As a serious travel writer, Young himself was a Fellow of the Royal Geographical Society.

CHAPTER 11

THE CAMPBELLS HAVE COME
1951–1958

During the summer holiday when the School was empty, the newly appointed Headmaster came to Middle Road to be shown round the buildings by Colonel Wilson, Deputy Head and the only master left whose experience of teaching at the Lower School had started under Mr Butt. It was a chance for Mr Campbell to familiarize himself with the layout and to get a feel for (a word he often used) the 'tone' of the School. As they crossed the yard to the New Building he said to Willy, 'Is this a friendly place?' The reply he received summed up the view of virtually every boy who ever attended the John Lyon School. 'Oh, you don't need to worry about that. Friendliness is built into the brickwork.'

Every organization benefits from a sense of continuity. That is part of the attraction of tradition. It enables those involved to feel they belong, to feel at home there, and it helps confer self-belief and a positive attitude to the world around. It is equally true that if tradition rules for too long and in too hide-bound a way, any organization be it school or club or business, loses impetus. It begins to atrophy and fails to adapt to changing times.

Philip Davies came to the view that Boyd Campbell's arrival was the most significant step forward in the School's history, that he was as it were the Lower School's equivalent of Dr Vaughan. This is to overlook the very positive contributions of each of his predecessors: J E Williams in moulding a school and imbuing it with an identity and a moral code from its rocky and argument-torn beginnings; Ernest Young whose energy and expansiveness came – appropriately for a rambler and good friend of Lord Baden-Powell – like a breath of fresh air; Mr Butt, without whose extraordinary determination, sheer grit and hard work, the School would unquestionably have gone under; and O A Le Beau who built on this foundation to see the School elected to the Headmasters' Conference, to extend its size dramatically and to give a new emphasis to science. Every one of these men, incidentally, remained deeply loyal to the School to the end of their days. The new man was far from unaware of this. One of his first actions was to have large framed photographs of all the previous Headmasters displayed on the east wall of the Memorial Library.

Nonetheless, it cannot be denied that Mr Campbell had a profound and lasting personal impact. As a former scholar and subsequent governor of several schools, Stephen Adamson has observed, it is the drive created by the Head which makes and shapes a school. Firm, clear and certainly headmasterly, Boyd Campbell instilled immediate respect and, in some boys, fear. Some of this was the teacher's mask. He was unquestionably caring and took pains to know the back-story of any boy who had emotional or behavioural difficulties. Despite appearances, his principal approach when term started was to listen. 'What do you usually do here?' He changed nothing without understanding what the existing process was. If it was good in his view, he did more than let it be, he encouraged it. He listened to staff. He listened to boys. But when a decision was made, it was made to be adhered to. At the same time, more than any of his predecessors, he encouraged initiative. Indeed, he expected it.

Most of the School's extra-curricular activities, and there were many, had been instigated by individual boys or groups of them. This was something Campbell was keen to see continue. He wanted to know what boys wanted and for them to go ahead and do something about it. Once a new club or activity was under way there would usually be, as before, a member or two of staff involved to give encouragement and provide oversight, the masters almost always being approached by the boys themselves. One of the traditions of the John Lyon School was and remained how unsparingly these same masters gave of their time and interest.

Almost immediately, three new clubs came into being. A Table Tennis Club occupied the Cloisters, now that the canteen had folded. Malcolm Ames, who had won the year's tennis competition, set up a Badminton Club, and a number of fifth- and sixth-formers founded the Classical Society, electing Brian Plummer, in later life to be Professor of Geography at the University of Wales, as its first secretary.

There were two immediate top-down initiatives, as well. Talks on careers, in association with the County Council's Youth Employment Service started and, very soon after, a Careers Prefect was appointed; in the Library, Old Lyonian R S Laurie, head of Wealdstone County Library, was brought in to give a short course on the skills and methods required to do the job properly. He later generously spent many hours cataloguing the books according to the latest system.

Then came two deaths. One, significant to Harrow and to education in

Middlesex: Ernest Young, who presided over two schools in the borough at critical times and later had worked for the County Education Authority, died aged eighty-two. Four days earlier, on 6th February 1952, significant to the whole country, the death of King George VI had been announced in the course of the morning. Boys were sent home at lunchtime. For all the sadness, that led too, to a sense of renewal. The accession of the young Queen Elizabeth engendered ideas of a second Elizabethan age, of serious attempts to shrug off austerity and any gloomy overhang from the war and to reach for something better.

Confidence affects performance and something of the upbeat feeling that was abroad affected the First Elevens of both football, where decisive wins were recorded, and cricket where the team enjoyed their best season, possibly ever. Playing twenty-one matches in the summer they lost only three; they won twelve and in all six draws the end came with the team well in the ascendancy. Against Harrow School, for example, John Lyon declared on 138 for 7; Harrow were 94 for 9 when stumps were drawn. Come autumn, they played an additional match, overcoming Mercers' by three wickets. Boys were now regularly coached during the winter at Chiswick Indoor Cricket School and Ames was selected for the Middlesex Schools Tour.

There were successes elsewhere. Michael Rose, the former School pianist, began accruing prizes and awards at the Royal Academy of Music at an amazing rate: LRAM, then ARCM and GRSM, the Langrish Prize for composition, along with the Cuthbert Nunn Prize, and the Silver Medals for both piano and violin playing. Jolyon Sloggett was awarded the Muir Bursary at the University of Glasgow and went on to gain a First, the Reid Birrell Prize and then a further four University prizes.

Over the years, a small number of boys had left to train for the merchant navy on HMS *Worcester*, the first being W Davis in 1899. Two who went there now were Bill Lucas and John Butt. In due course, Bill passed out as the *Worcester*'s Cadet Captain and joined P&O; John Butt joined Cunard. It did not take Bill Lucas very long to rise to professional Captain's rank and although he died unexpectedly in his early forties, it was not before he had written a witty and highly popular spoof maritime manual, *Sod's Law of the Sea*. Mr Butt, meanwhile, rose to be the Cunard Line's Cruise Director. When he left, after new owners took over Cunard, he was immediately head-hunted by the Fred Olsen Line for the same role and then, later, invited by Cunard to return as one of their consultants. In his seventies he continues to work for both companies when not at his home on St Lucia where he and his wife host the likes of Dionne Warwick during the island's annual jazz festival.

Other Old Boys were busy at Pinner View with a production in the grounds of *A Midsummer Night's Dream*. The three actors receiving the most favourable notices were John Learner as Oberon, Derek Wilson – in later life to become a popular and successful historian, having at Cambridge won the Archbishop Cranmer Prize for historical research, and currently still at the School where he was the first Careers Prefect – and, in the role of Egeus, a very recent leaver, Timothy West.

On the Hill, among the talks given to the Literary Society, the well-known broadcaster, Leslie Paul, spoke about poetry including the work of his friend the eminent poet, Roy Campbell; Paul Wilkinson spoke on the history and culture of Russia, 'described with admirable lack of bias'. Paul was a fifth former at this point. He went on to have a highly distinguished academic career as 'one of the world's foremost experts on terrorism and political violence.' 'A man of erudition and originality of the highest order', [37] he advised the governments of, among others, the USA, Canada, Germany, the Netherlands and the United Kingdom. He founded, after a considerable struggle to persuade others of the need, the first university department to study international violence, at St Andrew's in 1989 and was pleased to note twenty years later, that by then there were twenty British universities which had followed suit, the latest being Oxford. He published many books dealing with the responses of liberal democracies to terrorism and was a regular on British radio and television, especially in the twenty-first century. He received the CBE the same year he presented the prizes in the Speech Room, shocked to find it less than half full, owing to the decision that only prize-winners and their families should attend. He died three years later, in 2011. Paul Wilkinson was, quite simply, one of the outstanding men of his generation.

International awareness at the School was marked by the French Circle making a journey to the Royal Institute in London to hear Foreign Secretary, Anthony Eden, discuss relationships with France.

As the Queen's Coronation approached in 1953, the School held an Easter Fair. Opened by Sussex and England cricketer, David Sheppard, who was later to be Bishop of Liverpool, there were numerous events and exhibitions on the Middle Road site. A balloon race vied with bingo, a rifle range with Don Allan's art gallery; there were chemical demonstrations and every society put on a display, including the Yachting Club,

---

[37] The *Scotsman* newspaper.

which seemed to have been created for the purpose – or perhaps because the Headmaster was known to be a keen yachtsman. One entertainment which decades later might have fallen foul of the Advertising Standards Authority was *The Three Maries*. Billed as a Cornish Mystery Play, unsuspecting parents and friends arrived to watch what promised to be some sort an Agatha Christie set on the moors. Instead they saw a serious performance of a fourteenth century miracle play. Delivered in the fourteenth century Cornish language.

> Pandra wramavy ellas
> Ow Arluth yn beth gallas

might not have been quite the dialogue they had expected. Don Cowtan, who directed it with a cast of mainly senior boys, had a remarkable knowledge of Celtic languages and was one of only six living speakers of Cornish at this time. A well-known broadcaster, R Morton Nance, was another. Happily, he attended one of the performances, so at least a third of those in the world who could understand what was being said saw the piece. Everyone else felt highly culturally sophisticated and, as the phrase was then, 'very one-up'.

All these sterling efforts raised £650, the equivalent of maybe ten thousand pounds in 2013 value, towards the building of a new pavilion at Sudbury.

Among the items exhibited at the Fair was a copy of the Proclamation of Her Majesty, Queen Elizabeth II and among the performers at the Coronation itself was Old Lyonian flautist, C D Chambers and about-to-be John Lyon boy, Brian Graves, singing in the choir at Westminster Abbey. The whole School went to the South Harrow Odeon to see the colour film of the ceremony and the celebrations that went with it. The event had been shown on television for the first time in history, but only in black and white and anyway, many families still did not possess sets. In the honours announced at the same time, President of the Old Lyonian Association, H A Parker, was awarded an OBE.

A few days later, Major-General B C H Kimmins[38] proved very popular in what he said when he spoke to the entire School Cadet Force, having conducted the annual inspection at the Harrow School track and officially opened the Corps Hut at Middle Road. The latter had been there some time and had a biology laboratory one end, a classroom

---

[38] The Kimmins family were Harrow residents and Brian, later knighted and a Lieutenant General, was GOC the Territorial Army and Cadets. With his brother Anthony, a distinguished film producer, his early education was at Orley Farm School.

the other and in between the Orderly Room and another room where the
duty member of the Ambulance Section, who would have the senior
qualification of St John Ambulance, could administer first aid. All these
rooms opened directly to the outside. Underneath them were covered
bicycle sheds which were entered from the opposite side, lower down the
slope. The changes to the School lay-out have been so great that it is
difficult to envisage now where it was. Roughly speaking, it was in the area
now occupied by the rooms immediately behind the new dining area of
the Main Building, and it was approached by descending a dog-leg path
from the playground.

   With 'O' levels finished, the present writer approached Mr Campbell
to ask permission to mount a show in the School hall. He agreed. The
exchange that follows illustrates the Headmaster's customary style:

> HM: How many seats will you want in the Hall?
> Boy: I don't know. How many will it hold, sir?
> HM: That's not what I asked. I asked how many do you want?
> Boy: Two hundred, sir.
> HM: You'll have two hundred.

And we did.

   '*The Pride of Lyons*, a vaudeville entertainment by Burrell and his fellow
fifth-formers, gave a merry evening to a fair-sized audience.' So began Mr
Walker's review, accurately defining the nature of the evening and then
recounting it in detail. Jack Walker was a wizened man who suffered
appallingly from asthma and whose academic gown was green with age
and use. He was erudite and once a boy was a fifth-, or even better, a sixth-
former, he treated him with great courtesy and as an equal. Lower down
the School he held iron discipline using one of two methods. He would
simply stare at any recalcitrant youth, bring out his half-hunter, flip open
the glass and continue, unbroken, the cold hard look; then he would flip
the watch back into his pocket without a word spoken. If, on the other
hand, a boy was spotted glancing at his own watch, Walker would again
fix him with a baleful gaze and say, 'I don't mind a boy looking at his
watch, it is when he begins to shake it to see if it's still going, that I start to
worry'. At other times if he decided to speak he could, as one former pupil
remembered, be equally withering. 'There you sit, stodge to the eyebrows,
cement in the head, brooding upon the rising price of Brilliantine', the
same boy recalled, half-a-century later. Clearly Martial and the other
classical epigrammatists were close to Jack's heart. Though not a few boys
doubted that he possessed such an organ.

Mr Campbell approved of the show we had done and found me next day to say he wished us to stage a revue shortly before Christmas, to be given one afternoon to the whole School. All forces were combined for this. The orchestra played, Mr Cowtan gave a piano solo and Mr Boardman, newly arrived to the staff from Cambridge, equipped us with some genuine undergraduate comedy sketches. We had also our own material which included a joke about Monitors and the size of their heads, probably the highlight of the evening for many of our audience. Next morning, as I arrived at School with my good friend Phillip Mansley, I was mobbed by junior boys. Phillip took the role of the Roman soothsayer: 'You were good,' he said, 'but you weren't *that* good!'

From this beginning, drama was restored as part of the life of the John Lyon School. We formed a Drama Group with frequent play readings and with visits, such as had occurred regularly up to the late 1930s, to the Old Vic, only this time organized by a boy, in the same way that many of the existing societies had come into being.

Before the second revue, however, other things occurred. The previous year there had been a holiday trip to Quimper in Brittany; now there were two, to Biarritz, and to Fuegen in Austria. George Weedon started dancing classes for boys so that they could waltz or quickstep or foxtrot (the easiest) without trampling their partner. As a couple of sixth-formers observed, 'those who thought they couldn't dance now can, and those who thought they could realize that they can't'.

The new pavilion at Sudbury which Sir Stanley Rous,[39] Chairman of the Football Association, had promised to open was instead launched by one of the F A's vice-presidents, and one more sea-change in the School's life occurred. Colonel Wilson retired. Except he did not quite: for the next couple of years he returned twice a week to continue training the choirs. Nonetheless, it was a significant punctuation mark and lavish tributes were paid to Willy for his huge contribution to so many aspects of the Lower School's activities.

With the new year there was an emphasis on physical achievement, as much by chance probably as by deliberate design. Ian McIntosh, a keen sportsman when at School, was elected president of the Junior Common Room at Oxford's most sporting college, St Edmund Hall; at the Headmaster's invitation, two members of the first team to conquer Everest, Michael Westmacott and George Lowe, gave an illustrated lecture about the expedition to an audience crammed into the room;

[39] Often, including in School records, spelt Rouse. Rous is correct.

and John Lyon gymnastics took a giant leap forward. At the Metropolitan and Southern Counties championship, held at the Central YMCA in Great Russell Street, the School team won.

Jonathan Charles, at twelve the youngest member of the team, remembered the response among boys to George Weedon's leadership and enthusiasm. Numbers joining the Gym Club swelled and onlookers would stand on the hall's small balcony to watch the excitement. Inter-house competitions, where senior boys helped to train their juniors, proved popular with audiences. Crucially, George took schoolboy gymnastics onto a higher plane: the pattern was to be modelled on the Olympic programme. Instead of one-off floor exercises following each other, John Lyon boys gave an exhibition of callisthenics, flowing performances linking the disparate exercises into a whole. No other schools attempted this. Then, the Reverend Charles recalled, boys were introduced to more difficult disciplines: the high bar, the pommel horse and the rings. That resulted in another team success. Southern Counties champions 1956 in the Under-15 vaulting and agility competition.

Mr Weedon's influence went further than simply the School. Brian Graves, who had only recently left, came second in the senior competitions for both individual vaulting and agility, representing the Regent Street Polytechnic.

Although other sports results had dropped back a little, the programme of inter-house and inter-school fixtures increased noticeably.

British Railways remembered our founder's eminence and restored to use the name of JOHN LYON, originally seen on a steam locomotive and removed during the war. It now graced diesel locomotive number 1. When that was decommissioned many years later, the plate bearing the name was presented to the School where it remained for several years on display in the entrance to the Main Building.

It was at this time, too, that the bond between the two Schools on the Hill was cemented further. The use of several of Harrow's facilities by the day school – sports grounds, running track, swimming pool, Speech Room, rifle range – were long established. Now, the John Lyon School's Head and Deputy Head Boys were invited to Harrow School Songs, attended every year by Sir Winston Churchill and eventually re-named for him, Churchill Songs. At the 1955 concert, surrounded by eminent Harrovians including Earl Alexander of Tunis, he stood on the platform and paid emotional tribute to his old colleague and sparring partner Leo Amery, who had died a few days before. A little later, Earl Alexander was to conduct the annual review of the Cadet Force. In the summer, it became usual for forty or fifty John Lyon boys to attend the first day of the Eton and Harrow match at Lord's.

The Drama Group staged a composite version of Shakespeare's *Henry IV* plays, concentrating on the Falstaff story, and considerably helped by the folding triptych set created by Don Allan. The proscenium curtain was provided by Harrow, courtesy of Custos. Among the more than thirty boys in the cast, Michael Bogdanov was given his first part as Poins.

Raymond Jackson, whose reign as Head Boy was the shortest in School history, had gone before the performances. He had been appointed in September 1954, but left in the November to enter Sandhurst, along with fellow Lyonian, Alan Webb. Numerous ex-pupils were also commissioned as National Service officers, while Giles Bolitho, a senior NCO in the School's RAF Section, gained his full civilian pilot's licence.

Returning to sporting achievements, the Gymnastics team, captained by the same Bolitho, retained the South of England championship, the Sandle Shield, for a second year. Then for a third, fourth and fifth year. In 1958, the team toured Germany giving displays and meeting German Olympic heroes Helmut Bantz and Hardi Frenger who had been instrumental in setting up the trip. The John Lyon School in the 1950s was the country's outstanding school in this field.

Meanwhile, Clive Woodbridge was elected by his fellow Colours to be Captain of Cricket and was selected for the Middlesex Schools' Eleven, just one hundred and two years after the first members of his family entered the English Form. Clive remained faithful to his sport all his life, starting a cricket club in Spain when he eventually moved there. Which is why, outside Alicante, you will find the Woodbridge Oval, a ground named in his memory.

There were difficulties with the grounds at Sudbury, however. The pitches had been prone to flooding if there was prolonged rain. It was decided, therefore, to install mole drainage, as it was called. This entailed a good deal of digging up and re-turfing, or re-planting, and consequently for a time games could not be played there. Happily, the good relations between all the local schools meant the Lower School was able to stage its matches on grounds lent by Harrow School, the Old Lyonians, the Old Gaytonians and nearby Orley Farm School.

Shooting, too, was showing improved results. Under the excellent tutelage of Harrow's Sergeant-Major Moore, a former King's Cup winner at Bisley, the School VIII came twenty-eighth in the Country Life competition and first in the landscape shooting section. The latter an achievement they repeated the following year, although on that occasion they were joint top in the section and thirty-sixth overall. The total number of schools competing was of the order of a hundred and fifty.

Oscar Le Beau was busy writing the School's history and appealed for former pupils to send any information they could, especially about the earliest years. Unfortunately, however far he reached, no book resulted. Meanwhile Boyd Campbell revived two elements from times past and ended a more recent one: credit marks were no longer to be awarded, while Founder's Day was restored to the calendar with a longer service in the Hall. United Nations Day and Remembrance Day were marked in the same way. And when a service to commemorate the achievements of Thomas Blackwell was held at Harrow Weald, the Headmaster, accompanied by T W K Young, attended. Young was the holder of an unobtrusively restored Blackwell Scholarship.

Among the changes occurring, the new young English master, Geoffrey Thornton, appointed with responsibility to produce an annual play as part of his contract, also took over editorship of *The Lyonian* from Donald Cowtan, who was undoubtedly happy to hand it over after thirty years, if only to be spared the proof reading. Likewise, the highly qualified Michael Rose arrived to replace Colonel Wilson in training the choirs. At the same moment, making immediate use of the gift of a record player and records from Lord Somervell, boys, led by David Reeves, formed a Music Club. Annual School concerts continued and a group of boys from the long-established Christian Union went to Wembley to hear the American evangelist, Billy Graham.

One bright new idea failed to find favour. The seemingly endless indecision afflicting both schools on the Harrow Foundation as to what precisely the badge to proclaim each of them might be, irked Mr Campbell. Not a man to do nothing about it, he commissioned David Christie-Murray, a local resident and an experienced designer of coats of arms, especially for public schools, to produce a definitive blazon for the Lower School of John Lyon. This he did. A rampant lion on a silver ground, with three sets of crossed arrows in a wreath surrounding it in a regular-shaped shield. The design was published with full heraldic explanation and sold from the Harrow School Bookshop.

When proffered to the College of Heralds the response was a surprise. Although the College had granted arms to the Governors in 1929 for Harrow School's use, they now thought it was the Lower School which more properly had the right to them. Therefore that institution had no need to register anything different. Harrow, on the other hand, perhaps should.

It can be imagined what the Governors' reaction was when this came to their ears. The design was to be withdrawn immediately and copies of it destroyed.[40] The Lyonian *samizdat* ensured several copies were preserved. But nothing more was done about regularizing the badges the School used.

More positively, an Inter-Schools Debating Society was inaugurated with senior pupils from seven or eight schools taking part, including Harrow, Heathfield, Pinner and Harrow County. The subject, 'That toleration is the best answer to the world's problems' was proposed by the Head Boy of John Lyon and carried by 91 votes to 72. The previous experience of debating gained by the public-school-educated young people was clearly evidenced on this occasion, even if the result was not as overwhelming as that at one of the Literary Society's instant debates, back on the Hill. The motion there was 'That competitive exams should be abolished'. It was carried unanimously. It is quite something when even the opposing speakers vote for the motion.

Along with those who had survived the rigours of public examinations, the School reported that the new Lord Shepherd, a successful business-man who inherited his title and became a Labour Whip in the Upper House, had been at the School in the 1930s. Harvey Stockwin, a more recent leaver who had been an Exhibitioner at Queens' College, Cambridge was now appointed Lecturer in Economics at the University of Colombo.[41] War hero, Group Captain J Woodroffe DSO, DFC had been placed in command of RAF Wittering in Huntingdonshire. It was his misfortune to be killed in Florida two years later when commanding an RAF detachment in a bombing and navigation competition. The Bucknill Open Scholarship, tenable at University College London and University College Hospital, had been awarded to sixth-former Douglas Hems, the most brilliant boy of his year. It was his father, Dr Arthur Hems, whose combined business acumen and scientific skills as their Chief Research Chemist, was to take the small pharmaceutical company Glaxo and turn it into the giant GlaxoSmithKline. Sadly, his son Douglas who rapidly rose to be Reader in Biochemistry at St George's, was to die in early middle age and in tragic circumstances.

[40] The source for this account was Boyd Campbell himself at the time of the event. The present writer assured the joint owner of the Bookshop, Mrs Gwen Nunn, he had never had a copy of Christie's design. She sought that assurance, knowing full well she had sold him two. Mrs Nunn's son, Colin, was to join the School not long after and, in time, to be elected President of the Old Lyonians.

[41] Harvey went on to become one of the most authoritative commentators on Asian affairs. He is correspondent on the subject for the *Times of India*, for the *Japan Times* and has a widely respected and fearless weekly programme on Radio Television Hong Kong.

In response to the fact that eighty boys in the School were also members of the Scout movement and three of the Monitors were warranted Scouters, that is to say they either ran or assisted in the running of Troops, General Sir Rob Lockhart, Deputy Chief Scout, was invited to present the prizes at Speech Day in 1956. On this occasion I was invited to make the report on the School's sporting year and to thank the honoured guest. This was the first time a Head Boy had made a formal speech in the Speech Room. It was to become a tradition and the articulacy and effectiveness of Head Boys since has been most impressive. Among the successes I was able to recount was the Shooting VIII coming second in the Middlesex Cup and the Badminton Club retaining its unbroken record. They had so far not managed to find anyone with whom to compete.

This year saw an important expansion in the School's geography. The Governors acquired the Red House across the road. There, a day or two after term ended, a group of Old Boys whom Mr Campbell had traced gathered for a fifty-and-more-years-on reunion. The oldest gentleman there was Harry Burcham who had left the School in 1897. He recalled the not entirely successful introduction of rudimentary chemistry lessons in his day. He had also recovered one of his school reports. It read, 'He shows intelligence in his work, but allows his attention to be distracted far too easily', proving that boys do not change with the generations, neither do the comments of those who teach. Others among the seventeen present included Harry Phippard, who was almost certainly one of those small boys in the 1894 photograph of the Lower Division; Arthur Rackham, the accomplished musician who had taught as well as learnt at the School, and had combined this with being Borough Surveyor for Harrow; Edgar Rayner, School Captain in his day, and one of the three brothers who attended John Lyon and whose forbears gave Rayner's Lane its name; R J Bartlett,[42] the high-achieving scientist and educationist who had only just, aged 75, retired from heading the Psychology Department at Birkbeck College; and Sir Henry Turner who had joined the School on an early County Council scholarship (abandoned once the County School opened) and whose Civil Service career had taken him to the top. From early in the war until 1950, he had held the key post of Controller of Meat and Livestock at the Ministry of Food, the work for which he was knighted. Max Hofler, the painter, missed out as he was marginally too

---

[42] Throughout his life, the School could never make up its mind whether he was R H Bartlett or R J Bartlett. There is no question both versions apply to the same man and his name was Robert John Bartlett.

late a leaver and, anyway, the School seems not to have been aware of him. He was living, as he had been for decades, just a couple of hundred yards up the road at his Hill Studio, number 20 Crown Street.

The acquisition of the Red House, an elegant early nineteenth century building,[43] with a gable added when The Wheatsheaf public house next door had been demolished, allowed a number of developments to take place. Rooms in the existing buildings were freed up the moment boys moved across the road. As a result a science wing, with advanced laboratories, equipped with the aid of a grant from the Industrial Fund, could be developed in the New Building. For the first time, too, the School had a dedicated Art Room.

All first-formers and one sixth form, along with the Headmaster and his secretary, made the migration. Whether by design or not, this ended the long-standing initiation rites imposed on new boys. Near the entrance to the School there is a low Victorian wall, about a metre in length, slightly tilted by subsidence and topped by round-edged glazed bricks. Over this, The Whacker, each novitiate was laid by two or three second-formers, keen to pass on their own experience in their first days at the School. After a few slaps, mild if you were lucky, the new boy was deemed a fully-fledged Lyonian. Stephen Adamson also remembers boys being rolled down the bank as another form of initiation, and a rather riskier one. The bank that edged the playground on its western side would have been around three metres deep, at an angle steeper than forty-five degrees. It is now, like the view across neighbouring counties, invisible from the schoolyard, subsumed into the Lyon Building.

The practices ceased for the simple reason that, from this time, first-formers took their breaks in the garden of the Red House, so could no longer suffer indignities at the hands of their (only just) elders who were still on the original site. They were not free, however, from future corporal punishment, should their behaviour warrant it. The Headmaster and all four House Masters had the cane among the sanctions they could use.

For sixth-formers, too, there was an improvement. On my penultimate day at School, Boyd Campbell asked me, if there was one change I could make, what it would be. I answered, abolish caps for sixth-formers. Next morning, at the last Assembly of term, along with 'Lord, dismiss us with

[43] In answer to an enquiry from JLS boys, the Rev C E Prior who had been brought up in the Red House, and who with both his brothers had been educated at the School in the 1890s, wrote that the date June 29th 1815, found scratched on the window of the big room on the middle floor, was the likely date that the house was first occupied. The full text of the letter is in the Appendix.

thy blessing', the announcement was made. Sadly, of course, with the caps went the historic silver Monitors' cap badges, but the decision was unquestionably popular.

With Michael Rose now established as the first full-time music master, this pursuit became more and more central to the School's life. The first step came when he introduced individual instrument tuition. The orchestra and the Corps band had long awakened boys' interests in playing, but they either took private lessons or taught themselves. As had happened years before with gymnastics, what had been extra-curricular now took its place on the timetable.

School plays continued, Mr John Savage bravely producing Milton's masque, *Comus*, following the previous year's *Oliver Twist* directed by Mr Thornton. *Comus* was a large undertaking with a backstage support staff to match. The flaming torches, music and well-spoken verse all contributed to what was regarded as a triumph. Phillip Mansley, now Head Boy, was acclaimed for his brief and final School appearance as a shepherd: 'at the level of genius, he gave us a bucolic to end all bucolics'. Which sounds an unlikely preparation for his distinguished career as a diplomat and Arabist. Michael Bogdanov had earlier taken over as secretary of the three-year-old Drama Group. Michael was one of the outstanding athletes in the School's history. He won his colours for football, cricket, athletics and gymnastics. After his degree at Trinity, Dublin, and further studies in Europe, he took to directing and, naturally, emphasised the physical aspect of his productions, as a result falling foul on one occasion of the bile of Mary Whitehouse, the self-appointed conscience of the nation. With Michael Pennington, he founded and ran the English Shakespeare Company; he was the Director of the Young Vic Theatre and for a considerable time he was an Associate Director of the National Theatre. His career is international and has won him many awards, nominations, and honorary degrees, including Olivier Awards in 1979, 1989 and 1990. The twenty-first century has seen him enjoying further success as Director of the Wales Theatre Company, based at the Millennium Centre in Cardiff, while also being responsible for a string of productions elsewhere, including across Europe.

When Phillip Mansley came to make his Speech Day speech, he had some pleasing information to impart. P E Peck was keeping wicket for Middlesex Schools and for Young Middlesex played at Trent Bridge, while Brian Collins was captaining Buckinghamshire Colts. Perhaps even more enjoyable, because there are few things sweeter than defeating a friend, he was able to report that the Shooting VIII in direct competition with Harrow School had, unusually, trumped them by one point, 724 to 723; and, to rub in a little salt, at a rain-soaked meet, the School had defeated Harrow School's Beetlers on the athletic track.

It was decided to change the names of the School's Houses from the rather colourless cardinal points of the compass to those of former Head Masters of Harrow School, two of whom had been vital to the School's existence. It was also announced, only seven years after it had ceased as such, that 'first steps have been taken to equip the Cloisters as a canteen'. Access to Top Missus had ceased not long before. Top Missus was a tall, angular and elderly lady who appeared to run her little shop in Crown Street as a charity for the boys. Two-pennyworth of biscuits from her would take a full fifteen minutes to eat. When, for some reason, she was put out of bounds, her patrons were mightily disappointed. It is more than possible however that this saved her, not merely from her own generosity, but from a consequent life of penury.

Other genuine changes were on their way. Gordon Blyth was among the masters leaving and was soon to be Headmaster of Downham Market High School in Norfolk. Many boys, on leaving, donated attractively carved pine chairs, engraved with their name, to the Library. The Monitors of 55–56 had given a teak bench seat, engraved with their initials for the Red House garden and the Monitors of 56–57 did the same. The garden itself was beautifully maintained by a group of boys who chose horticulture in preference to the Cadets.

The following year, when Lord Somervell presented the prizes, Head of the School Peter Bell, or Pierre Cloche as he signed himself when writing up the activities of the French Circle, was able to report positively on the sports scene and a notably successful football season. The Headmaster announced from the same platform that plans were in place to accelerate the progress of some boys so that they reached the sixth form after only four years. Competition for places at the School had measurably intensified both at age eleven and among those sitting Common Entrance at thirteen. The standard that entrants reached was both higher and more even and it was this increasing level of initial achievement which encouraged his thinking. He would therefore be dividing the fourth and fifth forms into three smaller divisions, in place of the long established two divisions. Doing this also enabled him to take in a number of boys from Mercers' School which had been among our friendly rivals on the sports field for many years.

CHAPTER 12

THE SIXTIES AND MORE
REMEMBERED
1959–1968

Mercers' School had a history as fascinating as, and even longer than that of Harrow and the John Lyon School. Founded in 1542, and possibly even then the continuation of an earlier establishment in the City of London, it was – as its name makes clear – the offspring of the Mercers' Company. Initially, a schoolmaster Thomas Freeman taught thirty-five boys, some of them fee-paying, in a small City chapel. Over the years the numbers increased and decreased, hitting rock-bottom in 1721 when there were just four boys on its roll. The Plague of 1665 and the following year's Great Fire had seen temporary closure and then one of many removals to new premises for the school. By the late eighteenth century it was in Watling Street and soon after moved to Red Lion Court. Early in the nineteenth century the Company decided, as John Lyon had intended for his school and as the English Form was to embrace, that the curriculum at Mercers' should concentrate less on the classics and be broadened to include subjects useful to boys going into commerce. By the time the Lower School of John Lyon was on the horizon, Mercers' boys were spending less than half of their time on Latin and Greek in order to concentrate on English, French and mathematics. As the Middle Road site was opened, Greek disappeared completely from the Mercers' curriculum and German, more useful for international traders, was added.

Around now, too, Mercers' again changed location, made necessary by its continuing growth and success. Staff had increased to six and scholars to one hundred and fifty and in 1880 the school removed to Barnard's Inn to accommodate them.

Over the succeeding decades, the Company spent considerable sums improving the site and purchasing a sports ground away from the City. In response to the 1944 Education Act, the subjects studied were further modified and emphasis was laid on building a substantial sixth form. The Governors, however, were hampered in their plans for development by

The badge that never was. Designed by David Christie-Murray and suppressed on the orders of the Governors.

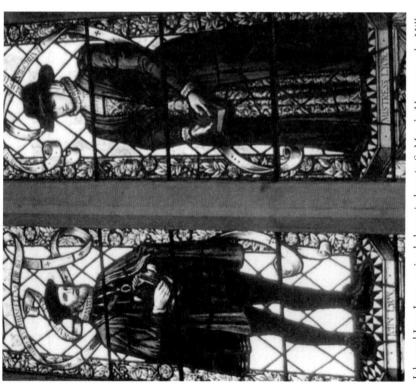

John and Joan Lyon, stained glass windows in St Mary's, Harrow on the Hill.

Crown Street in the mid-1930s. Watercolour by Old Lyonian Max Hofler whose studio was to the left of the figure walking along, carrying an artist's sketchpad. From the collection of the author.

The Duke of Edinburgh shares a joke with sixth formers, after opening the Sports Centre and the new Memorial Library, 1997.

Outward Bound course members test the raft they have built, 1994.

Year 8 pupil Ben Gill receiving the Junior Athletics Cup, on behalf of Vaughan House, from Tim Wright, 2001.

The Golden Mask of Agamemnon directed by Neil Pankhurst, 1997.

John Lyon boy Vladimir Kara-Murza with former Russian Prime Minister Sergei Kirienko,
Moscow 1999.

Portrait by Matthew Barker, 2007.

Self-portrait by Sonny Flynn, 2007.

Sixth formers in their suits relax in front of the Red House.

Ben Sehovic, Mr Graham Ryder, Head Boy Sameer Jethwa, Mr David Rimmer and Nasri El-Sayegh in the garden of the Headmaster's house, Association Day 2007.

The Art Mall, 2008.

Kevin Riley, Headmaster 2005–2009.

JLS footballers mount an attack.

The John Lyon School Musicals 2003 - 2010
Directed by
Deborah Gibbs

Photography : Graham Ryder

The country's first-ever woman Head of an independent boys' school: Katherine Haynes.

the physical limitations of the site. Acquiring more space in the post-war City of London was not financially feasible. Despite the school's high achievements and reputation, its applications for Direct Grant status were rejected by the government on grounds of the inadequacy of the buildings.

To the distress of all involved, its proud and long history came to an end with the last days of the summer term of 1959. One master and three boys had already come a year earlier, as an advance guard, to the John Lyon School. The master was William Stevens. One of the boys was John Hayes.[44]

John had been three years at Mercers' and was to remain four years on the Hill. The change for a fourteen-year-old was initially traumatic. Among many things, he missed the real organ which accompanied morning assemblies at his old school. Having been captain of both lower school cricket and football at Mercers', when presumably he would have played against John Lyon as the two schools had for decades been regular opponents, he had to start all over again and never achieved another captaincy. Modestly, he failed to mention that he did, however, gain full colours for football, cricket and athletics at his new school, though he missed the opportunity for competitive swimming, a sport at which he had excelled and which did not feature in his days at John Lyon.

It is reasonable to assume he did not miss too badly the much stricter discipline he had been used to at Mercers'. He was certainly pleased to find how close the sports ground at Sudbury was, compared with the long journey into mid-Kent necessary to reach Mercers' ground at Grove Park. These two responses might have surprised existing Lyonians (and even more, present-day ones) who would have regarded life during Mr Campbell's headmastership as strict and the walk to Sudbury as quite far enough.

John Hayes, and his fellow pioneers from Mercers', Tony Dawson and Graham Fermor, joined Four Alpha, part of the new arrangement Boyd Campbell had announced the previous Speech Day. There they found themselves with around a dozen boys who were a year and more younger and who had been accelerated into the fourth form. To begin with the Mercers' boys found this tedious. Their classmates were academically, physically and socially noticeably less mature. However as the months passed, it worked out well and John says the Mercers' boys found their

---

[44] Not to be confused with John Hayes, Old Harrovian and Chairman of the Governors of the John Lyon School, 2009– .

new school easy to fit into. Their cheerful assimilation is borne out by the fact that only a few years later Tony Dawson was elected Honorary Secretary of the Old Lyonian Association with John Hayes as Assistant Secretary.

One small help when they first arrived would have been the familiar presence of a master from their old school. Bill Stevens came to teach English. He took over as Careers Master and set up the School's system for processing University applications once UCCA came into existence. A year later, as Mercers' closed and more of its boys joined the School, so did their distinguished chemistry teacher, George Andrew. The author of several textbooks on the subject, he was a leading member of the Science Masters' Association. When he later retired after a total of forty-one years' teaching, Mr Andrew was elected President of the London and Home Counties section of the Association for Scientific Education. This was a signal honour. In the course of its existence, the Association had only once before appointed as President a man who was not a University Professor.

1959 saw another change, less important than the closure of a great school, but a change that has lasted to the present day. The thrice-yearly production of *The Lyonian* was reduced to an annual publication. Geoffrey Thornton, who had edited the magazine for the last several editions, was now joined by J R Potts who was to be responsible for its latter part which would be devoted to the OLA and the achievements of Old Lyonians.

For the first time, advertisements for local firms appear. The scope of these soon broadens as national companies, banks and the military see them as an opportunity to recruit promising boys to their cause. Happily, the seventy pages still have space for a good number of original contributions from members of the School, as well as reports from all the many clubs, on all the sporting activities and the full list of the School's Officers, from Head Boy C M H Sharp to the holder of Vaughan House Colours who, for alphabetical reasons comes last, H J Ramsay.

The devoted service of three long-serving masters is recorded as they leave: Don Cowtan and 'Spike' Hughes for retirement, 'Jack' Hogg the head of chemistry off to teach teachers. Also recorded is the revival of the Corps Band, led by Corporal Michael Wright. It had collapsed for lack of playable instruments, age and use having taken their toll. Happily, parents and Old Boys came to the rescue in the persons of OLA President Douglas Woodbridge and Mr Young, father of leading drummer Corporal N R Young. Keeping things in the family, Michael Wright's twin brother, Corporal J P Wright was the leading bugler. It was around now that it was found that there were twenty-one sets of brothers among the School's population. As the Wright boys and their friends left, they presented their successors with a brand new mace.

Music was becoming of marked importance in the School's life, an importance that continues to the present day. Richard Charles remembered not only orchestra and choir practices, but a string quartet and a chamber choir singing madrigals, all with increasingly high standards. Richard himself played the cello and used to cycle to School with it strapped to his back three times a week.

In 1960, the largest undertaking was a production of Brittten's *Noye's Fludde*, put on in St Mary's Church with girls from Harrow County School, the first time the School had – metaphorically speaking – embraced the opposite sex. Though, for the master responsible, it proved literally true: Michael Rose first met his future wife, the County School's music mistress, on this occasion. The lasting influence of good teachers is evidenced by Mr Rose making clear that the spur for his interest had been the brilliant teaching of Don Cowtan, and Michael in turn inspired Richard Charles to follow a career in which he was, for several years, chief recording engineer for Saga Records, subsequently spending thirty years at the BBC, much of it in the Music Department. There he would have found another of Rose's ex-students, Head of BBC Opera, Clive Bennett.

Shortly after the *Noye's Fludde* performance, another Britten piece was tackled by the School. *St Nicolas* was played and sung in the Speech Room as a charity concert to raise money for the Greater London Fund for the Blind.

As the sixties proceeded, Michael left to become County Music Adviser for Middlesex and then for Bedfordshire. The following century, he saw his 75th birthday celebrated at Bedford Corn Exchange with a packed concert in his honour given by John Lill and a full orchestra. Shortly after, he himself conducted two performances of the Verdi 'Requiem' in the same venue.

It fell to Tony Sloggett, who matched his substantially older brother Jolyon in becoming Head Boy, to note in his 1963 Speech Day speech that the planned ending of Saturday school would alter the sporting calendar. First and Second Eleven matches would continue to be played on Wednesday afternoons as they had been designated as sports periods for the entire fifth and sixth forms. All elevens would continue to play on Saturdays, but younger teams would, as a result of the change, have fewer fixtures.

The John Lyon School formally adopted this long-used version of its name in 1965, soon after another inspirational teacher arrived. Cited by several Old Lyonians as a positive influence on their young lives, Roger Williams took over responsibility for music. Under his direction the Motet Choir he developed became, and it remains to this day, internationally famous. Regular appearances in British cathedrals, at the Purcell Room of the Royal Festival Hall, on the BBC, led as years passed, to performances around the United States and across Europe.

The chain of inspiration commenced, as we have seen, with the persistence and enthusiasm of Donald Cowtan. A painful irony, given that he confessed to Geoffrey Thornton who succeeded him as head of English, that every day of teaching had been to him 'a kind of crucifixion'.

Before all this, however, in the early sixties, symposia on careers were introduced for fourth- and fifth- formers with half-a-dozen or more Old Lyonians, qualified in disparate areas, coming to discuss them. Meanwhile, repeating the pattern familiar in the early years of the School's existence, the experiment of accelerating boys so that they reached the sixth form after just four years, proved 'a complete success'.

School societies proliferated and among the activities going strong were the Christian Union which organized several outside speakers to address its members, as well as conducting Bible study sessions, visits and rallies at other schools and, as for many years, attendance at the Student Christian Movement Conference.

At this point an unfortunate habit started to creep into editions of *The Lyonian*, just occasionally at first and then more and more. It was of entries signed only with initials. For a magazine of record, this is not a route to take. As the years roll on 'PH' and 'CFP' become unidentifiable. Is 'MTR' different from 'MR', signatories to adjacent articles? Are they boys, are they members of the staff? There is no way of being certain.

The Duke of Edinburgh's Award Scheme was launched at this time and several boys signed up for it. One of the enthusiasts, 'RFM' writing, 'it is annoying to be unsuccessful . . . it is infuriating to knock the bar off at your seventh attempt, cook in a gale, and find your spare socks soaking wet. But we're glad we did it eventually.' A year later, John Mather[45] achieved the first Gold Award, twelve boys the Silver, fifteen the Bronze and a further thirty-seven were in training.

---

[45] John, who became Head Boy, went on to a distinguished career, becoming Chief Medical Director of the US Government's Social Security Administration and, incidentally, Secretary of the International Churchill Society.

.Glad of his achievement, too, the Headmaster was awarded a scholarship by the Headmasters' Conference and the English Speaking Union to travel around the USA. Mr Campbell wanted to see how schools operated in communities like that of Harrow Borough, how methods of selection were applied – not only for schools but for universities as well – and to meet again American boys who had been at John Lyon. With the headquarters of the USAF in Britain being at Ruislip, there had been several. Campbell managed to track down two: Stephen Laffey in Boston and George Blackburn who was now at Yale.

For two months he followed an amazingly dense schedule, spending time and making notes at schools and colleges of every kind, all over the States, including the South and discovering one, Gilman, a Country Day School in Baltimore, which in size and nature resembled the John Lyon School.

At home, more and more trips were being arranged for boys. As well as to the Outward Bound school on Dartmoor where 'all forms of subtle torture' were involved, groups went to Switzerland, to Heidelberg, to RAF Brueggen in Germany, to the Austrian Tyrol for ski-ing and on a walking tour of Scotland and a rather less energetic minibus tour of Wales.

Sport continued to feature, but with contrasting results. The first eleven soccer team, captained by Frank Bogdin, was remarkably successful as the decade began, registering only six losses from twenty-three matches, two of which were against adult teams from the Southern Olympian League. By 1962 results took a dip which lasted longer than anyone would have wished, reaching their nadir three years later when the team managed to avoid winning a single match. For some time cricket did not suffer in the same way. Wins greatly outnumbered losses and draws were often with the School in the ascendancy as, for example, the match drawn with Harrow Weald Grammar School. The score sheet read: John Lyon School 150 for 4 declared; Harrow Weald 76 for 8. Cricket Captain and Head Boy, H M J Stapley, and R E Perks were selected for the Middlesex Schools' Eleven. In athletics, Heryet became the first Lyonian, current or former, to run the half mile in under two minutes when he recorded a time of 1 minute 59.1seconds in a match against the Old Boys.

The slow process of the two schools on the Harrow Foundation getting to know each other better took an interesting step forward in 1963. Boys from Harrow spent a day further down the Hill and boys from John Lyon spent a day at the top of the Hill, sharing the experience of life in the other school and writing about it for *The Harrovian* and *The Lyonian*. Some things were radically different between the two: House Colours at the day school are awarded for all-round service, not simply for a sporting contribution; the fact that the Monitors' Room at John Lyon has a telephone earns an exclamation mark from the Harrovians; the fact that the Cadet Force is voluntary made the same boys sigh; and the prospect of two to three hours 'prep' after a school day ending at 4.15pm they regarded as 'formidable'. The John Lyon boys were first struck by the locational contrast: the buildings of the day school are all in close proximity, those of the boarding school, widely spread; the complexity of the privilege system at Harrow, based on the year you are in, seemed impressively byzantine; the range and nature of school societies seemed remarkably similar. The biggest contrast, of course, lay in the fact that much the greater part of a Harrow boy's life centres on his House. That is where he lives, sleeps, baths or showers and takes much of his recreation. A John Lyon boy would identify with his School to a much greater degree, with his House rather less, because he sleeps, does his homework, watches television and the rest, in his own family home.

There were of course a number of aspects of Harrow School that were familiar to the John Lyon boys: the Speech Room, the shooting range, the bookshop, the running track and some of the sports fields. What emerges from this small project is the idea that the two schools might benefit from knowing a little more about each other, given that they share not only a Hill, but a foundation and a founder, the same Governors and the same motto. Within a short period, the John Lyon Society was formed. Sixth-formers from both schools joined for its first meeting when a fine lecture was given by Professor Joel Hurstfield on the year that the original charter was granted, including an explanation as to why this is sometimes given as 1571 and sometimes as 1572.[46]

Possibly with the thought of peer inspection in mind, one fourth former, C J Street, offered a description of a typical John Lyon boy:

> Round-toed Oxfords with leather soles;
> Grey wool socks.
> Baggy grey trousers, creased to the hilt;
> Plain white shirt.
> Bold cut hair, clean white necks;
> Thin wire glasses.

[46] Put simply, at that time in history, the year started with March, hence September was named as being the seventh month. The charter was granted in January, then regarded as the previous year, which is how the discrepancy arises.

Flannel blue blazers with leathered elbows;
Rusty push bike.
Talking of Latin, cum et qui;
That's a Lyonian.

'Jack' Fish, who was laboratory steward at Harrow from 1924 and who filled the same role at the School for sixteen years from 1953, went on record to say he thought John Lyon boys were the more natural and had a greater respect for the individual than the boys further up the Hill where they seemed 'a bit far away'. He also thought discipline and self-discipline had declined with the current generation, though it is only fair to say every generation thinks that of the latest brood. Charles Lamb in the early 1800s makes the identical complaint and there is an ancient Egyptian text on exactly the same lines.

There may or may not have been a contrast between those at the two schools as to the pocket money available to them, at least in term-time. A survey at the John Lyon School found the average ranged from three shillings and sixpence a week for first-formers to ten shillings a week for sixth-formers. Fifth-formers were clearly better negotiators as they managed sixpence a week more than their seniors.

Unsurprisingly, the same survey discovered that 75% of the boys liked pop music and, not so predictably, that 120 of them (31%) played an instrument. The next architectural development at Middle Road was the opening of the Music School, a hexagonal performance space in the garden of the Red House, the ceremony performed by the eminent conductor and organist, Thurston Dart. Here, Roger Williams success- fully revived a once hugely popular burlesque opera, *The Devil to Pay*, not seen on a stage since 1750. In it John Barnard earned himself a good notice before leaving to take up a place at Selwyn College, Cambridge.

As the sixth form grew in size, so did the number of boys going on to university, notable successes including Malcolm Underwood who won an Exhibition to Oxford's Corpus Christi after just five years and one term at the John Lyon School, having failed the 11-plus. Not long after Martin Nelson won the School's first Choral Exhibition, to Cambridge's Gonville and Caius. There were many more scholarships, exhibitions and places achieved at Oxbridge colleges at this time, as well as young men going, on a regular basis, to Dartmouth, Sandhurst and Cranwell and to the newer universities. Usually the same boys were busy with many activities in addition to their academic studies: Underwood was playing Becket in *Murder in the Cathedral* while preparing for his Exhibition examination; Nelson and Stephen Janaway won themselves golden opinions for their performances in Mr Thornton's controversial production of *The Brass Butterfly*, as Janaway prepared to sit – and win – the Brisco-Owen Scholarship to Oriel College, Oxford.

Still other boys won scholarships in engineering to join Handley Page and other companies while the curriculum continued to broaden, with woodwork, Ancient Greek and modern Italian about to feature on the timetable. The Classics department suffered a sad loss when Christopher White, remembered by David Learner along with Roger Williams and Ian Whybrow as lively and influential, and described elsewhere as restlessly energetic, died suddenly of acute leukaemia at the age of thirty. Before Mr Sadler was appointed in his place, the gentle, scholarly retired headmaster, Dr Witt, filled in for two terms.

Art had for some time been a recognized 'O' and 'A' level subject and teaching it had long been in the hands of Don Allan. He had designed the colour combinations used in the refurbishment of the Red House; he had produced outstanding sets for numerous School performances and he had inspired more than one boy to take the not-easy path of a professional painter. A pupil at the School in the late forties, Michael Turner was already building himself a career. Staff at the time had complained of his schoolbooks being covered with drawings of racing cars and aeroplanes. His paintings of the same became extremely popular over the next sixty years, selling thousands of prints, and the originals have been bought by dozens of major collections. Hot on his heels came Roy Perry, painter of landscapes, golfing and cricketing subjects. Then in the late fifties/early sixties, Richard Berridge, professional portrait painter and book illustrator. He remembers two significant moments in his development as a student. The first when Allan, looking at watercolours Richard thought he had had made a mess of, said simply, 'all these highlights are too strong'. He took the painting, washed the highlights away under a tap and showed how much better it now was. The other was the sort of basic advice any professional loves and which is so obvious once you think of it. It was this: if you are drawing a figure, first establish where the light source is, do the shadows and leave the rest unshaded.

In sport, the glory in playing football remained in the taking part. Cricket was doing well with only four First Eleven matches lost out of eighteen played. Athletics showed promise after a close match with Harrow and beating both Preston Manor and Wembley County in a three-way match. Badminton was something of a triumph. The School team were Harrow and District champions, winning nine of their ten matches.

Then, in 1967, Boyd Campbell broke new ground. He appointed the School's first female member of the teaching staff. Mrs Alison Dillon had a double first in Maths from Cambridge and to describe her as doughty would be an understatement. Known among the boys as 'Ma' Dillon, she insisted on being addressed as 'sir' and being listed as a master. She saw the value board games could have in developing brain-power and started an Indoor Games Club, running it for several years and inventing a number of new games in the process. At the same time, she was not invulnerable to the spirited inventiveness of boys. Mrs Dillon was properly averse to pupils sporting scarves in class. When one boy did, she confiscated it, returning it at the end of the day. Next lesson with the same group, she found every boy was adorned with a scarf. She confiscated the lot. The third time she took the class it was again only one boy so clad. As she pulled the offending scarf from round his neck she found another tied to it, and another, and another; in fact all thirty-five in a near-endless chain.

Soon after her appointment, but quite coincidentally, Boyd Campbell had announced he would be leaving at the end of the 1968 summer term. Having served outside the School on the Selection Boards of both the Admiralty and the RAF and having chaired the Voluntary Service Overseas Board, he was now moving on, after seventeen years as Head-master, to be Director of the Public Schools Appointments Bureau.

During his final term, he and his wife Desiree gave a luncheon for everyone who had served him as Head Boy. Then, when most had left, he once more took the walk through the empty School buildings that he had made with Mr Wilson some days before his first term on the Hill began. A sentimental thing for a usually unsentimental man to do. As he reflected on all that had happened, it is unlikely he realized how permanently he would be remembered.

CHAPTER 13

NEW PRESSURES
1968–1982

The pattern of appointing the housemaster from a boarding school was repeated when Gordon Surtees, formerly in charge of a house at Malvern College, was installed in Boyd Campbell's place. He was to preside over the School for the next fourteen years, years that saw continuing and steady development, continuing academic progress and some remarkable sporting achievements, though after the first ten years rarely in the major game of football.

Exemplifying this, two boys, R G Lindsay and P J Cohen won the London Schools' Golf Championship within months of Mr Surtees' arrival. Tragically, Peter Cohen was killed in a road accident two years later. Football, having been in the doldrums, for a spell saw a considerable resurgence with Lionel Boardman's faithful coaching and oversight rewarded, the team playing twenty-seven matches with only four losses in 1971. At the same time they reached the quarter-finals of the Public Schools' Six-a-Side Competition. John Blake achieved a postwar record, scoring thirty-seven goals in one season. When Brian Holgate took over the training, success continued and the First Eleven won the Middlesex Championship Shield more than once. By mid-decade, the Second Eleven was maintaining excellent results – in 1974 they were Middlesex Schools Champions at their level – and the First Eleven reached the final of the Middlesex Schools' knockout competition, for the Brigg Cup, losing by one goal scored in extra time. Similar ill-luck beset the Six-a-Side team the following year when, having beaten Ardingly among others and drawn with Millfield, in the Public Schools' tournament, they lost the final in extra time, again by one goal, on this occasion to Forest School.

Cricket, too, after an initial slump was lively in the early 1970s, the first team, in 1972, completing a whole season undefeated under the captaincy of Simon Vessey. They remained in good form throughout this period, for example playing thirteen matches in 1979 and only losing one of them. Two years later they repeated the achievement.

What makes this remarkable is the increasing number of sports in which boys were engaged and the startlingly good results obtained, year in, year out, in one of the newest. From the days when sport at the School meant football, cricket, then gymnastics, athletics and boxing as well, the range had now grown to embrace badminton, basketball, squash, ski-ing, swimming, tennis, table tennis, road relay and cross-country, too. Boxing had been dropped and badminton, from the moment it was started, reigned supreme. The School now combined with the girls of Bentley Wood for the mixed doubles teams and were initially hampered as Bentley Wood did not have a sixth form. This meant that while every year from 1972 the School dominated the county competitions, winning the Under-16 Singles, Under-16 Doubles and Under-18 Singles Championships they lacked equally committed and skilled partners for the Under-18 Doubles. Until Bentley Wood started a sixth form, whereupon the John Lyon teams wiped the board, taking all four Middlesex championships.

This extraordinary level of achievement was maintained with one group of exceptional players following another as the generations of schoolboys moved on. The sport was coached and overseen by Mr Bill Podmore and after ten years of uninterrupted success he wrote, with justifiable pride, of the John Lyon players he had watched winning regional and national finals. 'So much of the enjoyment. . . . lies in the visible combination of skill and personality. The fierce competitiveness of Geelan, Foster, Saunders, Hughes, the elegance of Kerley and Fell, the combination of delicacy and power in partnerships like those of Biddle and Richards, the tumbling agility of Fields, Baulch and Melling, the occasional magical touch of Lamont and Parkinson, all come to mind.'

The county competition began in 1971 and from the off Jeremy Geelan and Steve Dunning worked hard on their preparation and won (aged 14) the first Under-16 League Championship. Ten years later the record was almost overwhelming: in the Harrow Schools Championships, John Lyon boys had won twenty-two out of thirty senior titles and all but two of the thirty Under-16 titles; in 1974 J R Davies had won all six titles: singles, doubles and mixed doubles at Under-16 *and* at Under-18 levels; the School had won eleven out of fourteen Harrow Youth titles; and out of thirty-three possible County League Championships they had won twenty-four. In all of these, when they did not win, they were usually the runners-up. Twenty-two boys in that time had been selected to play for Middlesex. It did not end there. As the new decade got under way, the John Lyon School won all four Middlesex titles for a second time and, with Chris Baron, A Ross, A Flude and C Bendell playing, all four titles in the Harrow Youth Tournament.

Several of the same boys were mainstays in other sports as well, Geelan, for instance, scoring 66 in a ninth wicket partnership with Vessey which rescued the School from certain defeat at the hands of Battersea Grammar. David Fell was another who featured outstandingly in several sports. He went on to win his blue for cricket at Cambridge, scoring a century in his debut match against Nottinghamshire at Fenners.

Among the other sporting highlights, athletics enjoyed its best season for years, beating Harrow School, Preston Manor and the Old Boys in different matches and having six current Lyonians selected to represent Harrow in the Middlesex Championships of 1970. A few years later the team was still doing well in competition. E K Moore won the County Junior High Jump, coming fourth in the National Championships. At Sports Day in 1976, eight new records were set, two them, the triple jump and discus, by the same boy, R M Harrigan. Cross-country enjoyed successes as well: in the 1969 Independent Schools' race, R B Jones came home first and broke the seniors' course record with A T Salloway third; while M A Reed in the junior race mirrored Jones's achievement and also broke the course record, with Simon Vessey in second.

Shooting, too, showed at least one remarkable result. In 1973, as the Harrow School Range was closed for much of the time, the Eight only fired in one competition: the international schools' one organized by *Country Life* magazine. The team achieved the outstanding result of coming second.

Not to be outdone, the Old Lyonians, always keen on the field of play, entered the *Guinness Book of Records* when the combined skills of Jim Anthony as thrower and John Wilson as catcher set a new world record for hurling an egg. And catching it! The distance recorded at Pinner View was 268 feet 7 inches. Or 88.6864 metres. The date: 25th May 1971.

Not all games were involved in external competition. Squash, introduced by Mr Kim Bruce Lockhart, was limited to hard fought matches within the School. Kim himself was a Cambridge Blue and Scotland's current number one international at the sport, playing for his country a record fifty-nine times. Highly popular and intellectually stimulating, it came as a stunning loss when he died suddenly, aged thirty-three, on court at the Herga Club, nine years after his arrival at the School.

There was, of course, another form of competitive game, mentally but not physically energetic, and the School in Mr Surtees' time had success in that, too. The Chess Club early on announced a surge of interest and fifty new members. After coming fourth in the Harrow and District League, the School's principal team went on to beat the champions and won a string of other matches, while the Junior team became the Harrow and District Junior Champions. Ironically, both teams were made up of first-formers.

In 1981, the senior team won, for the first time, the Harrow and District title, giving special pleasure to Sean Ringsted in his final year at School. He had played for the team every year from being one of those first-formers.

Unlike some public schools, John Lyon has never been principally about sport. The balance between teamwork and physical fitness on the one hand and academic achievement and intellectual development on the other, with an emphasis on contributing positively to the community added in, evolved from the earliest days to be the School's aim; and it is entirely in line with the Founder's plan for the school he had in mind.

The academic success of boys and former students reached an impressive level throughout Mr Surtees' headship. The increasing number of boys going on to university, the greater number winning open scholarships and exhibitions would make recital of their names soporific – except of course to the high-achievers themselves. In 1969, by way of example, the School gained only its second-ever Choral Exhibition when J A Fullerton was awarded it by Trinity College, Cambridge. The following year, S P Edwards obtained exactly the same award; while Fullerton's contemporaries won an Exhibition in Science to Peterhouse (R W Hiley), an Open Scholarship to Selwyn to read Engineering (N Stansfield) and a Scholarship to Oxford's Pembroke College to read Medicine (M G Spencer). At the other end of his reign, in 1982, again four boys went on to Oxbridge and a further twenty-four had obtained places at other Universities and Polytechnics with one boy going on to the Royal Northern College of Music and another to Guy's Hospital. Roger Beam, meantime, was leading the way, followed later by a number of Lyonians, as an outstanding journalist. Starting his career with the *Lancashire Evening Post*, he went on to write for *The Times*, the *Observer*, the *Mirror* and more, receiving the IPC National Press Young Journalist of the Year Award, then their Reporter of the Year Award. He branched out into television, producing and directing numerous documentaries for the BBC, ITV, Channels 4 and 5, including for the Despatches series. His book on the Special Operations Executive, the commandos who worked behind enemy lines in Holland during the war, won in 2011 the Jerwood Non-fiction Prize.

Back in Middle Road, there were minor changes to the curriculum. Drama crept briefly into the sixth form General Studies course; the new 'A' Level subject, Design and Technology, was introduced; and the Founder's demand that all boys should learn archery was finally acknowledged lower down the Hill as it had been further up, with the sport taking place at Sudbury. Plans were laid for an indoor range and for future external competitions.

There are other modifications, too. A Sixth Form Committee came into existence. Elected by boys in the lower and middle sixth, with a Monitor co-opted as its secretary, it acted as a sort of mini-parliament, proposing at its thrice-termly meetings changes it would like to see for itself, and for others in the School. Its existence illustrated the softer touch Surtees applied. Campbell regarded the Monitors as the body to filter suggestions to him, and his Head Boy in particular as the voice of the School. The difference between the two Headmasters may have been much less simple. Both had military backgrounds. But Surtees was working against a backdrop of 'flower power', sit-ins in colleges across western Europe including Britain and, in the wider world, the operation of the Baader-Meinhof gang and the Red Brigades. It no doubt seemed wise to try to loosen the reins a little. This was not something about which Surtees felt at all comfortable. To begin with it made it more difficult for him to establish himself. Among the staff, he was regarded as approachable, clubbable, but lacking in confidence, inclined to bluster. This presumably led to his reputation among many boys for irascibility and a perpetually short fuse. They did not necessarily share the staff's view that his bark was worse than his bite.

Nonetheless hair was now allowed to be very much longer and the sixth-formers suggested altruistically that caps for boys in the Main School, that is third-, fourth- and fifth-formers, should be abandoned. This left the first- and second-formers somewhat aggrieved, a survey showing that 65% of them thought the change should apply for them, too. The sixth-formers asked for, and after a year or two obtained, a room to work in where the Library rule of silence did not apply. R F B Campbell's photograph joined those of his predecessors on the Library wall, but would not be gazing down on these talkative students. The same boys also requested a coffee vending machine then, rather dodgily, requested that athletics should no longer be compulsory. It can have been no accidental slip that Mr Knott, head of the sixth form and of cricket, wrote of them, 'next year's sixth will, I believe, be a more interesting one.' It appeared they were, but Mr Knott did not stay to find out. He left for Alnwick, the other end of the country, to take up his appointment as Headmaster at Dukes Grammar School there. Come 1974, the sixth-formers not only had their silence-free workroom, they had a common room to boot, with armchairs for all, newspapers, magazines and soft drinks on tap. They did, however, administer it themselves and contributed a small regular subscription to pay for its upkeep.

The sixth form enjoyed more stimulation, as well as relaxation. The Sixth Form Union, now in its tenth year, attracted a range of top-rank speakers: in 1969, the Secretary-General of the Association France Grande-Bretagne and the Director of Industrial Affairs at the CBI, among them. Later speakers included Dr Rhodes Boyson, the controversial educationist and Mrs Mary Whitehouse, who was later to take legal action against Michael Bogdanov.[47] She failed, in the event, to obtain any kind of conviction. At the School, she impressed by her mildness. The same year as she came, so did James Firman, the liberal-minded Film Censor. Happily, they came separately or she might have tried to sue him, too. Another guest was the renowned and splendidly named explorer, John Blashford-Snell. He had led the first ever descent of the Blue Nile, among scores of expeditions to remote parts of the world. It was his use of inflatables to descend white water rapids that instigated what is now a popular sport and he was awarded the Livingstone Medal by the Royal Scottish Geographical Society for his exploration of the Zaire river, among the many honours he received for his work as adventurer and animal scientist. When he spoke, you can be sure the shades of Ernest Young, and probably Oscar Le Beau too, were there listening.

Generally, the staff were thought to be very personable and teaching methods were often exciting. Long evenings playing music and discussing anything and everything at the home of Mr Sydney McMinn; General Studies which entailed jumping into the School minibus and going to the Albert Memorial or to watch the Globe Theatre being built on the South Bank, and discovering the background and history involved in both. It was this sort of enterprise, and in particular the gifted teaching of Bill Podmore, that inspired Stephen Pollard, later to be a regular *Daily Express* and *Telegraph* columnist and editor of the *Jewish Chronicle*, Gary Gibbon, Political Editor of television's best news programme, Channel 4 News, and Liam Halligan, influential economist and winner of more 'Journalist of the Year' awards than can be reckoned, to pursue the adventurous career paths they have.

---

[47] She took Michael to court, alleging indecency in the staging of one of the scenes in *The Romans in Britain* which he had directed at the National Theatre. She lost the case, but gained for herself – and the production – a lot of publicity.

One young man in the sixth form had a unique story of his own. A Czech, he and his family had left their home in Prague in the aftermath of the Russian invasion of August 1968. Jan Knytl and his parents were able to escape because of the chaos which engulfed the city. Speaking very little English and wishing to study science subjects, he arrived at the John Lyon School, much as a rather younger Hungarian boy had in the 1950s, avoiding an earlier invasion of his native country by the same imperial force. Jan acquired the language of his new country with remarkable speed, but was surprised, even then, by the polarities of wealth he found. He was glad to know of England's political freedom, but he missed the mountains of his homeland.

Apparently no one thought to ask him to address the Geographical Society where his first-hand knowledge of a foreign country would surely have commanded an audience. And commanding an audience is something the two oldest School societies were clearly failing to do. Year after year during this period, the Geographical Society and the Scientific Society file complaining reports of their lack of support. A look at their programmes, nothing but film shows in both cases, no visits, no speakers, nothing involving participation from members, make it perfectly obvious why. Sadly whoever was running them lacked the ability to learn from experience. The same dreary programming was repeated, along with the complaints. Finally both societies closed.

By way of contrast, the Table Tennis Club announced many more recruits: it offered something a boy could do, just as the swelling Chess Club did. The Music Society flourished with a programme of quizzes, informal concerts, talks and recordings. Again, some variety and the chance to participate in different ways. The brand new Motor Club made a good start, despite showing films, because it also offered members the chance to do some practical mechanics. The Railway Club had their own adventure to occupy them. The loft at the front of the New Building, once the home of the Signals Section of the CCF, and for some time the site of the club's model track lay-out, had been condemned as a fire risk. As a consequence, members of the club were kept busy removing and relaying the track in the potting sheds.

Even the acquisition of a school goat – luckily Lyonians seem to have been unaware of Harrovian Lord Byron keeping a pet bear – excited a number of boys to care for her, on non-school days as well as on school days. But she did not arrive until after the demise of one proud and long-standing institution.

The Combined Cadet Force saw encouraging increases in its numbers in 1973 and '74 and had only recently been described by the officer conducting the Annual Inspection as the best he had ever seen. Then, quite suddenly its closure was announced, causing more than disappointment among its supporters. An editorial by the Old Lyonians attacked the decision. Many were, and remained, perplexed at what seemed a high-handed decision to axe one of the School's most successful activities. A defence of the action by John Barnard on the grounds that the Corps was being superseded by the Duke of Edinburgh's Award Scheme and that it was out of step with the age may have convinced some. It certainly did not convince all, including former student Colonel Keith Farnes of the SAS.

What was not said, and quite surely lay behind the decision, was that this period saw a worrying expansion of IRA atrocities on the mainland. In a fourteen-month period during 1974–75 more than forty bombs were set off in London alone, killing thirty-five people and injuring many more. There is evidence that school armouries and stores were being targeted for supplies of uniforms and weapons and, by their nature, such places were incapable of being kept secure twenty-four hours a day. Their existence, indeed, created a threat to the schools that housed them and to schoolboys walking around in military uniform. It is understood, moreover, that at least one school armoury in the area was successfully raided: that of Harrow School. For security reasons it was not information that could be broadcast at the time, but in these circumstances what had appeared capricious takes on a very different hue.

It meant, of course, no more shooting at the Harrow School Range and there is some small comfort that the John Lyon School's Eight had attained its highest-ever position in international competition not long before its closure.

With the Corps rooms emptied at Middle Road, Demelsa the pedigree goat took occupation. It can be presumed the IRA were not thought to be partial to feta.

Two of the busiest activities at the School continued to thrive. Drama involved more and more performances and, logically enough, more and more boys. A show called *Youth and Age*, put together by pupils in the middle years was performed in St Mary's Church and later taken to the Shenley Mental Hospital where the cast joined patients for conversations afterwards.

Then, in an innovation not always sustained, newcomer to the staff Ian Whybrow directed Frisch's *The Fire Raisers* with girls playing the female parts. The choice of plays for production was refreshingly varied: Beaumont and Fletcher's infrequently performed piece, *The Knight of the Burning Pestle, Everyman*, Pinter's *The Birthday Party* which in its sense of ever-present threat has something in common with Max Frisch's play. Revues cropped up now and again and names that recur of boys who make their mark include Larry Barker and Christopher Glynn, whether it is revue or Stoppard or Marlowe's *Dr Faustus*.

Larry went on to become one of advertising's most successful creatives, responsible for campaigns for Haagen Dasz and for the launch of Orange that won him awards in London, New York and Cannes. Having reached the top in his sphere as Executive Creative Director at one of the most innovative of advertising companies, he moved into screenwriting full-time, working more closely with performers, the role he most enjoys. Christopher Glynn, like Michael Turner more than a generation before, had covered his schoolbooks at John Lyon with sketches. Not entirely a surprise, therefore, that he went into design and animation for the BBC, Glyndebourne and for feature films as well as teaching at Cardiff's degree level School of Art and Design.

In 1977 an inter-house drama competition was inaugurated for the junior boys in the Red House. It comprised sixteen five-minute perform-ances. The following year a senior competition was added along the same lines. Instead of a single main production, the School presentation was a selection of pieces linked by Martin Esslin's misleading label, *Theatre of the Absurd*.[48] They included Beckett's *Endgame*, a favourite with John Lyon boys; N F Simpson's *A Resounding Tinkle* and a Pinter revue sketch written for Kenneth Williams, *Last to Go*.

Full-length plays returned to the stage in 1980 and having presented *The Physicists* some years before, another Duerrenmatt, *The Visit*, was produced, this time by Kim Bruce Lockhart. Then in Ben Jonson's *The Alchemist* the youngest of the three Geelan brothers, Christopher, won golden opinions for his performance as Doll, who is seen variously as slut, aristocrat and fairy queen: an invitation to any would-be actor. Christopher's own self-deprecating view is that it was his performance which ensured the decision that, in future, all female parts would be played by girls. The directorship of the annual production rotated among the English staff and there was an idea among the boys that it was viewed by them as a poison chalice, to be handed on as soon as possible. Not so, according to Ian Whybrow who insisted he thoroughly enjoyed the task.

---

[48] Esslin linked together a number of disparate playwrights under this title, including Harold Pinter, who resented it. Pinter's work was avowedly political, though in his early years he resisted admitting it. His dialogue brilliantly reflects everyday speech and his plots, the corrupted world as he saw it. Rather than the absurd, he is the playwright of betrayal.

It was exhausting on top of the other responsibilities of teaching, but entirely worthwhile, the main difficulty being that plays were presented in the Music School and there, a certain resistance to use of the space was regularly encountered. Christopher Geelan, incidentally, went on to found and run with his wife the Young Shakespeare Company, introducing a hundred thousand secondary school children every year to the works of the Bard.

The brightest jewel in the School's artistic crown, however, remained music and throughout this period it more than kept its high international reputation. The Motet Choir, after contributing to the soundtrack of the Bette Davis/Michael Redgrave film, *Connecting Rooms*, made its now customary tour of cathedrals, this time either side of the Atlantic. It joined Eric Robinson in his popular television programme. In 1970, John Gardner, a composer in the tradition of Vaughan Williams and Walton, wrote his *Mass in C* and his *Psalm 23* for the choir. Then, the next year, not long before he left, Mr Williams drew together Lyonians, recent leavers and boys from King Edward's School Birmingham in an epic production of Sophocles' *Philoctetes* which, under the auspices of the British Council, played in Berlin as part of British Week there.

Frederic Goodwin[49] who took over as Music master was a former member of the well-regarded singing group, the Clerkes of Oxenford. Under his baton the cathedral tours flourished: Chartres, Notre Dame, Ely, Coventry, Lincoln and Peterborough, performing evensong in each; and other times, with Harrow School Orchestra, entertaining at a conference of music teachers, or singing, at the invitation of Gervaise de Peyer, brother of the John Lyon English master, in St John's, Smith Square. The list of invitations taken up is almost endless and the standard of musicality was clearly maintained at the highest level.

On a later tour which again took in Peterborough Cathedral it became clear, however, that Mr Goodwin's skill at navigation was not of the same order. Taking a break on the river in Cambridge, he managed to ram his punt full of John Lyon boys into that being steered by the Dean of Peterborough who, by chance, was also enjoying a day's recreation, accompanied by his daughters. Enjoying it up to that point, anyway. But then, as Philip Davies commented, 'What do you expect from an Oxford man?' The Dean's comment is not recorded.

Mr Goodwin was keen to tackle major works and in succeeding years performances were given of *The Messiah*, Haydn's *The Creation* and the *St*

[49] Not to be confused with the individual who shredded both the bank he ran and his knighthood.

John Passion. Then, in 1977, two School choirs were formed, augmented by members of the choir at St Mary's, the orchestra was divided into two as well, and with professional singers in the major roles plus John Barnard on the organ, the *St Matthew Passion* was given a rousing performance in the Speech Room. A quite extraordinary achievement.

The Motet Choir tours continued, in 1980 led by Ian Burrell, across the Channel to the cathedrals of St Malo and Dol de Bretagne. A little earlier, a new group had come into being, the Calico Consort made up of around a dozen boys, basses and tenors, under the leadership of John Barnard. As with drama in the Music School, there was some contention here: Goodwin did not really approve of boys singing barbershop and the Beatles. It was not his kind of music, though he moderated his view later. They began by giving local concerts, and singing in old folks' homes, especially at Christmas time. The carols and readings service, an autumn term regular at St Mary's since the 1950s, now featured the Consort and this year was repeated in its entirety at St Alban's Church, North Harrow.

The following year, 1981, the Consort ranged further afield. There were several local appearances, at St John's Greenhill, in Windsor and at Harrow Arts Centre, no one noticing, apparently, that this last venue occupied the buildings of century-long rivals on the field, the Royal Commercial Travellers School, now defunct. This year, too, the Calico Consort issued the first of their three LPs, recorded at Pinner's Studio Republic.[50]

The boys also mastered a number of German folksongs and some Bach chorales, singing them in their original language to the delight of their audiences as they toured Baden-Württemberg and Bavaria. Among those present and most pleased were Friedrich Silcher, an authority on German folksongs and Josef Dahman, an old friend of Vaughan Williams, some of whose songs the Consort also featured.

Membership of the different singing groups, Motet, Calico and School choirs was not, of course in any way exclusive. A posse of Andrews, for instance, turn up in all of them: Andrew Ellis; Andrew Rintoul; and Andrew Carwood who will reappear later in this history.

Everything recounted so far in this chapter, though, concerns the daily manifestations of the School's life. There were two major physical developments, three if you include replacing the pavilion at Sudbury

---

[50] Founded and run by John Bales at Church Farm at the top of Pinner High Street, he was assisted by Old Lyonians, Peter Ballard and Richard Charles in the early days of the studio's existence.

which, after only twenty years, had decided to fall apart. In addition there were two socio-political threats to take up Mr Surtees' time and energies.

Numbers attending the School continued to increase and it became clear that, yet again, more space, more facilities were needed. The first response was to extend the New Building forwards, further onto the playground, and onto the land below and to the side. This did away with the small balcony, and with it the bell which, through the day, had tolled the knell of each passing lesson.

The plan, which came to fruition in 1974 when it was officially opened by former Chairman of the Committee of Management, Mr Seton Watson, was to create a new hall-cum-gymnasium, a new staff room and library and to provide improved laboratories. These were each put to use the moment they were completed, so the actual opening, performed from the inside because of pouring rain, was more ritual than reality.

The extension provided a new entrance, facing Middle Road from below a flight of steps, and familiar to today's boys and parents as the way into the Main Building, as it was now to be called. A plain doorway was considerably enhanced by Don Allan's large embossed version of the School arms which surmounts it.

The years immediately after the opening ceremony are well remembered for long periods of drought which threatened the new development as the building settled. Cracks appeared in the walls of the gymnasium and the library ceiling threatened to collapse, so remedial work had to be undertaken, as for many buildings across England, in 1977.

Then there occurred a fortuitous opportunity. The house and land adjacent to the School, beyond the Main Building, was acquired by the School from its owners, Harrow School. Discussions among the staff as to how the site could best be developed produced four principal needs: more classroom space for junior boys; provision of a proper art department; an additional assembly hall; and, the School playground having been reduced in size and anyway being some distance from this site, somewhere for the young boys to play. Increasing the number of rooms for boys in years one and two at John Lyon (or years seven and eight as they would now be termed) would allow Mr Surtees to improve the teacher/pupil ratio. Instead of two forms of thirty-one boys, there could be three forms of twenty-two boys in each year, slightly increasing the total admitted while decreasing the number to be taught in any one group.

Planning permission was granted, the existing house was demolished, and building got under way in the autumn of 1979. The initial plan was modified and the hall dispensed with, allowing for a junior library to be included and the art department to comprise both a large and a small studio, and a pottery room. Towards the end of 1981, it was opened by a smiling Mr Anthony Grant, Member of Parliament for Harrow. The gods of the weather allowed him to do it from the outside. The name of the original dwelling on the site, Oldfield House, was retained by the School and a full-scale reorganization of the rooms in the existing buildings answered many of the needs different departments had felt for some time.

While the School was clearly flourishing, there were two developments which gave the Headmaster and everyone in the independent sector substantial worry. Five years into his headship, the Boroughs of Harrow, Hillingdon and Brent decided to abandon free and assisted places at independent schools. Surtees wondered aloud who supposedly gained from this. He thought the effect would be the reverse of the one the local politicians intended. That it would reduce educational opportunities for bright girls and boys from humble backgrounds. The Governors intervened to provide two scholarships for boys entering at age eleven and two more for boys joining at Common Entrance age. While this was welcome, it nonetheless meant a reduction in the overall number benefiting and it posed problems for the families of boys already at the School on local authority scholarships who suddenly had their financial support removed.

More disturbing still was the threat from government quarters to end the existence of independent education altogether. With it came the suggestion that 'A' levels should be abolished, an examination where the School was currently achieving an 82% success rate. The attack ignored the simple fact that public schools were so called because they had for centuries provided the opportunity to acquire learning when the state, in whatever form, provided no education at all. To destroy some of the best establishments, having removed the opportunity to attend them from the less financially fortunate, and to destroy an accepted test of achievement, did not appear to many to be motivated by a desire to improve what was available to the public. As Gordon Surtees had urged back in 1972 to a conference of bankers, true academic achievement, healthy competition and training in leadership were values that should be promoted rather than attacked.

In the event, 'A' levels continued, largely because the government concerned did not. And only a year after its abolition, Harrow Borough Council took the decision to restore the Assisted Places Scheme.

It would be wrong to leave this period without recording that a noticeable degree of humour returned to the pages of the School magazine. Its editor Ian Whybrow reported hearing, at the conclusion of one of his classes:

> Second former: What have we got next?
> His friend: Biology. Human reproduction.
> Third boy: Is it a practical?

On a further occasion a different second-former asked a fellow pupil: 'What does *comment allez-vous* mean?' only to receive the reply: 'I thought you'd done your Latin homework.'

In an early film of *Tom Brown's Schooldays*, Dr Arnold is given the line: 'Boys may come and boys may go, but we go on forever'. It may sometimes seem that way to the boys, too, but of course, it is not true.

During the fourteen years of Gordon Surtees' reign the ebb and flow of staff saw several very long servers reach the moment for retirement. Joey Cummings left, and so did Fred Sibcy who worried about his nickname, 'Basher'. 'I don't hit the boys, you know,' he used to assure doubtful parents and it appears never to have occurred to him that he acquired the soubriquet from his long stint commanding the Cadet Force: 'square-basher'. Mr Jackson, the friendly and loyal groundsman at Sudbury completed his time, to be replaced by an equally popular successor. Sergeant-Major Moore, the excellent shooting coach retired and the School Eight had celebrated by winning every single match during his final year. Bill Worman left after thirty-six years, timing his exit so he could avoid sitting through tributes on Speech Day; George Weedon, whose three sons he had educated at the School, moved on after twenty-one years to Quainton Hall. There he did for prep school gymnastics exactly what he had done for secondary school skills at John Lyon.

Mr Ernie Webb the School Caretaker, a man of considerable patience, ingenuity and with a humour not always welcomed by the Headmaster, reached pension age, sadly dying not very long after.

David Latham, who for his last four years had been Head of English, who had previously edited *The Lyonian* and who had been instrumental in developing the School's substantial work in the community, left to teach handicapped youngsters. It was a shock when, at the early age of 43, he died half-a-dozen years later. An earlier shock had been the death in a car accident of Mick Stapley. A former Head Boy, he had returned to the School as a master teaching maths and French only to lose his life before he was thirty.

Alfred Dunhill, the eminent Old Lyonian, whose company was twice winner of the Queen's Award to Industry and held the Royal Warrant, passed away. So did former Headmaster O A Le Beau, until that moment the last living Englishman to have sipped vodka in the Kremlin in the time of the Tsars. Edmond Vernon, nineteen years Head of Chemistry and author of a staple textbook on the subject, died quite unexpectedly, three days after summer term ended in 1981. He and his wife lived on Middle Road and his avuncular manner won him the name among the boys of 'Nunky'. Phil Davies ended his tribute to a man who had an enormous sense of fun with a classical joke he would have enjoyed: 'Nunc Dimittis, Domine'.

But, of course, a school is about constant renewal. Along with the new buildings, the new societies, the Computer Club and computers, there came new boys, new masters. Among the latter who had joined were Mr David Rimmer, in 1977 Mr David Dixon and a year later, Mr Dudzinski who was welcomed with the public revelation that his first lesson as a chemistry teacher had started with a bang and, 'his attempt to inaugurate an annual cull of fourth-formers has been greeted with interest'.

CHAPTER 14

LIGHTER TOUCHES
1983–1991

Chris Geelan who was Gordon Surtees' last Head Boy found the morning meeting with him each day something of a trial. He had to be there at 8.38 am on the dot, a minute's lateness unacceptable. The Headmaster, he said, seemed always to be on the brink of anger and the short time he survived in retirement (he died aged 67) came as no surprise, given the tension he regularly evinced. Another boy said you could always tell when Gus, as he was known, was about to give you a roasting: his spectacles came off and he waved them to the side as with his other hand he beckoned the offender. A third, obliquely confirming the staff view that he lacked confidence, said he never set bounds clearly. He would give permission for some relaxation of rules, white shirts no longer necessary as part of school uniform for example, and then rescind it later, displeased with the result. Another instance can be found on the After Surtees Club website: after throwing chalk at a second-former, presumably with some accuracy as he was a regular chalk thrower, he gave the boy money for sweets, to make up. This kind of conduct weakened his authority at a time when it was his misfortune that authority was being regularly challenged in the wider world.

Boys who had an outside-school relationship with the Head found him easier, whether the connection was singing at St Mary's where he worshipped, or receiving his help in entering the Navy where Mr Surtees was an adviser to the Admiralty. Most, of course, simply accepted that is how Headmasters are and were glad of those moments when, for example, Gus saw a Sikh boy with facial hair and asked whether it wasn't time he shaved: he asked and accepted the answer, rather than waving those spectacles.

Gordon Surtees, himself, had always said he should like the last music he would ever hear to be *The Dream of Gerontius*. In that at least, his wish was granted. Having moved back to the Malvern area, he went to the Three Choirs Festival to enjoy a performance of Elgar's great choral work at Worcester Cathedral. Three days later he died of a heart attack.

David Dixon who succeeded him had quite a different style. More than one boy cited him as their favourite master before he assumed the headship and it was a popularity he retained. While not a man to be crossed, he almost never needed to raise his voice, his customary expression was a smile and he was felt to be empathetic and approachable. He was also clear in his objectives. Asked whether there might be a lull in building work, after all the recent activity, he was certain there should be more: the temporary huts which housed some forms should be replaced with a new permanent building; the School needed a theatre and it needed an all-weather practice pitch. He was not in favour of increasing the number attending the School. The intimacy that allowed all boys and all staff to know each other he regarded as a prime ingredient in its success. He was very clear that the pedagogic approach of continental teaching, which he correctly defined as simply the imparting of information, did not measure up to the English tradition, concerned with the whole pupil, with pastoral care as well as academic progress, and with the young person's present and future role in the wider community.

In one intention, that he should serve as Headmaster till retirement he was, sadly, mistaken. Events intervened and his reign, fondly remembered, lasted only three years.

Mr Dixon was at one with the School's first Headmaster, J E Williams, in his belief in the value of games as a positive force in the education of boys, increasing their confidence, building teamwork, encouraging competitiveness and, indeed, helping them to have fun and make friends. It was his good fortune to preside over the School at a particularly fine time in its sports history. In football the First Eleven won more than two thirds of its matches – thirty-five of them in 1983 – in each of his years as Head; and lower teams did as well or better, except in 1985 when there was an ominous hint of what might follow as the Under-12s managed to lose all ten of their matches. In 1984 the First Eleven lost only eight of its thirty-eight matches and five of the team were selected to represent the Borough. Michael McCarthy was appointed captain of both Harrow Schools' and the Public Schools' South of England sides. Two years later the senior team lost impetus although the Second Eleven were in line to win the Middlesex League for the third time in six years. They were deprived by bad weather and a teachers' strike in other schools resulting in several matches being scrapped. The football authority insisted that sixteen matches must have been played to qualify for the play-offs. The John Lyon School, despite having lost only three of its fifteen matches, was thus barred and a mere four teams (with poorer results) were allowed to compete. The Second Eleven captain, Tim Theobold, was especially disappointed. He had hoped the boys could make winning the trophy again a proper tribute to Bob Shaw whose last season it was as coach.

In cricket John Lyon had some outstanding achievers in players like Alistair Fraser, Simon Bird and captain David Fell, now a senior boy in the School, and the team continued to outstrip losses with wins and draws. The tragic death of First Eleven player Duncan Whichelo in a house fire was keenly felt and he is remembered in the prize his parents presented in his memory. In 1986 the team lost only three of its thirteen matches. It also provided four members to the Middlesex Schools Eleven including Chris Jenkins appointed as its captain; and for the Middlesex Under-15 Eleven, John Lyon's Paul Snelling was selected captain, a role he repeated leading the England Under-15 Eleven in two internationals.

In badminton, the School notched up years thirteen, fourteen and fifteen as County Champions, David Fell leaving in 1984 with the enviable record of 246 games played and 229 of them won. Given that as well as captaining cricket, he played basketball for the School and was an outstanding table tennis player, it is hardly a surprise that David Dixon described him as 'the conquering hero of Middlesex'.

Other sports had their moments, too. J Marsden, who came second in an inter-schools cross-country race, was selected to represent Harrow in the Middlesex Championships. He was selected again a little later, along with Mike McCarthy's younger brother Paddy, for the Middlesex Athletics Championships.

In that most sedentary of games, chess, the School dominated although the Harrow Schools League began to fall apart. In 1983, the senior players won all three of their matches, beating Gayton, Latymer and a combined North London Schools team; the same year the juniors overcame Gayton and Latymer in their only two matches. The following and final year of the League, John Lyon teams again achieved the maximum in their only four competitions. One of the boys who came from Gayton to play against JLS, Mehul Trivedi, recalled how envious he and his companions were of the facilities they found, a reversal of the situation when Harrow County, as Gayton had earlier been known, had been founded and a mark of how far provision at John Lyon had improved in the course of the twentieth century.

Other aspects of school life also shone brightly. The Motet Choir continued at the highest level with six concerts in seven days in Germany, while Harrow Borough Awards for Music were won by Andrew Carwood for singing and, coached by Nigel Springthorpe, the JLS string quartet for their chamber music. Playing 'cello in the quartet was Julian Rhind-Tutt. When the School staged *Hamlet* he won golden opinions in the title role, as did Adam Barker as Claudius. The production played first in the Music School and then moved north to the claustrophobic surroundings of a disco, audience on three sides, at the Edinburgh Fringe. Here, Julian's performance, in its passion and sincerity, was described as having touches of greatness about it and Philip Davies wrote that 'never, but never, have I found *Hamlet* so moving'. Julian went on to a stellar career as an actor and as one of the best voice-over artists, a popular choice to read Radio 4's 'Book of the Week'.

The impact of Fred Goodwin, a perfectionist whose passion was for orchestral and choral music, is evidenced by the achievements in the field of three of his students at this time. Andrew Carwood, after a successful career as a tenor when he often returned to sing alongside the Motet Choir at major events, became Director of Music at St Paul's Cathedral where he trains and rehearses the choristers and is responsible for the music at all the services, including some of the nation's most significant celebrations. His contemporary and friend, Michael McCarthy, has exactly the same role at Washington's National Cathedral in the United States, while Stephen Langridge has an international reputation, directing opera all over the world in the major houses, including our own Royal Opera House, Glyndebourne, Vienna, Chicago and many more. All three, too, acknowledge Syd McMinn's influence, introducing them to opera, listening to long-playing records at his home on Friday evenings. Stephen also inherits the values of David Latham. He combines his high-profile career with directing operas cast from the residents of HMPs Bullingdon, Pentonville and other prisons, and with working extensively with the disabled and the disadvantaged.

While the Motet Choir illumined more and more cathedrals, not to mention the Château at Carrouges, the regular School Choir continued to give a variety of demanding concerts in the Speech Room and elsewhere, singing works such as Haydn's *Nelson Mass*. Lower sixth-former Julian Cable distinguished himself by winning a composing competition organized by Boosey & Hawkes. The task was to produce a piano piece to be used by music teachers and his *Nocturne in D Minor* took first prize.

The energy apparent in the School and in its staff was truly impressive. The extra-curricular activities already mentioned demanded a great deal in time and commitment. Then there were the multitudinous trips. In one year alone, exchanges with boys in the German Rhineland and in

Paris; holidays in Rouen and Paris; in Berne in Switzerland; visits for outdoor pursuits in the Southampton area; to study biology in Pembroke; and another to study both biology and geography on the Welsh coast; and there was the annual sailing course down at Poole. Then there was Expeditions Day when masters took groups of boys of all ages to fourteen different destinations: to Boulogne, to Guildford Cathedral, to see *Antony and Cleopatra* at Chichester, to Brownsea Island or Broxbourne Lido; to the Planetarium and more. Messrs French and Sanders took thirty-five boys who were Duke of Edinburgh Award candidates to the Chilterns.

Roger French had been educated at Haberdashers' Aske's and his brothers had gone, one to the John Lyon School and one to Merchant Taylors'. The consensus among the three of them was that David, at John Lyon, had had the most fruitful time. That is why Roger chose to teach here, joining the staff in 1973. He retired – technically at least – in 2007, spending one term at Wycombe High School for Girls and then one term at Harrow School, while regular teachers at each took a sabbatical. After which he 'unretired' and came back to the Biology department at JLS and, once more, to head up Outdoor Education. In 1958 the School had been granted Operating Centre status for the Duke of Edinburgh's Scheme. This was run by Roger. He also chaired the Award Scheme's Harrow Standing Conference and oversaw its start and continuation to the present day at Harrow School.

In his Speech Day report in 1984, Mr Dixon said 'I cannot mention all our many activities. . . . [and] the John Lyon School stands or falls by its academic excellence. We are determined to achieve the highest possible standards. But a school that diverts all its educational effort into the classroom is giving its pupils a poor preparation for life.' In saying this, he could be fairly confident in the School's academic standards knowing that one Old Boy, David Punter having taken a Double First at Cambridge had just received his PhD there and that thirty-three members of the upper sixth were about to move to higher education, six of them to Oxbridge. One of the last was American boy, Daniel Slifkin, who was to take two first class law degrees at St John's Oxford and was to reach such eminence as an attorney in his native country that he was featured on the cover of *Newsweek*.

There is an ever-present darker side to any institution's life and three deaths marred the prospect at this time. Marc Escoffey, latest in the line of promising painters was going on to art school, but only a couple of years after completing the course, he was killed on Majorca. Recent leaver

Darren Shutie died of leukaemia. In his memory, numerous events were organized by boys at the School, raising a total of seven-and-a-half thousand pounds for cancer research. Equally tragic, Billy Harford, a lively debater who bravely and uncomplainingly fought Hodgkin's Disease throughout his years at the School and won a place at Queen's College, Oxford, died before he could take it up.

Then, as a result of his divorce and planned remarriage to the former wife of a Harrow master, the Governors took the view, urged it is believed by Harrow's Head Master Mr Beer, that Mr Dixon should resign, a view shared by very few, if any, of the John Lyon staff or pupils at the time. Many, including parents, still voice the opinion that John Lyon lost one of the finest Headmasters in its, or any school's, history, owing to this puritanical reaction. It was, perhaps, in the same spirit that the Governors then appointed in his place the only clergyman to serve as a John Lyon Headmaster, the Reverend Tim Wright.

Liam Halligan, Head Boy for Mr Wright's first year later recalled the new Headmaster's consternation at arrangements for morning Assembly. Teams of boys laid a tarpaulin on the gymnasium floor, then benches were fetched from the Cloisters for boys to sit on, this process taking longer than the twenty minutes of the Assembly itself. On its conclusion another half hour was spent returning the benches and tarpaulin. This was soon changed. Though quite why someone had thought boys could not stand for Assembly as they had for the first century of the School's existence remains unresolved.

As he mused on the need for physical expansion, Tim Wright, nonetheless, found the atmosphere at the School 'fantastic and friendly' and years later, as this book goes to press, his grandson is one of its pupils. A further sea change occurred around now: two masters who had spent their entire teaching careers at the School and whose contribution had, in contrasting ways, been enormous, retired. Phil Davies, Deputy Head, sparky, humorous, the leader on many foreign adventures, occasional cricketer and singer in every available choir from St Mary's to the Royal Choral Society, was to return regularly to School and Old Lyonian events, often to sit at a piano and accompany all present in a rendition of 'Forty Years On'. He continued as he had begun, singing to almost the end of his days in Guildford Cathedral Choir. Don Allan, quietly spoken, quietly persistent, had created and broadened the Art Department as the subject was incorporated into the examined curriculum. His influence on design within the School was practical and effective, extending from paint colours in the rooms to illustrations in *The Lyonian* and including the creation of sets, and sometimes masks and props, for every School play from 1954 until 1986. The influence of both men was to be long and fondly remembered.

In Mr Davies' place, Tim Wright appointed popular Old Lyonian John Barnard, efficient, energetic and good humoured, as Deputy Headmaster. Wright was clear that if you have a good deputy, the School runs well. The equally popular Bill Podmore was asked to become Director of Studies, with responsibility for the large number of curricular changes that were coming in, a role he filled outstandingly.

Among boys leaving at this time was Andrew, the younger of the Harrison brothers both of whom attended the School. In due course he graduated from Sandhurst and when the United Nations intervened in the civil conflict in Sierra Leone at the beginning of the twenty-first century, as Major Harrison of the Parachute Regiment he was awarded the MBE, always a high honour when won in the field, for his courage and leadership.

A demographic change in the Harrow area had been under way from the time that the dictator Idi Amin expelled the Asian community, whose wealth and success he coveted, from Uganda. Several families settled in the borough. As often happens, with years passing, more joined them, and the ethnic mix broadened impressively. It was, to a measurable degree, the commitment of these new arrivals to the best education for their sons, to hard work and enterprise, that helped sustain the John Lyon School through the recessions of the seventies, eighties and later, when some schools struggled or shut down. Occasional sports rivals the Royal Masonic School for Boys, for instance, had closed its doors in 1977. The John Lyon School, in contrast, grew, as did the competition for places. By the late eighties, Mark Gifford reckoned the School's make-up was highly diverse, being roughly one-third historically white British, one-third boys of Jewish descent and the remaining third Asian, with more Hindus than Moslems.

Mark's take on the School during his time there, between 1986 and 1993, was positive. If he felt that sport was neglected, just one afternoon of games and one period of P E each week, and, though he allowed it may have been down to what as a boy he chose, that the food available was neither interesting nor healthy, he nonetheless regarded his time as trauma-free and blessed with some wonderful teachers. The influence of individual staff members, as so often, is exemplified by the effect Religious Studies master Keith Noakes had on him. After taking a degree in Theology at Durham and then studying Law in London and at Oxford,

Mark returned in later life to take yet another degree, this time in Indian religions at the School of Oriental and African Studies. He contrasts his experience with that of his brother who went to boarding school where he was successful both academically and on the sports field, but where he felt miserable and confessed that the day he left was the day he had longed for.

In similar vein to Mark Gifford, a boy attending the School a little later in Tim Wright's reign, cited several masters who profoundly affected his later career and his ability to follow it. Sadat Edroos gave credit to Mr Bailey whose excellence as a maths teacher enabled him to take his GCSE in the subject a year early and, again because of him, to take two 'A' levels in maths after that. Messrs Sanders, Holgate and Ryder all gave 'really good' support to Sadat in his desire to pursue medicine. Indeed, three of his contemporaries took the same path, one becoming a surgeon in New Zealand, two becoming general practitioners as well as Dr Edroos, himself, a cardiologist doing research work into the causes of heart attacks. True to the School's tradition of lasting friendships, thirty members of his year keep in regular touch and, every Christmas Eve, they all meet at 4.00pm at Cafe Cafe on the Hill.

Cricket results declined around this period and football at the School started a steep and depressing downward trend from the laudable seven matches lost of twenty-eight played in 1987 to just one win out of twenty-seven played, five years later. There were, initially, some gifted boys in both sports. Allan Camp, Robert Lawler, Paul Snelling still at John Lyon, Andrew Rees and Stephen Hallam featured in both teams and, while the School Badminton team lost its county supremacy to Hayes Manor, Camp still scored some notable victories on court.

There was also some solace in other sports. The School had taken, in 1986, to competing against Harrow for the Silver Arrow Trophy and won it every year until 1990; and even in 1991 when they lost for a second time, John Lyon had fielded the highest scorer in Jon Poley, after which five of the six boys selected for the Borough team to take part in the London Youth Games were from the School. There they won the gold medal, by the impressive margin of 1,236 points, a tribute to the coaching of Nikki Abbott. At tennis, the School team beat both Harrow and Latymer Upper while the Under-13 and Under-15 teams were chosen to represent the Borough in the Midland Bank National Schools' Competition and won all their matches. Further success over Harrow School came in the annual triangular swimming match, also involving the boys of Felsted School, when the John Lyon team emerged top in 1988.

Although Tim Wright is remembered principally for the building development he brought about and is sometimes said to have been more of an organizer than an intellectual, it is undeniable that the cerebral side of School life prospered under his leadership. Debating continued as a major aspect of life at Middle Road and articulacy was highly regarded and encouraged, Mr Wright himself quoting one boy's complaint that 'you bring us up to think for ourselves and then expect us to share your opinions', a criticism which he recognized to be pertinent. In the same vein, reading and reciting competitions, which continued as a regular feature, encouraged confidence and ability in public speaking. Taking part in the London-wide Youth Speaks contest, organized by Rotary, both senior and junior teams were well placed.

As plans were being laid for the School's next physical development, the examination results improved every year until, by 1990, the 'A' Level pass rate was 96%. Just a year before, when a then record 92% pass rate was achieved, the *Today* newspaper surprised everyone by descending on the School with a photographer. A happy moment, it proved, for some nationwide publicity. And, while at the beginning of his time, preparation of candidates for Oxbridge was not prioritized, perhaps because any result depended on 'A' Level grades and a single interview, as against the three days of examination and two interviews at each and every college of thirty years before, this was soon corrected by the Headmaster. Each group of leavers again included half-a-dozen or more boys moving on to the ancient universities, as it had the year he took over when eight sixth formers, including Head Boy Liam Halligan, had made the journey.

The new building envisaged was to be sited on the western edge of the playground, straddling the bank and obscuring the view of distant horizons. It was to contain a large hall for performances, finally ending the competition for use of the Music School, some classrooms and smaller seminar rooms and a Senior Common Room for the increasing number of staff. Named the Lyon Building, and the theatre space, the Boyd Campbell Hall, it was in full use by 1990.

The same year also saw *The Lyonian* go into full colour with higher quality photographic reproduction than it had featured for many years. Oddly, the black and white photographs in the nineteenth and early twentieth century, though few in number, were usually sharper than those that followed for several decades. At this time, too, original artwork by the boys returned to its pages after an absence of some years; and boys were now usually referred to with both first and surname, after a century of surnames only, with an added initial only when needed to avoid confusion. Original writing, poems and stories, had been revived a few issues earlier after languishing in separate, roneo-ed[51] publications using the title *Unicorn*. The reason, presumably, was that the more workaday stapled sheets could accommodate much more material at little cost and could be produced in-house; that was surely an advantage, but as publications they looked what they were: cheap.

One area of School life, however, now reverted to something of the confusion that had pertained in the late 1920s, if anything to a greater degree. For most of the School's life, there had been two ranks of School Officers: Prefects and, senior to them, Monitors. The pattern had been to have two Prefects to each of the forms prior to the sixth, so around twenty, a few more as the School increased, and a dozen Monitors, four of whom would be House Captains, and two of them Deputy Head Boy and Head Boy. They were recognizable by the badges described in Chapter 8. With the proliferation of different sports, boys awarded colours no longer added a defining letter to the large gold blazer badge, but Monitors retained the 'M' on theirs. Except, if photographs are to be believed, some Monitors did, others had the badge blank and at least one, named in the caption beneath the photo, is shown still wearing what was the regular blazer badge. Pictures of Oldfield House Prefects confusingly include recognizable Monitors and the number of Prefects escalates to a degree that makes the title almost meaningless: in 1988, fifty-eight of them; later still, sixty-nine. It must have been a greater distinction to get through the sixth form without attracting promotion. In reality this was not possible, because the change from previous usage was deliberate. It was to make every upper sixth-former responsible for some area of School activity and to call him, therefore, a Prefect. It was a way of engaging every senior boy and, by placing the more difficult ones with a staff member they respected, to encourage them to give useful service. It was viewed at the time as a commendable project.

Each year boys gained valuable experience taking part in Young Enterprise, a well-named competition with local, regional and national finals, designed to give young people a taste of the business world in an entirely practical way. A small group of senior pupils, of either sex, would constitute themselves into a company, elect a chairman and other officers, plan and create what they intended to market, and then do just that, including raising the necessary capital. The sums of money involved were

---

[51] The process was to type material onto a skin which the metal keys of the typewriter punctured. The skin was then transferred to a machine made by either Roneo or Gestetner when inked rollers printed what had been typed as single sheets of paper lay the other side of the skin. The quality of what emerged was variable.

small, but real. The profits and losses were real, too. All aspects of commerce were involved: market research, design, budgeting, production, advertising and actual selling. One or more members of the Board would be called upon to make a public presentation about the product, and this would be judged by experienced business folk at the same time as the product itself and its profitability would be weighed in the scale. The JLS team did notably well in 1988, producing and selling a worthwhile number of clock/penholders, partly as a result of striking a deal with the City of London Girls' School. In return for the girls ensuring their writing implements were neatly stored in a timely way, the boys bought quantities of the girls' product: boxer shorts. There is no record of the market research undertaken by the girls. The boys divided their profits between the workers involved, the shareholders who had put up the modest capital required and, admirably, charity.

The same year, the British Association of Young Scientists started an 'ideas into action' competition. Boys from the School constructed a water tower – this was their unaided work – using only cards, straws and pins. It was judged the best engineered structure in the competition and they became the London Region champions, an achievement another group from the School were to better the next time. This team of Sagar Das, Alex Monsey and Gareth Payne beat Mill Hill Comprehensive, Godolphin and Latymer School and Radley College to win the London Regional Final. They then competed at the Science Museum, seeing off the champions of Scotland and Northern Ireland, to take part in the Grand Final where they came third, one point behind Haberdashers' and the holders, King's School, Worcester.

Then another team of Lyonians won the Ladbrokes Racing Trophy as the most successful company of the eleven taking part in the Harrow area of Young Enterprise.

Service to the community still flourished as an important aspect of School life. One autumn, a hundred and six boys became blood donors; the following spring, a hundred and forty-three did the same. Record sums were regularly raised for charity, staff, parents and boys, for example, combining their efforts in 1990, to raise nine thousand pounds for Action Research into Multiple Sclerosis. The Physiotherapy Unit for this was to be located at Harrow School Farm and, in light of the School's substantial donation, it was named The John Lyon Room.

The Motet Choir meanwhile carried on at the highest level, touring Strasbourg and singing Fauré's *Cantique de Jean Racine*, 'discovered' rather later by Classic FM, in venues as various as St Alban's Cathedral and the Guild Chapel in Stratford-upon-Avon.

There were striking drama productions, too. The musical *Oliver* staged with a huge cast of boys, girls and staff, directed by the ever-enthusiastic Ian Whybrow and musically by David Arkell; and, a little earlier, a fascinating interpretation by John Bell of Peter Shaffer's *Amadeus*. All the cast, excepting Mozart and Constance, were made up to have a mask-like deathly pallor, conveying both a sense of dreamlike ritual and the sort of bleak, embittered view of the world taken by Salieri.

As the new decade dawned, academic results were impressively high and with the unflappable Clem Reed, Old Lyonian, House Master, Head of Geography, Head of Sixth Form to guide the candidates, the number of Oxbridge successes in a single year reached ten. The only Lyonian in the School's history to be elected to the Commons, Michael Shersby, later to be knighted, having just presented the prizes on Speech Day, it seemed to Tim Wright a good moment to think again about the School's facilities and what might yet be done.

CHAPTER 15

SETTING THE BOUNDS WIDER
1992–2000

The years leading up to the millennium in many ways replicated the pattern of the years immediately preceding. The Reverend Wright's 'safe pair of hands' – a description used of him by both boys and Governors – served the School well. Examination results were impressively high: a pass rate of 90% at 'A' Level, with fifty-seven boys going on to university, seven of them to Oxbridge in 1992; and 82% of GCSE results for the year being As or Bs with a 95% success rate in all subjects sat. By the year 2000, 'A' Level results showed over half of the grades achieved to be As or Bs and a similar majority of GCSE grades to be As or A*s. All forty-five sixth-form leavers were going on to university, three of them to Cambridge including the remarkable Vladimir Kara-Murza, of whom more later.

The examinations set by the Associate Board of the Royal Schools of Music were now taken by a large number of boys and they, too, showed remarkable successes in the course of this period. The diversity of instruments played and the number of Merits and Distinctions achieved demonstrate how central to life at the John Lyon School music had become.

Sporting results, despite the Headmaster's personal support at nearly all matches and competitions, were as varied as it is possible to conceive.

To begin with, football showed a small improvement on recent form, not difficult given the poor season of 1991, and offered future hope in that the Under-15 team lost only three of their twenty-two matches and reached the final of the Middlesex Cup. From this team, Michael Shaw played for the County and for the Chelsea FC junior eleven, while Jason Wilmot put the ball in the net twenty-seven times in twenty matches. This level of play, however, was not maintained. The following season all the School's football teams lost more matches than they won. Later, promise appeared to be fulfilled as the Under-15 boys matured and the First Eleven won more than half their matches, the midfield player and captain Michael Shaw again being selected for Middlesex. Once more, though, it was a false dawn, football remaining in the doldrums for the rest of the decade until some encouraging wins for the First Eleven raised hopes in 1999, only to dash them again in 2000 when the team lost momentum.

Cricket, while hardly vintage, thankfully offered rather more positive signs. Early on these came principally from the younger elevens, while the First team discovered, like England Test teams, the difficulties of playing on pitches quite different from our own when, captained by Geraint Hughes, they toured Barbados. As the decade proceeded, wins and draws well outstripped losses. By 1995, the School's eleven were semi-finalists in the Middlesex Cup, inspired perhaps by Middlesex and England bowler, Angus Fraser, opening the latest pavilion at Sudbury, the previous year. In 1996 Barbados again set its snares for the First Eleven, though two wins were managed this time, and at home the team did well, losing only four of its seventeen games; and the Under-12s had a similar level of success. A little later, it was again the younger boys who led the way, Rhodri James proving outstanding with bat and ball as the Under-13s played twelve matches with only three losses. The decade ended with the First Eleven managing more draws than wins or losses, but with apparent ambition: taking on an MCC side containing seven County players was asking a good deal and the result was predictable. Making his mark as bowler and batsman was Neil Packianathan.

Other sports, among the many undertaken by the School, had moments of greater glory. In several cases because of the initiative Mr Wright, 'TJ' as he was known to the boys, pressed home to make a major improvement in the facilities available. The Main Building was to be extended again, to this purpose.

Meanwhile archery, well established as a success zone for John Lyon boys, achieved the ultimate with the School, led by Daniel Weber, becoming British Schools' Champions in the national indoor competition of 1992. Every member of the team took a gold medal. Unsurprisingly, the same team reclaimed the Silver Arrow from Harrow and two of its members, Daniel Weber and Jon Poley were selected to represent Middlesex. The next year, they narrowly lost to Harrow, despite the individual successes of Robert Kendrew, with the highest score, Rishi Shah with the highest number of hits and Adrian Roberts scoring the highest number of golds. They immediately won it back by the massive margin of nearly a thousand points and the School provided the entire Borough team in the London Youth Championships of 1994. Thereafter the John Lyon team beat Harrow School every year for the rest of the century, that is, seven times in succession. In 1998 the boys won numerous medals in the Postal League and in 1999, Jeremy Shere, taking 500 points out of a possible 540, made the highest score ever achieved in the Silver Arrow competition.

The same period began with an unbeatable partnership in badminton, M Hodgson and S Patel playing fifteen games in a row without loss, recalling the glory days of the seventies and early eighties. This level was not immediately maintained, although by 1996, thanks to the coaching of Lindsay Irvine, the School teams were once again Middlesex County Champions in both age-groups. The next year, the Under-19s lost a thrilling final against City of London School, 13–15 in the final set. The senior team were again runners-up in the County final of 1998, while the juniors found themselves in the same position in the Middlesex League. In the County Closed Championships, Bartlett and Overy won the doubles and went on to represent Harrow at the London Youth Games. At the end of the decade, the youngsters again finished runners-up in the League, having enjoyed victories over Park School, UCS and Harrow School on the way, while the senior team were easy group winners in the Middlesex Cup and reached the final where, having just lost two of their main players, they were again bested by the City of London School.

The allied game of tennis had a number of successes, too, throughout this time. To begin with, the first team won four out of its six matches, beating Harrow School, St Paul's, Latymer and Merchant Taylors' while the Under-15s became London Area champions and reached the final of the Midland Bank National Championships losing to the team representing the East of England. The following year they lost none of the matches they played, again beating Harrow, Latymer and Mill Hill among others. Even with an inexperienced team, the boys of 1997 managed to reach the third round of the annual Youll Cup, held at Eton College; and by the year 2000, they were able to beat Merchant Taylors', Haberdashers', Aldenham and Eton to reach the final of the Youll Cup, where this time, despite beating them earlier, they lost to Eton.

Athletics had its moments as well. Among many good cross-country results at all ages, the senior team beat nine schools to win the York House race, repeating this success in the St Martin's Road Relay and coming second of eight in the Belmont 'Oti' Relay. Over the years a number of boys were selected to represent the borough in county athletic competitions and discus thrower Michael Garcia ended the decade as County Champion. At the same time, Alex Ofosu-Adjei retained for a second year the Harrow championship for the triple jump.

As a result of the opportunities presented by the splendid new Sports Centre, opened in 1997 by HRH the Duke of Edinburgh, basketball, volleyball and swimming enjoyed increasing popularity. Fixtures for the first two were not easy to come by, but highlights included a victory for the volleyball team over Hatch End High in their sole match of 1997. The swimming teams did more than hold their own: that same year, Simon Colwill, Andrew Karim, Giles Matthews and Josh Dmochowski made up the Under-12 team to win the Harrow Schools' Sports Association Junior Gala. The following year, the School won two of the three age groups at the same Gala.

Karate swiftly became one of the School's most successful activities. In the first ever inter-school competition for John Lyon boys, against Mill Hill, Sam Bellringer came first and Alex Tolani second. By 1994, four Lyonians, Tim Sadler, Adam Stuart, Greg Wise and Sam Bellringer were black belts and the previous year the team had won the UK Annual Championships of the Karate Governing Body as well as several individual cups and medals. These were achievements they were to repeat three years in succession. Then, in 1996, David Forman took first in the Kata and second in the Kunaite, retaining his national title and the next year winning a further medal.

The improved sports facilities in the Main Building, and the popularity of the sport among boys contributed to the outstanding success of karate at the School. The most important factor, however, has to be the coaching of Mrs Brenda Wise, a formidable competitor herself and clearly a gifted inspirer of others. In 1997 she was Great Britain's National Champion and travelled to Milan to represent the United Kingdom at the World Championships. Here, with ninety countries competing, she took bronze, beaten only by the champions of Japan and China.

As in every sphere of endeavour, whether academic, commercial or physical, the combination of good equipment in whatever form, with talented students and talented mentors, both willing to commit and put in the hours, is what is required to reach the highest goal; borne out again and again in the School's history and in the lives and careers of individual boys.

Unquestionably the major event of the period was the visit to the School by Prince Philip. Greeted by a fanfare specially composed by the then new Director of Music, Stuart Miles, he unveiled a plaque to declare the splendid Sports Hall open. He then repeated the process – unusually again without hitch, the Duke commented – opening the New Memorial Library, substantially larger than its predecessor, equipped with computers as well as thousands of books, a place of purpose, where both the Book of the Fallen in its glass case and the First World War memorial on the wall above command its far end.

The Sports Hall complex comprised three badminton courts, a 25-metre swimming pool and a weights room. This, however, was not the whole of the development. There were also new Science Schools, already in use, and a suite of rooms for maths and technology in addition to the Library.

As back in 1876 with the construction of the Old Building, the contractor in charge of this important development was an Old Lyonian. The late twentieth century architect and builder was Andrew Reed. As well as designing new developments, Andrew is responsible for overseeing the care and maintenance of all the buildings on the Hill belonging both to the John Lyon School and to Harrow School. As a boy at John Lyon he gained the Duke of Edinburgh's Award Scheme Gold Award. It was the School's eminence, it might be said pre-eminence, in this field that persuaded the Duke to come to Middle Road. In area presentations John Lyon School award winners were not merely the largest contingent, they regularly outnumbered all other club and school winners put together. Three years earlier, for instance, fourteen boys survived – by their own account – rain, hail, snow and a farmer with a shotgun as they spent a week trudging the Welsh mountains, sleeping in wet tents pitched in muddy fields, in order to complete their Gold Award assignments. They declined overmuch sympathy for this, though, claiming the sight of fifty sheep and having a pub meal on their last night were treats enough. And these same boys found the time to train the School's forty-four Bronze Award candidates. Add to these two groups the Silver Award competitors, all taking part in the same year, and the School's domination is evident.

As the variety of available sports increased, so the number of School clubs had decreased. There were now the Aquarium, Chess, Photographic and Sixth Form Societies and the Young Scientists. From the last named, three boys, Matthew Hodgson, Samir Mehta and Matthew Welch took part in the British Physics Olympiad of 1992. This meant participating in a three-hour test. All three achieved Silver Medal standard, the first from the School to do so. Later in the decade the mix of clubs had again changed: Aquarium, Chess and Photographic were still there, now joined by Art, organizing visits to galleries and collections, Bridge, Computer Room and, a perennial School interest, a Debating Society.

The reduction in the number of clubs did not signify a reduced range of activities. Music still played an enormous part in School life. Two senior boys, Nicholas Danks and Jeremy Llewellyn, both already entitled to put ARCO after their names, gave an organ recital at St Mary's, raising money for the church and the Motet Choir. As organ scholars at Cambridge University, they returned more than once in later days to add lustre to School concerts. The Motet Choir itself continued to thrive, touring Normandy, singing in cathedrals all over and, in keeping with the royal interest, at St George's Chapel, Windsor. It thrived, that is, until the moment when Fred Goodwin, its phenomenal catalyst, took retirement in 1995 and the choir made a final triumphant trip to Prague. There had been numerous other concerts of all sorts before Mr Goodwin left. Marking the four hundredth anniversary of John Lyon's death, the School joined with Harrow School's musicians in a shared event in the Speech Room. Harrow boys played two concertos while Nicholas Monsey took the solo piano part in Gershwin's *Rhapsody in Blue* and the School's Brass Ensemble gave Walton's *A Queen's Fanfare* and Mendelssohn's *War March of the Priests*.

Won over to the pleasures of barbershop, Mr Goodwin organized a concert of tenors and basses to sing in Pinner United Free Church to raise money for charity; and the many other concerts he staged included providing entertainment for a two-day conference in the Speech Room of the Armed Forces Association. In the twelve months before he left the array of performances he arranged and conducted is awe-inspiring: yet another charity concert with Harrow in the Speech Room; two chamber music events in the Music School; more barbershop, this time in the Harrow Hotel; Christmas Music in St Mary's; Haydn's *Creation* in the Speech Room; numerous summer concerts involving all the School's different instrumental groups; then the finale, Dvorak's *Mass in D* in Prague. It is hard to believe any school in the kingdom could rival the range of music with which he engaged boys and audiences, or the quality of performance he obtained. His influence continues to the present day.

A year or two earlier, Nicholas Danks, before leaving for Corpus Christi College joined with Paul Simons, about to depart to St John's, Oxford, in producing an impressive, week-long John Lyon School Festival of Music. Concerts were given in St Mary's, again in the Speech Room and all the musicians had a School connexion whether as parents, boys or Old Lyonians; among the latter, Andrew Carwood returned with The Cardinall's Musick, the professional choir of which he was founder and director. The following year the Festival included Britten's opera involving young people, *Noye's Fludde*; again picking up on the repertoire of the one-time Calico Consort, there was a jazz and barbershop evening; and a classical concert given by the School's orchestra and choir, joined by boys from feeder school Quainton Hall.

Although the Motet Choir did not outlive Roger Williams' and Fred Goodwin's presence on the Hill, music continued to feature in a major way. Interestingly, music prizes for different instruments often went to the same boy. In 1998, for example Adam Street won both Junior Piano and Junior Strings; Prabhat Malhotra won Senior Piano and Senior Wind Instrument. Prabhat was the latest in line to apply for an organ scholarship and he gave an informative account of the process involved. He travelled to Oxford to sit a paper in mathematics, his proposed degree subject; at the Music Schools there he was interviewed – over two days – and given keyboard tests, including playing his chosen piece by Buxtehude. Then he had to conduct a short choir practice at the college where he was applying. To everyone's satisfaction, including undoubtedly his own, he was awarded the Organ Scholarship at Balliol College.

Drama continued to flourish. Productions included *The Resistible Rise of Arturo Ui* directed by incoming Head of Drama, Neil Pankhurst in 1993, the same year Drama became a GCSE subject. Two years later, sixth former Chris Brown penned and presented a spoof on the Brecht classic, *The Resistible Rise of Julian Austin* about a money-making, mobile-toting, public school Head Boy who has given permission, without consultation elsewhere, for a French film director to make a movie at the school. The staff, the real staff that is, meanwhile, and perhaps less adventurously, had fun reviving the hardy old farce, *See How They Run*. Other productions covered Shakespeare with *A Midsummer Night's Dream*, musicals like *Smike* and *Little Shop of Horrors* and, early on the specially concocted revue, *Lyon's Fruitcake*, a title playing on the name of the then ubiquitous Joe Lyons restaurants and cake shops, which later went the way of F W Woolworth, vanishing suddenly from the landscape of every town. House play competitions, junior and senior, continued as did all the other confidence-building in-school competitions: for reading, debating and recitation. In the year 2000, twelve months after its first Drama Studio was created, the School saw thirteen different plays produced within its walls.

Young Enterprise also thrived and the group who participated in 1999 was regarded by its mentor, Mr Carr-Hill, as the best he had known at the School. The Sixth Form Union attracted a number of excellent and challenging speakers and debates. The forty-minute format, introduced in 1994, worked remarkably well, leaving everyone wanting more. Among the stimulating events that year were talks by Brian Gilbert, director of the

film *Tom and Viv* about T S Eliot, the art critic Anthony Slin, Claire
Rayner and the director of the charity helping the native populations
produce their own food, Ben James of Farm Africa, as well as holding
debates with regard to AIDS and drug abuse.

At this stage, politics, so rarely focused on as a subject in the past,
started to feature. Early in this period, Conaghan and Christopher,
possibly one boy doubling his impact by employing both of his names,
produced a strip cartoon lampooning the exit of Mrs Thatcher from
power, with John Major and Ted Heath making very recognisable
appearances. Mark Gifford led in a debate, complaining of the lack of
proportional representation in the United Kingdom and, the same year,
among the leavers, was A I Morris, going to university to read Political
Science. In the mid-nineties, Edward Glynn, retiring from teaching
science, was elected Liberal Democrat County Councillor for Sunbury.
Towards the end of the decade, just as politics was introduced as an 'A'
Level subject, the School held mock elections for the European
Parliament. The three main parties were represented and their candidates were allowed to campaign within strict guidelines: 'Vote Vlad'
posters, in support of Labour candidate Vladimir Kara-Murza, were
ruled out and a very different result from what might have obtained
half-a-century before emerges. The Conservatives get almost 32%,
Labour more than 25% and the Liberal Democrats just short of
22%. With a less than perfect grasp of the way things are structured
in Brussels and Strasbourg, the Labour and Liberal Democrat parties
form a coalition with Vladimir as Prime Minister and third-former Lib
Dem Mark Gettleson as Foreign Secretary.

What is fascinating about this is the career portents revealed and even
the precocity evidenced at that precise moment. For Vladimir Kara-
Murza, John Lyon schoolboy, son of a Russian journalist and descendant
of the first Latvian Ambassador to the Court of St James, had already been
for two years the London correspondent of one of Russia's two most
significant newspapers, *Novye Izvestia*. A little later he obtained a First in
History at Trinity Hall, Cambridge while acting as London correspondent for *Kommersant*. He has gone on, still a young man, to be
elected to the Council of Solidarnost, the pro-democracy movement in
Russia, and to be responsible for its international relations. He is a
principal opponent of Russia's perpetual (it seems) President, Vladimir
Putin. Young Mark Gettleson, meanwhile, went on to be elected a Liberal
Democrat Councillor in Southwark and to work as assistant to Simon
Hughes, the party's Deputy Leader and former President.

If politics, in the party sense, was not the most regular feature of interest in the School, awareness of the outside world, something day boys are likely to possess, always had been. It is worth observing that while some staff complained of the road bisecting the School, others, including several boys, welcomed it as a precursor of how university life would be and a healthy reminder of that world beyond. A committed attitude to the community had long been fostered in the School and many events, often involving parents as well as staff and boys, were organized to raise funds for this charity or that. Virginia McKenna came in person to accept a substantial donation to the Children of the Andes Fund, of which she is Patron. The sums involved continued to be impressive: more than £10,000 in 1995, some of it to provide an infusion pump for a pupil with visceral myopathy who had, for eight years, spent up to fourteen hours a night hooked up to a drip. Now he would be able to move around during treatment. A similar sum was raised the next year for Great Ormond Street Hospital, as well as more than £9,000 for gym equipment. By 1999, the annual sum realized had reached £12,000. More than this, boys regularly visited old folk on the Hill, giving practical help with chores where needed; and each year the School gave a festive dinner for a hundred pensioners living in the area, boys helping to serve and providing the entertainment.

The School magazine through this period became ever more sumptuous, in full colour with a high gloss cover and an increasing number of pages. The editors, Nicholas Parsons and Patricia Waldron, in consequence were able to include not merely copious photographs of the different teams, but to exhibit much more visual art and creative writing by the boys. The quality was high: along with portraits of heads and figurative work, impressive metal sculptures by Sam Foster, inspired perhaps by Giacometti and Lowry, are illustrated while the writing includes a wide range of material. Two pieces nicely define School life. The first, by Jagjit Kalyan, would be guaranteed to give at least modest encouragement to any teacher, depending on the recipe being taken as the cure, rather than the cause:

A Recipe for Boredom

Take a fourteen year old boy,
Add him to a classroom,
Stir in a textbook, ruler, pencil and calculator.
Mix in Pythagoras, trigonometry and algebra.
Leave to bake for forty minutes.

> Remove from oven at ten to four,
> And leave to cool for the rest of the day.

The second, a haiku by Christopher Farrant, suggests that even in these days of laxer discipline, the spirit of Colonel Wilson still lurks (cf. the opening paragraph of Chapter 9):

> All that remained of
> Paul when he got detention
> Was a speck of dust.

In the evolving way of things, School numbers grew from five hundred at the beginning of the period to five hundred and twenty-three a couple of years later, entirely accounted for by a larger sixth form. Staff retired, Bill Podmore among them, or moved on as Ian Whybrow did to concentrate on his successful career as a writer. Three masters, Michael Sadler, Peter Sanders and David Philpott, completed thirty years of service. Two women, stalwart supporters of the School, Mrs Baron the Appeals Secretary and Mrs Hull the Librarian, took their leave. New teachers came. By 1998, eight of the staff were women. Though one new female member found a problem. She publicly announced she disliked being called 'Ma'am', the courteous form of address used by John Lyon boys, in preference to the often inaccurate 'Miss'. Given the Queen is happy with the same appellation, it might have been thought acceptable by a young teacher. Over the years the School had recruited a number of Old Lyonians, including Deputy Head John Barnard, to the staff; now, in the shape of historian Ted Savill, it recruited its first Old Harrovian.

Other changes occurred. Sports colours, signified by different ties, were now given for Second Eleven members and for teams representing every age group. Intended to encourage, one boy observed there were so many of them that they failed to register. House colours were still designated by plain coloured ties, blue for Butler, red for Vaughan and so on, in a way that would have been immediately recognisable to boys of half-a-century before. In 1997, Monitors were still wearing the impressive gold badge on their blazer pocket. Two years later they disappeared, with all Sixth Formers looking smart in suits, even as they had to face the newly imposed 'AS' Level examinations. The Head Boy could be distinguished by his unique tie, blue with a pattern of red lions, and by the authority the position naturally gives to its holder.

If the changes that recently occurred seem extensive, they were nothing to what was about to happen.

CHAPTER 16

TEMPORA MUTANTUR
2001–2009

The new century saw the final year of Tim Wright's fifteen-year Headship. His period at the School had been positive, summed up by one boy whose entire time had been under T J's headship, Sadat Edroos: 'I have nothing but good things to say about the John Lyon School'; while another made clear how much he liked a Headmaster 'who lived and breathed' the School.

Some signal events marked this particular year. Music continued as strong as ever, with the Orchestra, Salsa Band, senior and junior Wind Bands, Jazz Band and Jazz Ensemble all performing; and with a special 125th Anniversary Concert held in the Speech Room. At the same time, fifty-eight boys sat and passed their Associated Board examinations, at various levels, twenty-one of them gaining Merits and a further nine, Distinctions. The highest mark of all was obtained by Owen Peachey, playing the euphonium.

Mr Wright must have been pleased, too, with the remarkable success of the Sports Centre on the Middle Road site. It was prolifically used by the boys, but it was also hired by IMS Health, Northwood Badminton Club and Ealing Swimming Club, among others. When British Telecom decided to stage a Secondary Schools' Swimathon to raise money for cancer research, they chose the School's indoor pool to host it.

Other sports varied in their degree of success. Football was disappointing, although the younger teams all did well, while in cricket, the First Eleven reached the semi-finals of the Middlesex Cup. The outstanding players in both sports were, again, Rhodri James and Neil Packianathan. The badminton team suffered a narrow defeat playing Harrow School in their opening match and then won every other contest for the rest of the season, the leading pair being chosen from Andrew Bird, Aneek Sarkar and James Silvester.

Results in tennis were excellent. Almost predictably, the School retained the Silver Arrow and, providing the bulk of the borough team, came fifth in archery at the London Youth Games. Cross-country also produced excellent results: the School, led by Ben Gill, won every team event entered bar the London Independent Schools' Championship, where they finished second. The same sort of success was to be found elsewhere in the School's activities.

For the first time, John Lyon featured in the *Daily Telegraph*'s list of schools in their recently devised academic first division. The School team reached the national semi-final of the Worldwide Geography Quiz where they came second of the four teams, only because of an error made by the question master. This sadly robbed them of the chance to contest the national final. In *The Times* chess competition, JLS easily beat Merchant Taylors', narrowly overcame Haberdashers', but then lost comprehensively to one of the strongest teams in the country, Queen Elizabeth School, Barnet.

The wealth of other activities continued as ever. A fine production of *Macbeth* ingeniously incorporated swathes of slit black latex into the set so that the witches could, almost literally, vanish 'into thin air'. The relatively unsung Aquarium Society was going strong, reliant on a posse of boys who came in early each day to feed the fish and to clean and maintain the tanks. There was a mock General Election which produced a result very similar to the European version of a couple of years before. And Oliver Hymans continued the tradition of lowering the spirits of any successors, by writing a report of his gripping adventures on an Outward Bound course in Scotland, guaranteed to chill the blood.

In the annual magazine, tribute is paid by the editors to the unstinting and unselfish application of Nikhil Amin, the Charity Monitor whose efforts, both personal and in galvanizing others, have raised nearly £11,000 for meningitis research. The same edition, as is now usual, carries impressive artwork including some able portraiture by Vishal Luther and a Munch-like prone man painted by the multi-talented Josh Dmochowski.

There were, of course, comings as well as goings and, among the new staff interviewed by boys, Carl Gladwell emerged as a man of tact and wit. Asked by Mark Gettleson what had attracted him to the place, he replied that 'it represented everything good about independent education'. When asked where he saw himself in twenty years time, he said, 'Still waiting for Mark Gettleson's history essay'. And when asked who he hated, he said did not hate anyone but, somewhat more prescient than the country's political masters, he added, 'I am immensely irritated by Rupert Murdoch. Have you read *The Sun*?!'

The response of boys to staff retains a remarkable measure of constancy. Throughout the School's history a wide range of teachers are remembered, not merely with affection, but as having a profound influence on careers, interests and confidence. Again and again, boys will mention as their favourites men and women who are approachable and – and this may be a surprise – strict. Boys like to be stretched, to have demands made of them, to be given boundaries that are enforced and at the same time to know that they, themselves, are valued. The John Lyon School has adapted as public fashion, technical advances, educational theory and employment opportunities have changed and developed. Its core values, however, have remained unchanged. They were set out by almost every Headmaster from John Williams on and they were surely there before, when the English Form was led by Messrs Hutchinson and Gregg. In the words of David Dixon, back in 1985, the staff were and are 'custodians of that most precious tradition that is responsible for the liberal education' of the boys who attend the School, and 'we aim therefore by study across the curriculum; by our sport, music, drama, service to the community and the various other activities boys are encouraged to take part in, to foster in them that wholeness of manhood. . . . which is the hallmark of real education'.

Among the custodians, one boy singled out Lyndon Budd, teacher of English, and Lindsay Irvine, Modern Languages master and with whom he still exchanges emails, as especially effective and influential; for another, his extensive list included the widely popular John Barnard, 'the fantastic and very approachable character' David Rimmer, the 'apparently stern but excellent' Roger French, the similarly described Jo Rowley-Jones, Stuart Miles too, and as on nearly every boy's list, 'one of the first adults who talked to us as adults', Syd McMinn. For Mr McMinn, his extraordinary contribution to the School and to numerous boys' lives, also came to an end in 2001. Both he and Tim Wright would be moving away, but leaving a tremendous record of achievement behind.

As a new Headmaster was appointed so, in 2002, a new Chairman of the Committee of Management was elected. The eminent conductor, Dr Owain Arwel Hughes, whose son Geraint had earlier been a pupil and captain of cricket, succeeded Professor Michael Edwards. More changes were in the pipeline. Dr Arwel Hughes and his colleagues were able to establish more autonomy and, in that sense, a higher profile for the School. The Committee of Management changed status to become Governors, replacing the arm's-length Governors of Harrow School. The relationship between the two original schools on the Harrow Foundation was as close as ever, but now the Headmaster of John Lyon was a Governor of Harrow, just as the Head Master of Harrow had long been and remained, a Governor of John Lyon. The School had its own Bursar, rather than a share in Harrow's. The number of Old Lyonians among the Governors increased and there were, not for the first time, parent Governors including Angus Fraser, both father and brother of Lyonians[52] and Sue Symonds.

The new Headmaster was Dr Christopher Ray. He had held a variety of previous jobs as banker, publisher with Oxford University Press, school-master and university lecturer. In contrast, say, to Boyd Campbell's listen and learn, then decide and enforce, approach to change, Dr Ray embarked on radical change from the start, and with great energy. His ambition for swift development was clear.

The management structure within the School had an extra layer added in the form of Faculty Heads. The curriculum was shaken up to the benefit of some, but not all. Spanish and Italian were added as examination subjects and one boy was impressed by the new Head's setting down a marker in every area of School life, from food to study, but less happy when he found that physical education, which he was planning to take for GCSE, was removed as an examination option. Another, John Breakell, later to be Head Boy for Ray's successor, welcomed the new opportunities offered throughout his time at the School. There was an added emphasis on academic achievement. Psychology, taught by Grendon Haines who some years later joined Harrow School as its resident psychologist, was added to the syllabus. Seminars and coaching sessions took place as staff gave up lunch breaks, and the number of boys going on to Oxford and Cambridge showed a resulting increase. Based on the Inspectors' recommendations in their 1998 report, Dr Ray sought to develop the sixth form further and to establish a School Council, chaired jointly by a sixth-former and by one of the, by then, two Deputy Heads, long involved in the pastoral aspect of the School's life, 'Lord' Rimmer. Around now, too, a computerized Library management system was installed and Prefects were trained to operate it.

The widespread changes, refreshing to some, created tensions and Head Boy Atish Lakhani described his position as being 'caught in the middle', never a comfortable place to be. Speech Day was moved to September; the thinking behind this was that prizes for senior boys had long been awarded on the basis of GCSE and 'A' level success and so could not be given in the summer term; conversely, the autumn date

---

[52] But not, as some sources state, an Old Lyonian himself.

meant that boys in the very first weeks at the School were confronted by an occasion that summed up the past, which must have seemed a little alien to them, and the occasion itself lost the feeling of a summation, a moment of completion when the whole School came together as a community in celebration, before starting over again.

Many of the regular activities, nonetheless, continued as before. Sport in particular spun its usual web of highs and lows, happily more of the former than the latter. The weather affected football badly but did not prevent Ryan Dale from being selected for the England Independent Schools' Under-19 Eleven, nor did it prevent, in 2004, outstanding young sportsman Ben Gill graduating to the Arsenal Soccer Academy.

If, to begin with, the first team in cricket had more losses than wins, the teams representing younger age groups enjoyed considerable success, the Under-14s losing only four of their fourteen matches and the Under-12s, suffering only one loss from thirteen matches. Anek Mhajan, who led the younger team, was described by Jeremy Preston as captaining them 'with intelligence and shrewdness'. These two teams maintained their standard as they moved up the School: the now Under-15s in 2003 recording excellent victories over Aldenham, Berkhamsted, and St Benedict's, for example, and Hawes achieving a remarkable triple wicket maiden bowling against Rooks Heath. At the same time Ian Read, writing of an exciting Under-14 team, counsels, 'Enjoy your cricket and continue to search for perfection; and remember, you will enjoy it more by winning with good grace and style.' Advice that, hopefully, was taken. Certainly Anek Mhajan's team, coached by Ian Parker triumphed all the way as they progressed through the age groups, being Middlesex Champions 2005, 2006, 2007 and 2008. Kabir Toor, meanwhile was selected for the South of England Under-14 eleven and several boys were playing for their counties.

In other sports, the School became swimming's joint champions for the Harrow area, while in 2003 Samuel Steel, representing his Ealing club in an international competition between clubs from twelve countries, won three individual gold medals, three bronze medals and one silver, at the Olympic Pool in Munich.

A new development was that archery became a prescribed sport for all first-formers. At dinner after Speech Day in 2003, an Old Harrovian complained with mock anguish to an adjacent Old Lyonian that the Headmaster had managed to mention three times in his speech that the School had beaten Harrow in the Silver Arrow competition. He was not greatly assuaged when he was told it was probably because John Lyon had enjoyed the victory for each of the last three years. He would have been even more disappointed had he heard the truth that it was more like the last ten years that this had been the case. It might have comforted him to know that in cross-country the following year, John Lyon had come second to Harrow in the borough championships. At the same time, three JLS boys were selected to represent the borough in the county championships and the School's junior team won the St Martin's school relays. This year, too, the School provided three champions in the borough athletics competition: Kofi Asante in the triple jump, Robert Clarke with the javelin, and young Arran Ahmed throwing the discus in the Under-14 category. The same Rob Clarke also swam for England.

At the end of Dr Ray's first year, six members of staff left and double the number were recruited. Among those leaving were John Barnard who acquired an additional honour at the same time, being awarded the Associateship of the Royal School of Church Music in recognition of his body of achievement as composer, organist and choirmaster. He was replaced, as already mentioned, by two Deputy Heads.

Among newcomers to the staff was Deborah Gibbs who took over as Director of Drama. She was shortly to direct a magnificent production of *Guys and Dolls*, the first of the School's shows to be staged in the splendidly equipped Ryan Theatre. For this, Stuart Miles added conducting a pit orchestra to his numerous musical adventures, then he handed over to Jo Rowley-Jones as Director of Music, so as to concentrate on his other role as Academic Deputy Head. When the next School musical, *West Side Story* was put on, eminent actor and Old Lyonian, Tim West and his wife Prunella Scales attended. Tim commented that he was 'astounded by what he saw'. The quality of drama at the School, which had long been high, reached unprecedented levels of excellence under Miss Gibbs's stringent eye and ability to enthuse.

Where drama and actual examinations met, matters could not have been taken more seriously. Ishil Mehta recalled the GCSE practical day in 2004. There had been a break-in at the School through the back door to the drama studio. The drama office had been severely vandalized and the floor of the studio itself was covered with tiny shards of shattered glass. The boys were to perform *Snake Man* which entailed, as the title might suggest, a good deal of crawling about. This they did, ignoring with Captain Oates-like *sang-froid* the pain and the actual *sang* they shed. Every member of the group was rewarded with an A*. The School was deservedly Number One in England and Wales for the study of drama.

The visual arts expanded with the establishment of a fully equipped printmaking studio; ceramics and photography were now undertaken as academic subjects, all part of the newly defined Art and Design Faculty, headed by Caroline Harrison.

Then, in 2004, Dr Ray resigned to take up the attractive post, for a Rochdale man, of High Master at Manchester Grammar School. This left many matters unexpectedly unresolved. As Mr Rimmer, who took over as acting Headmaster, commented at the Speech Day that followed hotly after Dr Ray's departure, 'Having vision is one thing: turning it into something tangible is another.' Other views from both boys and staff were less mild.

Happily, the sense of community and family which earlier pupil Xuan-Zheng Goh had identified as one of the School's strengths, survived the perceived coldness of Dr Ray and it fell to David Rimmer, briefly, and then to Kevin Riley, appointed from the Bristol Cathedral School where he had been Head for eleven years, to resolve that which had been left undone.

Two long-serving masters left along with Dr Ray. Michael Sadler, Head of Latin and of Lower School, Registrar and more, retired after thirty-seven years; so did Head of Science until he became Senior Master, Peter Sanders, having served for just one year less. The man who came in as Headmaster, Kevin Riley, had an approach quite different from that of his predecessor. His own first impressions that the staff of the School gave outstanding pastoral care, that there was a desire to do well and a willingness to try things, were borne out by the following year's Ofsted report which praised the staff's 'great dedication and great commitment'. Most satisfying, too, the report noted among many positives, the School's 'quietly celebrating its multi-cultural composition'. The tragic and appalling events of 7th July 2005 when 52 people were killed and 770 were injured in a series of terrorist attacks in central London, in the Headmaster's own words, only served to bring boys coming from a 'wide range of ethnic and religious backgrounds into increased togetherness'.

The importance of this atmosphere is hard to overstate. To quote just one parent, she chose the School for her son for a number of precise reasons and the pastoral care offered and the ethos which made it 'a lovely place for a boy to grow up', topped her list. She found John Lyon less impersonal than the rival schools she visited. At the same time it provided a springboard, exposing him to the widest range of opportunities. The son, himself, Alykhan Kassam, concurs entirely and is clear that the abilities he has were greatly strengthened and encouraged at the School.

He, too, had his list of great teachers and among them, Bob Shaw and maths master, Mr Clarke.

Mr Riley has been described by many boys as being always around, approachable, very smiley. One boy, who talked about him at length, said he tightened discipline which in some areas had become alarmingly slack and, although always giving a second chance, made a number of necessary expulsions. The same boy said the atmosphere in the School was transformed by his arrival; and of the four Headmasters he experienced in his time as a pupil, he was the only one he would, and did, go to with his problems.

Among those in the know, Riley was also recognized as a street fighter when it came to getting rid of staff who, despite their loyalty and their merits, could no longer be afforded. He also worked to repair fractured relationships with some of the feeder schools. Years later the Chairman and Headmaster of Orley Farm School spoke feelingly of their appreciation that two weeks after being in post, Mr Riley visited them, rather than inviting them to come to him, to encourage a renewed relationship between the two schools.

Much of the envisioned development went forward under Mr Riley's leadership. Japanese was added to the curriculum, and then Chinese. A Gifted and Talented programme was introduced to advance the work of small groups of exceptionally able boys. For them there was an emphasis on Ancient Greek and Mandarin, visits to a range of interesting places, from historic sites to the British Library, from the Sigmund Freud Museum to the Building Research Centre, and to special conferences. Internet technology mushroomed across the School and interactive whiteboards were introduced which enabled the teacher to display information as he or she wrote it on an iPad. Kevin's specialist degree was in drama and yet another extension of the Main Building was undertaken. Once again the architect was Andrew Reed and the development comprised a new science and drama block, at a cost of three million pounds. Bright and airy, it provided eight laboratories, three preparation rooms and three additional classrooms as well as a second drama studio, equipped with a high quality lighting rig. All the other new rooms had energy-saving automatic lighting.

As well as being out and about amiably chatting to boys at break time and at the end of the school day, Mr Riley was regularly on the touchline or the boundary at the many sporting events. Football initially was less than exciting but at least showed signs of improvement, and the School returned to playing against more independent schools. By 2006, the First

Eleven were winning more matches than they lost and results included wins against Westminster, Dr Challenor's and Harrow, while the neutral referee at the Second Eleven's game against Aldenham described it as 'one of the best advertisements for schoolboy football [he] had seen in thirty seasons of refereeing'. Shortly after this, Louis Lavers joined Watford FC as a player. A couple of years later, younger boys were doing well, the Under-14 team winning the majority of their matches. The same team, when Under-15, reached the semi-finals of the Rensburg Trophy,[53] losing – by inescapable irony – to the eventual champions, Manchester Grammar School.

Cricket, as often in the School's history, fared better. In 2005, both the Under-14 and Under-15 Elevens were finalists in the Middlesex Cup, while Kabir Toor, playing for the First Eleven, scored centuries against Mill Hill and Westminster. He was still a youngster and played for Middlesex and for England in their Under-15 teams. A year later he was playing for the England Under-17 eleven and the School were Under-19 Middlesex champions, having won all but one of their seventeen matches. Kabir and Avinash Morthy both achieved the admirable average of more than sixty runs with the bat, and the former just beat his captain, Anek Mhajan, with a bowling average of 9.06, taking sixteen wickets for 145 runs. After which the addition of a batting cage to the practice facilities helped Kabir increase his batting average to a quite remarkable 85 in the 2008 season, top scoring with 165. While still at School he was signed for Middlesex and subsequently has followed a career in first-class cricket; at the time of writing he plays for Kent. The future, too, held promise: in 2009 the Under-12 team were finalists in the Middlesex Cup while the Under-15s were Middlesex Champions.

Other sports had their highlights during this period. Early on three boys, Elliott Bertram, Michael Betts and Sonny Flynn, represented the county in athletics; Matthew Barker took an amazing thirteen seconds off the School 800 metres record, which had stood since 1970. Two years later Sonny Flynn, who emerged as an ace sportsman, was still representing Middlesex and paid tribute to the coaching he received from Cliff Jones and Ian Parker.

In tennis, after a year of whitewash victories including over Millfield, where sport is little short of a religion, to reach the final of the National Independent Schools Cup at Eton College, there followed another outstanding year. Having overcome Latymer Upper in the quarter-

---

[53] The name of the Independent Schools' Football Association Cup.

finals and University College School in the semis, the John Lyon team beat Langley Grammar School to win the Glanville Cup. They reached the quarter-finals of the National Competition, prevented from going further by the unavailability of all four principal players. The Under-15s lost their quarter-final in the same competition by the narrowest of margins after a sudden-death play-off, while the Under-13s met a similar fate in their semi-final. That three teams should get so far in the same year was a considerable achievement.

Other School activities not merely flourished, they increased. There is a photographer-in-residence as well as an artist-in-residence. Excellent work is displayed in the Mall and on the pages of *The Lyonian*. The range of work produced at this time reflects influences as diverse as Renoir, Klee, Warhol and Van Gogh, while the paintings of Matt Barker bring to mind the fascination Joseph Wright of Derby had with light sources. Interesting to note that two of the School's outstanding runners were also accomplished artists, as the work illustrated here of Matt and of Sonny Flynn shows. Stephen Rhodes, meantime, had entered Central St Martin's, coming in the top five of 3,900 candidates for the Art and Design course there.

In 2005 the School created a music studio, Music Technology now being an 'A' level subject. There were four full-time music teachers and an array of instrumental specialists who visited on a regular basis. Among the numerous concerts presented, the School performed, in 2007, Karl Jenkins' *The Armed Man* and two years later the newly revived Motet Choir shared the platform with the legendary Black Dyke Band for the annual Speech Room concert. This occasion celebrated the sixtieth birthday of the band's composer-in-residence, Philip Wilby, who happened also to be the father of JLS music teacher, Anna Wilby. The CD of the concert proved popular.

Drama remained, arguably, pre-eminent. The number and variety of productions was extraordinary. Musicals *Anything Goes, Grease, Copacobana, Oklahoma* all achieving a quite unlikely standard for school shows. Female parts were all taken by girls from a range of other schools. Competition to get into John Lyon School productions was fierce and the standard of the girls' performances was as remarkably high as that of the boys. Then add a *Hamlet* that was almost revolutionary for this time in that the cast wore accurate Elizabethan costumes; and plays as various as *Epsom Downs, Teechers*; several by Deborah Gibbs herself, including *Prizefighter, Was It All Worth It?* and *Tritton House*; *Arturo Ui, Twelve Angry Men*, Ayckbourn's *Revenger's Comedies* and *Oliver Twist*. This list is far from exhaustive and in the same five-year period, there were work-shops conducted by principals from the West End shows in question on *Hairspray* and *Phantom of the Opera*. The workshops were held at John Lyon with student participants coming from ten different schools. In addition there were inter-house competitions and two films directed by staff member Dom Roy. The first was a version of *Unman, Wittering and Zigo*, Giles Cooper's 1958 radio play, already professionally filmed twice; the second was an original screenplay, *Losing It All*, focusing on a boy, played by Sonny Flynn, devastated by the sudden loss of both parents. As he fails to cope, he descends into a world of drink, drugs and theft. Reminiscent of the work of Ken Loach, the film was leavened by a note of optimism in its conclusion.

Just as this particular history ends, young Tom Barker was featuring as the Boy in the stellar production led by Sir Ian McKellen and Roger Rees of *Waiting for Godot* at the Theatre Royal, Haymarket, while outstanding dancer Alex Tranter had moved on to Italia Conti and the commence-ment of his professional career.

Academically the School continued to enjoy notable successes, Krish-nan Patel (later to be an effective leader of the School Council), who came in the top ten of the 43,000 entrants for GCSE Religious Education, being among the outstanding results Mr Riley was able to report. And the School continued to be especially imaginative in designing its extra-curricular activities. The wide array of trips organized every year, for example, included the football team going to a Spanish training camp, to improve their language skills as well as their tackling and defending, while at home, a twenty-four-hour fast was organized to raise money for the starving in Sierra Leone.

There was one change that proved unpopular, even shocking, to many Old Boys. Speech Day, now unaccountably dubbed Speeches, was demoted to being a curtain raiser for Association Day. With cricket in the afternoon, it was held on a Saturday morning – admittedly in the summer term once more – and concerned only prize winners and their parents and those sixth-formers who chose to attend. Professor Paul Wilkinson, who was the Guest of Honour in 2008, was perplexed and upset to find he had been invited to address a two-thirds empty Speech Room. Nick Smart, who had been Head Boy only a few short years before, could not believe it when he heard about it. He said one of the principal spurs when he was a boy was to watch fellow pupils who had worked hard go onto the platform and to vow that next year he would be among them. As with the vast body of Old Lyonians, he regarded Speech

Day and Sports Day as the two major events in the calendar, when the entire School would come together as a community.

Of course, there were other changes, too. Ben Marsh joined the School in 2005. At that time Monitors could give detentions or lines to boys who broke the rules. As the years passed the impositions evolved into being required to do a litter pick or something similar and then, Ben remarked, Monitors lost the powers to punish altogether, partly resulting from parental objections. That neither Monitors nor Prefects could impose discipline marked a radical departure from the system embraced by Dr Arnold and which had characterized public schools for a couple of centuries.[54] So had the effects of European law and evolving attitudes to bringing up children. Corporal punishment by staff members had been banned in all schools in England and Wales by law in 1999, though when, somewhat later, Mr Riley said to a group of elderly Old Boys that dealing with an offender these days you had to stroke him, one of the party replied, to much laughter, 'I think I'd rather have the slipper'.

There was still pride and the effects of leading by example and exhortation to make being a Monitor attractive. Richard Symonds, later to be the Country Manager in Uganda for the Bujagali Trust, a charity devoted to helping desperately needy children and young people, said he gained tremendous satisfaction as House Captain of Moore. His own particular interests ranged through sport, music and drama and he paid tribute to young sports master Arthur Brammer, who was also Youth Coach at Watford FC, to 'super music teacher' Stuart Miles, to the impressive skills of Joseph Nolan who was the Royal Organist, in post at the Chapels Royal and frequently playing in Buckingham Palace and at festivals the world over. He taught singing at John Lyon, from barbershop to motets. Richard also acknowledged a debt to 'one in a million' Deborah Gibbs who was able to 'get such commitment on everyone's part'.

The School badge, worn on the blazers of boys up to Year 11 changed to a regular-shaped shield holding a large rampant lion, rather bolder than the unique, but small badge it replaced. There were no crossed arrows and no School motto, though both featured on the various sports kits boys wore.

---

[54] '. . . boy freedom and boy rule grew up accidentally, and. . . . once there, it was accepted and justified. One of the complaints against [Headmaster] Gabell at Winchester in 1818 was that he had abandoned the "English Method" – masters trusting boys, and boys having self-government under prefects – for the "French Method", where the boys were not trusted and government was by masters.' Jonathan Gathorne-Hardy *The Public School Phenomenon* Chapter 3.

Other positive developments included the production of a DVD introducing the School for prospective pupils and parents; the publication of an attractive termly news sheet, *The Standard* and the appointment of a Development Director and Assistant. Among other improvements this meant the School's archive, long in shambolic disarray, began to be rescued, organized, catalogued and in due course, many items including historic photographs, restored. It was to be a long but satisfying process: the present is always more comprehensible if there is an accurate knowledge and understanding of the past. And the past of the John Lyon School is in many ways both intriguing and encouraging.

The DVD, shot on an Open Day, provides a visual tour of the School site, though not Sudbury, and features the Headmaster and Head Boy James Caldecourt addressing young candidates and their parents. Mr Riley poses the likely questions of any new boy: 'Will I be happy there and will I make friends?' The evidence of the whole history of this School and reiterated by James Caldecourt when his turn came to speak, is over-whelmingly positive in response. Add to that that the School is academically in the top twenty of independent boys' schools, that it has just received awards for the levels achieved in both English and Drama and that the facilities now rival any school in the land and competition for places is understandable.

It was a surprise, and something of a disappointment, that Kevin Riley announced he would be resigning in 2009. Taking the advice he so often gave to boys, namely when there is an opportunity, you should seize it, he was accepting the offer to go to Bangkok as Headmaster of Harrow International School there, the 'Harrow of Siam'. In association with Harrow School, the Bangkok school is co-educational, twelve hundred strong and caters for all ages up to eighteen.

As Kevin left, so did veteran staff members David Rimmer and Nick Parsons. The new chief was appointed, putting John Lyon at the cutting edge: the first independent boys' school in the country to appoint a female Head. Katherine Haynes had been Head of Mathematics at Warwick School and the pattern of improvements and developments would continue. So too would the increasingly close relationship with Harrow School. Old Harrovian, John Hayes, was Chairman of the John Lyon Governors, a choice he made because he wanted 'to find out how the heck they did it when they only had the boys during the daytime', a tribute to the many achievements of John Lyon schoolboys. Two years down the line, a magnificent service in St Paul's Cathedral celebrated the bond shared by all the elements of the Harrow School Foundation and it was attended by all the boys of Harrow School and all the boys of the John Lyon School. Among the composers whose music featured was John Barnard and the entire event was musically directed by fellow Old Lyonian, Andrew Carwood.

When Miss Haynes, as one of a strong field, was waiting to be interviewed for the appointment as Head, she was surprised that a small boy passing down the corridor stopped to say, 'Good luck'. She was even more surprised when a moment later he popped back to add, 'You'd enjoy it here. It's a lovely school.'

As another of her pupils, later to be Deputy Head Boy, said of the place, 'That's the thing about John Lyon: it's not like other schools.'

POSTSCRIPT

There are thousands of boys and scores of teachers not mentioned in this book, many of whom deserve mention.

Every boy and every staff member contributes to the quality and ethos of the School and it is fascinating to have seen how, through testing times and easier ones, there has clearly been a definable spirit characterizing this particular school. The vast majority of boys who have passed through its doors have gone on to fulfilled lives, making a positive impact through their achievements at work, their contributions in voluntary organizations or, like David Routledge, who a handful of years ago was elected Mayor of Hillingdon, by using their energies in the service of the community.

The long gone Mayor of Westminster, quoted in one of the three epigraphs at the beginning of this chronicle was surely right: John Lyon, and his wife Joan, would be proud of what goes on in Middle Road. And disbelieving at the amazing results of their generosity.

APPENDIX 1

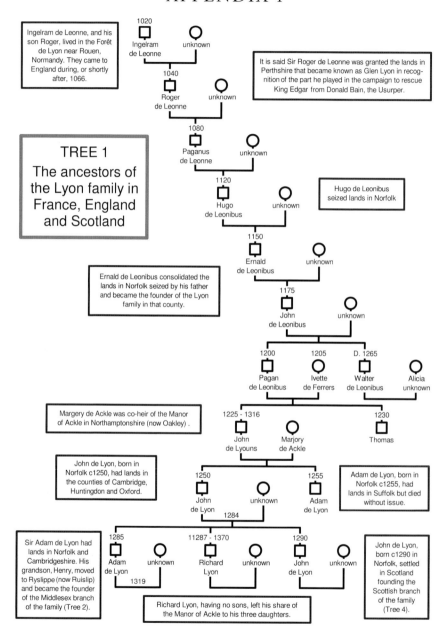

Ingelram de Leonne, and his son Roger, lived in the Forêt de Lyon near Rouen, Normandy. They came to England during, or shortly after, 1066.

1020
Ingelram de Leonne — unknown

It is said Sir Roger de Leonne was granted the lands in Perthshire that became known as Glen Lyon in recognition of the part he played in the campaign to rescue King Edgar from Donald Bain, the Usurper.

1040
Roger de Leonne — unknown

TREE 1
The ancestors of the Lyon family in France, England and Scotland

1080
Paganus de Leonne — unknown

1120
Hugo de Leonibus — unknown

Hugo de Leonibus seized lands in Norfolk

Ernald de Leonibus consolidated the lands in Norfolk seized by his father and became the founder of the Lyon family in that county.

1150
Ernald de Leonibus — unknown

1175
John de Leonibus — unknown

1200   1205   D. 1265
Pagan de Leonibus   Ivette de Ferrers   Walter de Leonibus   Alicia unknown

Margery de Ackle was co-heir of the Manor of Ackle in Northamptonshire (now Oakley).

1225 - 1316
John de Lyouns — Marjory de Ackle

1230
Thomas

John de Lyon, born in Norfolk c1250, had lands in the counties of Cambridge, Huntingdon and Oxford.

1250
John de Lyon — unknown

1255
Adam de Lyon

Adam de Lyon, born in Norfolk c1255, had lands in Suffolk but died without issue.

1284

Sir Adam de Lyon had lands in Norfolk and Cambridgeshire. His grandson, Henry, moved to Ryslippe (now Ruislip) and became the founder of the Middlesex branch of the family (Tree 2).

1285
Adam de Lyon — unknown
1319

11287 - 1370
Richard Lyon — unknown

1290
John de Lyon — unknown

John de Lyon, born c1290 in Norfolk, settled in Scotland founding the Scottish branch of the family (Tree 4).

Richard Lyon, having no sons, left his share of the Manor of Ackle to his three daughters.

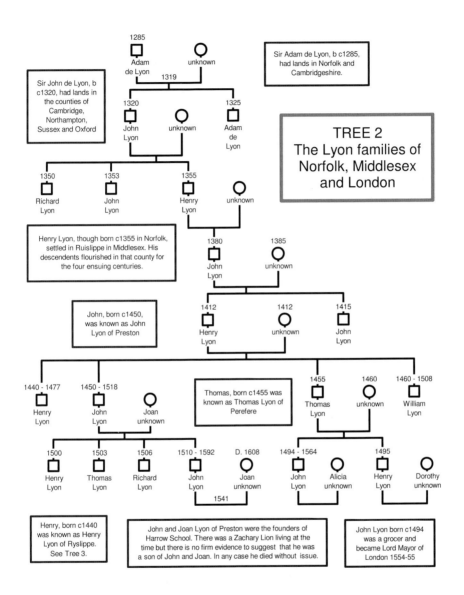

1285
Adam de Lyon — unknown
1319

Sir Adam de Lyon, b c1285, had lands in Norfolk and Cambridgeshire.

Sir John de Lyon, b c1320, had lands in the counties of Cambridge, Northampton, Sussex and Oxford

1320 John Lyon — unknown — **1325** Adam de Lyon

TREE 2
The Lyon families of Norfolk, Middlesex and London

1350 Richard Lyon **1353** John Lyon **1355** Henry Lyon — unknown

Henry Lyon, though born c1355 in Norfolk, settled in Ruislippe in Middlesex. His descendents flourished in that county for the four ensuing centuries.

1380 John Lyon — **1385** unknown

John, born c1450, was known as John Lyon of Preston

1412 Henry Lyon — **1412** unknown — **1415** John Lyon

1440 - 1477 Henry Lyon **1450 - 1518** John Lyon — Joan unknown

Thomas, born c1455 was known as Thomas Lyon of Perefere

1455 Thomas Lyon — **1460** unknown — **1460 - 1508** William Lyon

1500 Henry Lyon **1503** Thomas Lyon **1506** Richard Lyon **1510 - 1592** John Lyon — **D. 1608** Joan unknown **1541**

1494 - 1564 John Lyon — Alicia unknown **1495** Henry Lyon — Dorothy unknown

Henry, born c1440 was known as Henry Lyon of Ryslippe. See Tree 3.

John and Joan Lyon of Preston were the founders of Harrow School. There was a Zachary Lion living at the time but there is no firm evidence to suggest that he was a son of John and Joan. In any case he died without issue.

John Lyon born c1494 was a grocer and became Lord Mayor of London 1554-55

Researched by Robert Cutts OL

APPENDIX 2

Letter from Rev. C E Prior Concerning the Red House

Oxford Mission Barisal East Pakistan
(Undated)

Dear J A Hill,

My sister has forwarded to me your letter of 19th November 1958. I can give you some information. The big room on the ground floor was our dining room, the small room was 'the boys' study'. My elder brother Arthur Venn left the school in August 1895.

My younger brother Cunningham joined the school in April 1895. So for one term, the summer term of 1895, we were all at the school. My name is Carlos Edward. So that dates pretty decisively the cutting of the initials. May I suggest that it is not A-P as you have written, but **AP** the A P being joined together to make a V. He always wrote his initials so. In the big first floor room of the old house, which was our nursery on a pane is scratched the same date October 1815 I think, which is generally supposed to be about the date that the old house, 3 stories (sic), six rooms was built. It was enlarged in 1883 by my architect uncle Edward S Prior. The initials JTP, John Templer Prior, my father, used to be under the gable of the new part, but even in my day they had become obscure.

Roxeth Mead was originally called Trafalgar Cottage (before enlargement in 1856) which seems to date it. Arthur died in September 1950, Cunningham is still alive. We lived before in what is now called Buckholt, and my grandmother was living in Roxeth Mead. So the move in 1884 was simply a trek across the gardens. The back door, the door next to your room, had an oaken box inside the letter slip with a sliding side to pull out to get the letters out. When the box disintegrated, I took the sliding side and made it into a paper weight, which is still on my table.

We have a school here of rather over a hundred boys – boarders – Christians – they all live in the villages beyond Barisal. School opened 2 days ago. Tomorrow I suppose I shall sell at least 1000 exercise books. Has your room still got tiles of the signs of the zodiac over the fireplace?

Yours very sincerely,
(Signed) C E Prior

APPENDIX 3

Letter to the *Harrow Observer*
dated 4th November 1972

Dear Sir

JOHN LYON SCHOOL ON BYRON HILL

I was very interested in the front page illustration of Oct 27 showing the original Baptist Church and Hall in Byron Hill as, from 1910 for some ten years on this Hall was used to house the two junior forms of John Lyon School.

I myself spent three carefree? years there from 1904. There were some forty pupils aged ten or so who then proceeded to the main school. The form master was Mr E C Blomfield (Beaky) who at regular intervals administered the cane but I do not recollect any violent demos by the boys or parents in protest thereto. It was of course accepted as an inevitable part of the curriculum. A large proportion of John Lyon School consisted of farmers' sons as the whole area surrounding Harrow was farmland. In fact the view from the bottom of Byron Hill was entirely meadows and trees with never a building in sight.

The school fees (believe it or not) were two guineas a term for Harrow parishioners and three for outsiders.

I am sure there must be many Old Lyonians who received their early education here and who like myself would be very sorry to see this pleasant little part of old Harrow with its period architecture spoilt by the introduction of modern and no doubt unlovely buildings quite at variance with the environment.

Yours faithfully
Gurney A Higgins

Mr Higgins copied this letter to the School where it was displayed on the board in the Masters' Common Room

INDEX TO INDIVIDUALS
AND SCHOOLS

Wherever first names or initials could be established they have been given. Surnames for teachers where the first name is unsure have Mr against them; for boys, the surname only has been given.